Rick Jolly is a Surgeon Commander in the Royal Navy, and is currently serving in London with the Ministry of Defence as the holder of a Defence Fellowship. His professional interests lie in the subject of Battle Stress and its particular effect on Command, and he has spent the majority of his Naval service with either the Royal Marines or the Fleet Air Arm. Following active service in Northern Ireland he wrote the novel *For Campaign Service* in 1975, using the pen name of *Christopher Hawke*. This was followed by *The Red and Green Life Machine* in 1983, which recounted his experiences commanding the Ajax Bay Field Hospital during the Falklands Conflict. Married, with one son, he lives near Plymouth in a house which is ruled by the former ship's Sick Bay moggie from RNAS Culdrose, a splendid grey Leading Seacat called *Pusser*. Appointed OBE in 1982, he also holds a Diploma in Aviation Medicine.

Tugg Willson spent twenty-four years in the Royal Navy, seventeen of those on the lower deck as an Armourer. He retired in 1971 to pursue a second career as a cartoonist, a decision which has been brilliantly vindicated by his success. His reputation in the fields of aviation and offshore engineering is unequalled as an illustrator who can bring punch and well-remembered humour to important safety messages, and his annual Fleet Air Arm flight safety calendar is awaited as eagerly as his monthly contributions to *Navy News* in the form of the *JACK* cartoon strip. Tugg's three children are grown up, and he now lives in Northumbria with his wife, Elizabeth.

Jackspeak

THE

PUSSER'S RUM®

GUIDE TO

Royal Navy Slanguage

By Rick Jolly & *Tugg*

A dictionary and reference to the slang, euphemisms, idiom and usage — past and current — of the Royal Navy and Royal Marines

PRINTING HISTORY

Charity Edition July 1988
First Edition April 1989

Text © Rick Jolly 1989
Illustrations © Tugg 1989

ISBN 0 9514305 0 5
Registered at the British Library

Set by Palamanando Press in Century P.S.
using an Acorn Archimedes 310 driving
Pipedream Software

Phototypeset and printed by
Deltor Communications Ltd.,
Torpoint, Cornwall.

Additional copies may be obtained
(£8.95 inclusive of P&P in U.K.
and Europe) from:
Palamanando Publishing,
P.O. Box 42
Torpoint
Cornwall PL11 2YR

For *JACK* and *ROYAL*

*on whose broad and willing shoulders
the destiny of this island nation
has so often depended*

and for Miss SLM Eaton

with very best wishes from

Lt Cdr Rupert Craven Rn ...

[signature] 1989

PREFACE

This book is the direct result of a hobby which began on a sunny Mediterranean morning in 1971, very soon after I had joined the Royal Navy as a rather young and green Surgeon Lieutenant. My memories of that first patient are still embarassingly clear; a tall and very fit-looking Royal Marines Corporal told me he had **caught the boat up**. As Mr. Dom Mintoff was then in the process of kicking us all out of Malta, I presumed that my customer was delighted to have been chosen for a sea voyage back to England - or had he been selected for service in submarines ?

Those of you who are familiar with Naval slang will no doubt understand his total confusion at my proferred congratulations ! I had to excuse myself rather hurriedly, then pop out to to the front office and question the Sick Bay 'tiff. This splendid character slid under his desk for laughing, and then dined out on the story for the rest of his career. I returned to the consulting room, sorted my patient out in the conventional manner, and then decided never to be caught out again. What you are about to read is the final result of those highly enjoyable labours, and the computer-collated presentation of those hundreds of scribbled prescription pads and bar chits that have been accumulating since Day One in Sliema.

During a very recent two year stint as the Principal Medical Officer at the Royal Naval Air Station, Culdrose, I finally had a chance to sit down at the keyboard and punch this data in during the long hours that the airfield remained open for night flying. Of course, if I'd known then how much work was going to be required for completion of this little project, I would have baled out there and then ! It therefore says a lot for the resilient humour of my Sick Bay manager, *Chief Petty Officer Medical Asistant Sam Parker*, that the Boss was never allowed to flag. A constant stream of new suggestions came in, from him as well as the other stalwarts of the Chief's Mess at HMS SEAHAWK, and I owe him a great deal for that cheerful support and encouragement.

My Commanding Officer, *Captain **Paul Bootherstone** DSC*, also played a vital part - by writing to the 2000 plus UK members of the Fleet Air Arm Officers Association. This round robin led to an unprecedented response. Nearly 700 copies of the book were purchased over the Christmas period, and the limited charity edition of 1000 was soon sold out. We now had a figure of £2300 in the bank towards a special building project, but then the letters started coming in, from people who had enjoyed the book but wanted to help in the never-ending task of correction and improvement. I remain particularly grateful to *Lord Kilbracken DSC, Commander David Yates, Captain David Husband OBE, Captain Derek Oakley MBE RM, Major Alan Marsh RM, Hector Mackenzie* and *Alan Jefferson* who all provided good advice. My Brigade Commander during the Falklands campaign - *Major General Julian Thompson CB OBE* - also came up with the goods (again !), as did *Hugh Layton, Bill Morton, Alan Clifford, Ted Whitley, Commander Derek Shone, and Lieutenant Commanders Peter Bracelin, Terry Jane, Rick Sandover and Nick Butler.* For the Submarine Service inputs I am totally indebted to *Commander **Howard McFadyen** RN.*

Tugg's wonderful cartoons need no real introduction from me. They sum up, in just a few sharp pen strokes, the very essence of Jack's wry, witty and often self-mocking observations about life in the Andrew. Some of the drawings are originals, the others are taken from the **JACK** cartoon strips that have been appearing continuously in the *Navy News* since the first in February 1973:

I am very grateful to the Editor of *Navy News, John Tucker,* for his permission to use these, and for the arrangements that we have made under the laws of copyright.

In revising the text I found that the number of words and entries had nearly doubled - from 47,000 to 92,000 and from around 2,000 to nearly 3,500 respectively ! The problem has still been what to leave out - gross obscenity of course, because the sort of mindless swearing in which every seventh word must be copulatory in order to communicate is a form of speech that has no place in an anthology of this kind. However, neither Jack nor Royal are angels, and they still display a healthy interest in the nether regions of the opposite sex - which accounts for the many relevant phrases and descriptions that are in daily usage !

I was also guided by the working principle that this book should contain something for everyone, from the grizzled veteran of the Murmansk convoy runs, to the fresh-faced new boys and girls just starting their careers in the oldest and finest fighting service in the world. In this respect I am grateful to my professional head of Branch, *Surgeon Vice Admiral Sir Godfrey Milton-Thompson KBE*, for drawing my attention to a number of words and phrases with a maritime or Naval origin that have since come ashore to a wider general usage. Any analysis of Naval language is also a potted history of the British Isles; no doubt the new entries will also bring with them the slang terms of their own area and upbringing, expressions which may suddenly catch on and spread like wildfire - or just sputter away in one ship or establishment without making that crucial jump into the dark-blue vernacular of the future.

What worries me more is the prospect of our slang and usage falling into oblivion as a direct result of neglect. In the good old days of the Tot, messdeck conversation was witty and vital, stimulated by the daily infusion of *Nelson's Blood*. Now, that inevitable glass eye in the corner projects its mind-numbing videos and game shows to an equally-glazed audience, and four hundred years of living, dynamic and constantly-changing history is in danger of withering by atrophy.

May I ask your help in continuing to prevent this ? Please let us know if there ae any significant errors of fact or omission, and Palamanando Publications will try and incorporate all valid suggestions into a future edition. There are a small number of blank pages at the back to help you in this task. Tugg and I are now working on further cartoons for this, as well as drawing up preliminary plans for an edition of *TOT TALES* that stemmed from a competition run by *Michael Fogg* of *Messrs. Pusser's Rum Ltd*. Like the *Pusser's Rum* donation to the Tot Fund, we also intend to continue reserving a royalty of 10% for Royal Navy and Royal Marines charities from the sale of this, and all future books.

Finally, may I thank the hard-working people who helped to bring this First Edition of *JACKSPEAK* to press. Responsibility for the design of the cover has rested on the talents of *Anthony Denham*; the remainder of the *DELTOR* team, ably led by *Alan Shannon*, have always been the model of kindness and tolerance to this amateur enthusiast. *Janet Locket, Judy Martin* and even *James Jolly* helped with text preparation, and all the staff at Palamanando Publications, without exception, have been most supportive.

University College London
January 1989

ALPHA

A 25 (*FAA*)   Aircraft accident / incident reporting form which requires considerable detail for its correct completion. The effort involved in this (plus the actual survival !) is celebrated in the refrain to each of the **A 25** song's verses, which describe some of the hair-raising crashes and escapes of the past:

> *They say in the Air Force that a landing's OK*
> *If the pilot gets out and can still walk away -*
> *But in the Fleet Air Arm the prospects are grim*
> *If the landing's piss-poor and the pilot can't swim..*

> **(Refrain)** *Cracking show, I'm alive -*
> *But I've still got to *render my A 25..*

Some of the other verses celebrate traditional enthusiasms among *Fleet Air Arm* aircrew, such as:

> *My CO has promised me an old Tiger Moth,*
> *An appalling contraption made of string, wood and cloth,*
> *He says its performance - like mine - is fantastic*
> *Because we both go like crazy on knicker elastic..*

A's and A's   Older abbreviation for *Amendments and Additions*; the business of incorporating these corrections into a book of *JACKSPEAK* promises to become an unending task, but all comments are welcome and all suggestions will be considered ! See also Preface

AB   The rate (rank) of Able Seaman; often used in the expression *three-badge **AB** denoting a sailor, usually of great experience and character, who has not sought promotion during his naval career

abeam   Adjacent to, or just opposite something

ABC *(RM)*   The rather resigned response to any alteration of an official plan: *"Tomorrow is ABC - it's All Been Changed !"*   There needs to be some awareness however of the possibility that things will **ABCBA** in the fullness of time - *All Be Changed Back Again* !

accommodation ladder   Technically correct name for any stairway or flight of steps leading from one deck to another inside a ship; although the proper description for a temporary rope ladder used for boarding at sea is a *gangway ladder*, in practice and in daily *RN* usage the term **accomodation ladder** has crept in to replace it !   Note that the correct routine when accompanying a senior officer on *Rounds is to allow one's superior *up* a ladder *first* and *down last*, in contrast to the small boat etiquette of *last in and first out

ace   Two applications:
   1. Something or somewhere that impresses Jack as being of really high quality: *"Hey, seen Lofty's new tranny ? It's really ace.."* Or else: *"Newcastle's an ace *run-ashore.."*
   2. The *Flagship in a formation - the **ace** that must be protected

ackers / ackies   Corruption of the words *piastre* (Egyptian money) or *drachma* (Greek) which then became descriptive in the old Mediterranean Fleet for any form of foreign cash.   Overtaken in current usage by its further adaptation to *ickies, but see also *klebbies, *shrapnel and *washers

acquire   Euphemism for the illegal (or barely legal) process of obtaining a *Naval stores item that is in short supply.   See also *proff

across the Pond   In America, since the *Pond concerned refers to the Atlantic Ocean, as opposed to the *Ditch of the English Channel

Acting Unpaid   A rating who for good reason is granted (*local) permission by his Commanding Officer to wear a badge of rank when he is not strictly qualified to do so, but needs to have some authority over others of the same *rate

Action Stations !   *Pipe made when contact with the enemy is imminent

Active Service   An officer or rating of the Regular *RN* forces, as distinct from those on the Reserve, Retired or Emergency *Lists.   A national emergency or specific shortages can lead to recall to **Active Service** from the latter categories

actual
   1. *(FAA)* Flying in real cloud rather than simulating this experience under a helmet-mounted hood
   2. *(FAA)* Sleeping in a bunk during an operation or exercise instead of simulating this *kip by lying on the counterpane, exhausted

3. **Actuals** refer to actual expenditure, an accounting process authorized in countries where the cost of living is very high, and where fixed allowances would probably prove inadequate

Adam and Eve on a raft   Two fried eggs on a piece of toast

Adam's ale   Drinking water

addled   Old sailor's term for drinking water that had become stale or putrid; hence the term **addled eggs** for those that have gone off, or **addled brains** for someone getting a bit *handcarted !

ADDLS *(FAA)*   Acronym for an *Assisted *Dummy Deck Landing Sortie*; Naval aviators would do simulated carrier approaches to a specially marked runway with the help of a *Bats, in order to develop or retain the special skills required. When the mirror-landing sight was developed (in Britain !) these flights became **MADDLS** instead

Admiral of the narrow seas   Jack's historic nickname for someone unkind enough to vomit stale beer all over his *oppo

Admiralty clown   Physical Training Instructor; see also the terms *club- swinger and *springer (*RM*)

Admiralty Fleet Order   Precursor of the *DCI and originally abbreviated to **AFO**; in the Mediterranean and Far Eastern Fleets, *****Egyptian AFO**s were poorly printed and laughably misspelt pornographic texts

Admiralty ham   Suspicious description of any kind of tinned meat; see also *fanny for further explanation

Adrenalin's brown !   Fundamental discovery about one's personal physiology on being seriously frightened, especially when this happens for the first time. See also *drop a brown for an older version of exactly the same sentiment

adrift　　　Late for work or duty: *"Comin' back off *Crimbo leave,
Shiner got *legless an' missed 'is train - five hours adrift and *in
the rattle.."* The phrase **adrift to hell** (or stronger) implies being
very seriously late indeed, as depicted on page **D** -94

aerobatic teams *(FAA)*　　　The *Sharks helicopter display team is
the only officially constituted *Fleet Air Arm* outfit presently on view
to the public, although the *Historics continue to delight airshow
crowds around the the country each summer, and the *Pusser's Pair can
also be seen augmenting the solo displays by *SHAR, *Lynx, *Sea King
and *Wetdreams (Jetstreams) at various shows, Air Days and Navy Days.
In the past era of conventional fixed-wing jets there were some really
famous teams, including *The Ace of Diamonds* (Sea Hawks), *Fred's Five*
and *Simon's Sircus* (Sea Vixens) and the *Blue Herons* (Hunters). The
latter group was particularly smooth and proficient; because of its
very experienced but rather elderly pilots, it was also known locally
as the *Phyllosan Four* ! See also the *Crimson Crabs

Affirmative !　　　Jack and Royal's way of saying: *"Yes !"*

aft through the hawse-pipe　　　Descriptive phrase for a *Special
Duties List Officer promoted from the *Lower Deck. The traditional
seamen's *messdeck was up in the forecastles, ie. before the mast; the
hawse-pipes were openings in the forecastle deck through which the
anchor cables ran, and the Officer's *wardroom and accomodation was
generally situated **aft**. The expression is therefore heard sometimes
with **up** substituted for **aft**. See also *Upper Yardie and *Corps Commish

afternoon watch　　　The period between 1200 and 1600 hours

afters　　　Pudding: *"Woss' fer afters ?"*

Aggie Weston's　　　The network of Royal Sailor's Rests begun in 1876
by the formidable *Dame Agnes Weston*. These Homes from Home still exist
and flourish in Portsmouth, Gosport, Rosyth, Devonport and Plymouth.
Their emphasis remains on home comforts - and temperance. Such was
Jack's genuine affection for his Sailor's Friend that when the warship
HMS *WESTON-SUPER-MARE* was launched, she was immediately labelled
Aggie-on-horseback !

agony bags　　　Bagpipes; see also *porridge guns

Airship　　　The Royal Air Force equivalent of a Sea Lord,
because the *Crabfat model of Their Lordships of the Admiralty Board is
called The Air Board - hence ***Their Airships of the Air Board*** ! Jack
also has his own ideas about the Junior Service - see also **Per Ardua
Ad Astra*

Air Tragedy / Air Tragickers *(FAA)*　　　The professional skill
of *Air Traffic Control*, and thus a group nickname for practitioners of
this secret art. **Air Trumpeters** is an occasional alternative

A -4

airy fairy   Derogatory term for a person serving in the *Fleet Air Arm*. Can also be used as an adjective: *"Most airy-fairy *kit ain't nowhere near *bootneck-proof.."* See *Wafu in addition

Aladdin's cave   Any over-stocked *compartment full of stores

Alert
1. Bugle call played to mark a specific occasion such as the arrival or departure of an important personage: *"Sound the Alert !"*
2. *(FAA)* Aircraft's readiness state to *launch - **Alert 5** or **Alert 30** describes the number of minutes that it will take to get into the air and on task
3. Be **alert** - because the country needs **lerts**

all about   Someone who is *switched-on: *"You'd have to get up pretty early in the morning to catch him out - he's really all about, just like shit in a fanshaft.."*

all above board   Older description for anything above the deck of a sailing vessel, ie. visible to everyone; this has led to the more general meaning of fair and open business dealing

all fart and no shit   A noisy but basically ineffective leader

all for it !   Older term that can still be heard as a piece of lovely cynicism: *"The Job Evaluation team felt that my work here was absolutely vital to the security of the nation, but two of my three assistants had to go. Then they asked me what I thought about that. Of course, as you'd excpect, I said I was all for it.."*

all gait and gaiters   Nice description of *Guns and his staff when dressed and prepared for the parade ground

all nighters   Contraction and misapplication of the term *All Night Shore Leave* to describe an episode of intense overnight (and indoor) activity with a lady friend. Can also be used as **all night in** to describe a watchkeeper whose sleep, for once, has been unbroken

all of one company   Very important and oft-quoted sentiment applied to the conditions of service in the Royal Navy. Attributed to Sir Francis Drake in 1578 when quelling the discontent that existed in *The Golden Hind* between his professional seamen and the attached gentlemen of Court: *"..for I must have the gentleman to haul and draw with the mariner and the mariner with the gentleman. What ! let us show ourselves all to be of a company.."* See also *happy ship

all parts bearing equal strain   Classic Naval expression describing how everything is under control and giving no cause for any concern or anxiety. This may also mean no strain at all if the person making the statement: *"I'm going to put all parts under equal strain.."* intends to *slope off for a *kip

A-5

all-singing, all-dancing   Sarcastic description of any piece of *kit that is supposed to solve some previously impossible problem

all teeth, tits and toenails   Deflating description of an individual who is full of his own self-importance

Ambit   Rough, cheap, strong, red Maltese Marsovin wine, barely drinkable even when mixed with 7-Up or lemonade

amen wallah   A Naval padre or chaplain. See also *Bible basher, *Bible puncher, *bish, *Devil dodger, *God botherer, *God walloper, *Holy Joe, *sin bosun, *sky pilot

anchor-faced   Someone, usually an officer, who lives and breathes the *Royal Navy* even when retired, as on page **B** - 19. See also *Corps-pissed (*RM*)

anchor watch   A special watch kept while at anchor during a storm, to detect a dragging *pick; also used to describe Jack's anxious and frequent examination of his *toggle and two following success on the previous evening's *run-ashore

..and like it !   Older expression, usually tacked on the end of an order to perform some unpleasant or dirty job, and which forestalls any complaint: *"Right lads - you two, leap away to the top of that mast, clear the jammed halyard..and like it !"*

Andrew (the)   Widespread nickname for the Royal Navy used by all ranks within the Senior Service, especially when referring to length of time in uniform: *"Fifteen years in the **Andrew**, and most of that spent at sea.."* Nothing to do with the Duke of York (despite his being a serving *RN* officer) but said to be named after *Lieutenant Andrew Miller*, a highly successful press-gang officer of the 18th century, and thus also more completely referred to by older *hands as **the Andrew Miller**. See also *Impressment

Angels whisper   A *Defaulters parade, nicely depicted in this sense by Tugg on page **B**-49

angles and dangles *(SM)*   High speed manoeuvres in a submarine, involving large *trim angles of rise and dive

angry palm tree   A *burning and turning helicopter

animal   Half-admiring description of an individual whose social and sexual activity would be considered excessive in most quarters: *"Five pints of Old *Doobrey an' Ginge turns into a right **animal**, 'e does.."* Can also be used as an adjective (esp. *RM*) to describe an outstanding or memorable *run-ashore

ankle biter / ankle snapper   A small child that has just started to crawl. See also *rug rat and *carpet crawler

ante-
 1. A *Wardroom **ante-room** usually adjoins the dining room itself
 2. **ante-up** - make payment, usually of the stake money for a bet
 3. **up the ante** - increase the stakes in a deal or discussion

any fool can be uncomfortable *(RM)*   Splendid and sensible advice given by instructors at *Lympstone to recruits learning the business of fieldcraft. All it takes to be warm, dry and happy in the field is a correct attitude and the determined application of some acquired knowledge

ape-shit (esp. *RM*)   Descriptive adjective for someone who is extremely angry or upset: *"The *Boss went totally **ape-shit** when he heard about that missing weapon.."*

apples
 1. Rough cider or scrumpy
 2. Older term for pay - perhaps derived from the **golden apples** of mythology

Appointer   Naval Officer working in the *Madhouse who is responsible for the career development of officers in various specializations, in turn reporting to to the *Naval Secretary*, who is a Rear Admiral. In the old days, *NavSec* was *Naval Assistant to the Second Sea Lord*, and was said to take a keen interest in what the young chaps wanted - in order to be able to disappoint them !

Arch Tiff   The senior Artificer (Engineering Warrant Officer)

Arctic fox *(RM)*   A frozen turd lying in the snow

arduous duty tot   A special *tot awarded to men who have completed some particularly difficult or unpleasant operational task, such as the *seaboat crew recovering dead bodies, or First Aid teams exposed to unpleasant or hazardous conditions while tending injured survivors. This issue of spirit is still authorised in *QRRN 4924 para 2; the author utilised this provision in the Ajax Bay field hospital on twelve occasions during the land battles of the Falklands campaign

Argyll Bowl *(RM)*   Challenge cup for an annual Rugby Football competition; the trophy was presented to the Corps by the *Argyll and Sutherland Highlanders* to commemorate the close and happy association between Royal and the Jocks, particularly during the fighting around Singapore during WW2. See *Tunney Cup for the Association Football equivalent

ARK   HMS *ARK ROYAL*, currently the sixth ship to bear her famous name

Armstrong patent   Nice expression used at the turn of this century which almost boasts of the absence of any mechanical aids on a sailing ship, in that all the hard work is achieved solely through the strong arms of her crew. *Handraulic and *mandraulic are the more modern versions

arrigones   Tinned Italian tomatoes; one of the major suppliers in the early days of this commodity was a gentleman named *Signor A. Riggoni* who had his name in large letters all over the labels. The eponymous term persists to this day

arisings   Material left over after the completion of a task; these may be valuable and require accounting for, but they may also be worthless, as in: *"This *civvy *chippy didn't bother to tidy up as he worked. The whole *compartment was knee-deep in **arisings**.."*

arrival *(FAA)*   Understatement for the hard touchdown of an aircraft on landing. Fixed-wing carrier aviation remains a supreme test of piloting skills; conventional jet aircraft like the *Toom and *Bucc had to be placed accurately, at high approach speeds and sink rates, onto a relatively tiny area in order to pick up one of three arrester wires. Each landing was in effect an **arrival** - or a barely-controlled crash. Although the amazing *SHAR is now operated on the *"Why land and stop - when you can now stop and land ?"* principle, the older term persists in the *FAA*. Getting a *Lynx down in severe weather onto a pitching and rolling frigate flight deck requires native ability, some training - and a *navalised undercarriage

Arrows !   Exclamation of admiration and congratulation derived from the game of darts, but can be used in a wider context to mean *Well done ! or* Good shot !

arse   The familiar, although crude slang word for the buttocks or posterior, employed by Jack in a number of particular phrases:
my arse ! - expression of disbelief
arse about - to waste time in an ineffective manner
arse about face - back to front
arse bandit - a homosexual
doesn't know his **arse from his elbow** - he's rather unsure of his job
tear the **arse out of it** - overuse or exhaust a good thing
arse over teakettle - head over heels (*Wardroom)
arse over tit - as above (*messdeck)
tear him up for **arse paper** - give him a really hard time
arse-up duck - any bottom-feeding bird (eg. a swan)

arseholed   Vulgar term, often prefixed with the adverbs *absolutely* or *totally* to imply extreme drunkeness

Arthur, Martha or Mabel   Another amusing term for someone unsure of his job, or a little confused: *"He'd had that many *wets he'd forgotten whether he was **Arthur, Martha or Mabel**.."* See also *punched, bored or countersunk

Articles of War   Formidable 17th century document laying down the duties of Royal Navy personnel and the draconian penalties to be suffered by those who fail to carry them out. They have now been ratified by Parliament, and incorporated into the Naval Discipline Act. A copy is secured at some highly visible place in every ship of the *Fleet. The final **Article** is also known as the *Captain's Cloak because it even authorises punishment for any misdemeanour or offence not mentioned in any of the previous **Articles**

as long as (your) arse points downwards   Expression used to reinforce some definitive statement: *"As long as his arse points downwards, young Robin won't make it as a *Looker.."* This implies that some rather radical changes will have to take place if this opinion is to be proved wrong

ascend   See discussion at *scend

ashore   Anywhere that is not *on board, or anything on the shore side of the *brow. Jack will also describe the action of passing through the main gate of a Dockyard or Naval air station as **going ashore**, whether he does so by car or on foot. See also *run-ashore

A-9

Bag shanty

ashtray on a motorbike   Label for some poorly-designed piece of *kit: *"Honestly, it's about as much use as an **ashtray on a motorbike**.."*   See also *chocolate fireguard / teapot

assault with a friendly weapon   Sexual intercourse; in this context, see also *receiving swollen property

assy *(FAA)*   Abbreviation of **assymetric**, and applied to an individual with ears of different sizes or position

astern   Behind the stern, or if moving astern - going backwards. The advice to an officer that he or she is **going astern** means that his or her shoulder rank badges have been (incorrectly) reversed. The phrase **astern of station** can also be used to describe a programme that is running behind time, as well as something that is to the rear of its correct position

at the rush   As fast as possible; this expression was memorably abused once when a cavalry regiment was billetted in the Belfast accommodation ship HMS *MAIDSTONE*, manned in part by Royal. A *pipe was made for a certain *Corporal of Horse* to go to the *brow at the gallop !

Auction of kit   The sale, by open bidding as at an auction, of the personal kit of some deceased member of a ship's company or RM Unit. Outrageous sums of money can then be offerred for the most useless items, with the article often returned to the pool for re-auction. The proceeds of such a kit auction are then passed by the *Jaunty, via the ship's ledger account, to the deceased's widow or family. The older term for this procedure was a *sale before the mast

auto   Two meanings:
  1. Abbreviation of automatic, usually implying loss of temper: *"If you mention the Secretary of State for Defence's name to the Captain he'll simply go off in **auto**.."*
  2. *(FAA)* **Autorotation** of a helicopter, the process of descent following loss of engine power; the resulting airflow through the rotor disc keeps the blades turning. The aircraft glides down, but limited pitch control is still maintained - and then used to cushion final *arrival on the ground

Avast !   Dated but still used command to cease an action or procedure, and stop immediately

Avquack *(FAA)*   Aviation medicine specialist

awash   Half-submerged. Sometimes employed graphically with food or drink: *"No thanks, Yorks..I couldn't *hack another mouthful - me back teeth are **awash**.."*

Away lifeboat !   Verbal order to lower the duty *seaboat and crew as quickly as possible in order to save life. In older times the *seaboat would be manned by the nearest seamen to it when this order was *piped

Awkward   Standard name for a ship's defensive operational procedure in harbour when facing attack by underwater swimmers

Aye Aye !   Technically correct reply to a challenging ship, on being hailed, when there is an officer on board. See also *No No !* and *Flag !*

Aye aye, sir !   The *seamanlike reply given in acknowledgement of an officer's order, sometimes with a slightly sardonic emphasis on the second syllable to indicate Jack's opinion of its worth

BRAVO

B 13   Form of notification from *Drafty that a rating has risen to the top of a promotion *roster and that when medical fitness is confirmed, he or she will be promoted on the date specified

B's (pronounced *Bees*) *(SM)*   Reference to **Mrs. Beeton** and her celebrated cook-book - **Mrs. B's and thickers** is a rich sponge pudding topped with evaporated or condensed milk

babies' bag rations   The female breasts. See also *BSH, *lumpy jumper and *double bumps

babies' heads   Steak and kidney puddings

baby spanner   The male sexual organ; this device dispenses *baby gravy*

back-afty *(SM)*   Propulsion machinery *Tiff in a submarine, working **back aft** in the nuclear reactor control area or diesel machinery spaces

back in date *(FAA)*   Recently successful in sexual terms, because most *Fleet Air Arm* professional skills require regular inspections and checks, with the need to be **in date** for their currency; another phrase, with an identical meaning, refers to *getting your logbook stamped

back in the saddle *(FAA)*   Descriptive phrase for the refamiliarization flying undertaken by aircrew following a leave period

back teeth awash *(RM)*   See also *awash, but Royal also uses this expression for someone who is very drunk indeed

backside of the drag curve *(FAA)*   Expression denoting a fairly hopeless situation in which a wing's increasingly high angle of attack is creating more drag than actual lift. In this state, no matter how much thrust is applied, the wing will eventually stall: *"Running an elderly sports car is like being on the **backside of the** drag curve **as** far as my wallet is concerned.."*

backy dips　　Extra swimming lessons for backward swimmers

badgeman　　Any rating with one or more *Good Conduct badges* on the left sleeve of his uniform suit. Each gold (or red) chevron indicates four years of completed service. Fifteen years of what Jack tends to describe as undetected crime leads on to the *Pea-Doo or *Blue Peter; see also *three badger

badger *(FAA)*　　Aircraft handlers on a carrier flight deck wear different coloured surcoats for easy identification. In a previous generation of carriers like the *ARK, the stokers (*steamies) responsible for her catapults and jet-blast deflectors had white ones with a broad black stripe, resembling a **badger's coat.** Sad to relate, such skills are no longer relevant in the *SHAR era, and there are no **badgers** to be seen now *topsides alongside the other *roof rats during *flying stations

Bag　　Nickname for the *AEW (Airborne Early Warning)* version of the *Sea King helicopter, whose development was hastened greatly following lessons learned in the 1982 South Atlantic conflict; this aircraft carries a retractable radar aerial outside the fuselage, housed in an inflatable and pressurised rubber **bag**

bag and hammock   Jack's traditional nickname for his wife, but it can also be used to describe the sum total of Jack's personal possessions: *"She kicked him out, bag and hammock.."*

bag mealies   *Fishery Protection Squadron* nickname for the minehunter vessels which *day run from port, whereas the *FPS* ships may stay out on patrol for two weeks at a time

bag off (esp. *RM*)   Sexual intercourse; note also its application in the phrase *beer, big eats, **bag off** and back on board

bag rats   Light snack meal (usually packed in a cardboard box !)

bag shanty   A brothel or red-light district bar (see cartoon on page A -10); this also used to be the nickname of HMS *BACCHANTE*

bagger   Common unit measure of female beauty - or the lack of it:
1. A **one** (paper) **bagger** implies an unattractive face
2. A **two bagger** / **double bagger** indicates some anxiety that one bag might fall off
3. A **three bagger** / **triple bagger** ?   Heaven forbid !
See also *bulldog, *coyote, *stumper, *wildebeeste and *wolverine in this particular context

balbo *(FAA)*   Large formation of aircraft, usually for a fly-past, thus preserving the memory of *General Italo **Balbo***. Between the two World Wars this distinguished (and rather pro-British) aviator was responsible for the development of Mussolini's air power, and is especially remembered for a round-the-world seaplane expedition that he commanded

ballast   Material used to maintain the trim or stability of a ship but of little other use, hence a description of someone's worth:

"He's reliable, but not very bright - ballast really.." There is another special usage: *"He can't half **carry some ballast**.."* in the description of someone who can hold his liquor well

ball-bagged *(RM)*　　　　Alternative version of *chin-strapped; extremely tired as a result of physical endeavour, lack of sleep - or both

ballistic　　Similar to *banzai or *ape-shit, but used to indicate some senior officer's especial anger: *"If you dare to comment on the quality of his paperwork, our senior *schoolie tends to go a bit ballistic.."*

balls-ache (esp. *RM*)　　Something tiresome or very time-consuming

balls-out　　With maximum despatch, or as fast as possible

balls-up　　An error of quite significant proportions

banana boat　　　　Older affectionate term for an aircraft carrier, stemming from the *MAC ships of WW2 that had been hastily converted from general freighters. Now used also as an extra name for the *canteen boat in a minesweeper squadron

bandstand　　Several applications, depending on context:
1. The protective framework around an upperworks gun mounting
2. A cruet holding salt, pepper and mustard
3. *(SM)* Waist-high circular guardrail or support for the *Officer of the Watch* in a nuclear submarine, allowing him to remain steady behind the seated planesmen if the *boat heels at high speed underwater. See also *angles and dangles in this context

bandwagon *(RM)*　　Tracked oversnow vehicle - the Bv 202 or 206

Bandy　　Traditional (older) nickname for anyone called Evans

bandy *(RM)*　　Any member of the Royal Marines' Band Service

bang　　Sexual intercourse, esp. when used by Royal in conjunction with the adjective *belt-fed

bang box　　Gun turret

bang on / banging on　　Boring everyone to death about some subject very dear to the speaker's heart

bang out *(FAA)*　　Use an aircraft's ejection seat - its **bang seat** - or else leave a party that is still going strong

bang stick　　A rifle; may also be a corruption of the Arabic word *bundook* for rifle

banjo   Two meanings:
1. Hit someone or something very hard
2. Sandwich, originally created from all (or most of) a French loaf, and then filled with a variety of contents. A common variant is the **egg banjo** involving a fried egg

Bank of Israel   The spiritual home of all financial acumen in the world. Someone clever with money or knowledgeable about investments may be described as *drafted to the **Bank of Israel** - *for instructional duties...*

banyan   Tropical picnic held ashore by a ship's company while deployed at sea. Often the beach chosen is on some deserted island, so clothing becomes bright and colourful - **banyan rig** - and the informal tone of proceedings is both relaxed and refreshing for Officers and ratings alike. Its origin lies in the meatless **Banyan days** of the old Navy which were abolished in 1825 - and not with the pleasant shade that might be afforded by a **banyan tree**. Jack would try and keep some sort of cooked meat provisions aside to *tide himself over these *bare days

banzai *(RM)*   Frenzied, half-crazy: *"When 'e heard about his missus and the milkman, Chalky went banzai.."*

bar chit   An all-purpose piece of paper supplied in booklet form in *Wardroom bars, exchangable (when signed !) for drinks. It can also be used as loose-leaf diary, address book, note-pad or *(FAA)* an instructional medium for explaining tricky principles of flight, usually after about five pints of beer

bare Navy   Older term for a poorly *victualled ship in which the food conformed to the laid down scales of issue - and no more. Later on it was applied to someone without any additional financial means who had to live **bare Navy** on his pay alone

barge   Ceremonial, much-gilded and oared vessel of olden times; the term still applies to more modern methods of transportation. The Captain's personal motor launch is his **barge**, while any helicopter or aeroplane used to carry a *Flag Officer automatically becomes an **Admiral's Barge** - when not described by its more usual nickname of *Green Parrot ! The term may also be used to describe a flat wooden serving dish, such as a **biscuit barge** or **bread barge**

baron   A legendary source of gratuitous issue or generous hospitality. Anything free in the Navy was said to be **on the baron** rather than on the house; the process of taking advantage of a well-off *civvy individual or organization is known as **baron strangling**. See also the terms *beer, *rum and *tickler baron for a slightly different application and meaning

barrack damages   Financial charge levied against the pay account of whoever is responsible for the misuse or breakage of furniture or decorative items, even if these are actually in a Married Quarter !

barrack stanchion   Derogatory description of someone who deliberately avoids sea duty, or who has had a seemingly endless succession of shore jobs in his career

barracks   That part of a warship's *messdecks occupied by her Royal Marines *Detachment

Barracuda *(FAA)*   Important WW2 *Fleet Air Arm* aircraft of great ugliness which attracted criticism and affection in equal amounts. Designed as a torpedo carrier and dive bomber, early prototypes of this high-wing monoplane had an unpleasant tendency to flick inverted when the dive brakes were extended and flaps lowered. This was cured eventually, but these lethal habits - plus the ether-based hydraulic fluid that could anaesthetize the pilot silently in his enclosed cockpit, and the rivets which had an alarming tendency to spring from over-stressed wings, led to a famous *FAA* song being composed to the tune of *Any Old Iron* ! Despite all this, carrier-borne *Barras* did enormous damage to *TIRPITZ* in Tromso Fjord, before high-level bombing by the *Dambusters* of 617 Sqn *RAF* finished off this German pocket battleship

barrel fever   The hangover caused by a beer *sesh; see also *CSB **rash**

barrico   Pronounced *breaker*; a small wooden water cask stored in a lifeboat that could also be partially *broken out or *scuttled in an emergency as a water butt

base over apex   Politer conversational version of *arse over tit

bash the bishop   Masturbate

basha *(RM)*   Any temporary shelter constructed in the field, usually out of naturally available materials; the origins of this term lie in jungle warfare, a highly specialized art in which *RM* *Commando *jungle bunnies maintain significant and continuing expertise

basinful (of that)   Sardonic response to a person using some long or learned word; now also employed in admiration of a particularly busty or curvaceous female: *"Wow - I'll have a basinful of that !"* Note the term *BSH as well

Batch *(RM)*   Nickname for the annual intake of Young Officers entering *Lympstone for their officer and *Commando training. The members of this grouping will always identify themselves for the rest of their days by that **Batch number**, and usually meet for a celebration dinner at *CTCRM twenty-five years on, whatever their subsequent destinies turn out to be. The Guest of Honour on these occasions is always their **Batch Nurse**, who is usually delighted to find that the **Batch spirit** still prevails - unless of course they were a bunch of particularly *dank hands ! See also *YO

Anchor-faced

Bats   Nickname for a small ship's Flight Deck Officer, who guides helicopters onto a frigate using bats made of wire frames and brightly-coloured cloth strips. He is the direct descendant of the aviator who, long before helicopters or mirror-landing sights, was crucial to the process of *recovering aircraft on board. The **Bats** of that era stood on a raised platform with dive-nets all around in case some *Bloggs got it all wrong !

bats   Naval heavy shoes or *(FAA)* flightdeck boots with steel toecaps: *"'E was wearin' this bloody great pair of *pussers' **steamin' bats**.."*

batting on a sticky wicket   *Two's up in the coital sense

battle bowler   Older name for a tin helmet

battlewagon   Older nickname for a capital ship; see also the term *****pusser's battlewagon**

bazzy   Abbreviated use of the word *bastard* when referring to mood or demeanour: *"Watch out for the Chief, Sunshine - he's got a real **bazzy on** this morning.."*

BDV *(RM)*   *Blue Drinking Voucher* - a £5 note. Interestingly, a **BDV** was also the name of a between-wars cigarette that came with free coupons towards a range of gifts. One correspondent still has his clockwork Basset-Lowke railway from that era

bean stealer   Someone who is *RA but slips back on board early for a breakfast that he is not really entitled to. Now used also for the kind of person who never buys torch batteries, but always *acquires them from *Pusser instead

Beano   Jack's nickname for a certain type of Commander or *Jimmy who is always adressing the ship's company in a negative sense: *"There will **be no** (this) until further notice, and until (such-and-such) improves there will **be no** (that) either.."*

beans in a row   Phrase used to indicate a form of general agreement: *"If anyone should raise this point, then we've all got our **beans in a row** on the subject.."* *Singing from the same hymn sheet is an alternative version

bear pit   A stokers's *messdeck, or *(SM)* the lower aft section of a diesel *boat's engine room

***Beastie** (FAA)*   Nickname for the Supermarine *Attacker* jet aircraft of the early 50's which was heartily disliked by its pilots for tricks like folding its wingtips in mid-air, or its engine stalling when the guns were fired

beasting *(RM)*   Heavy physical training designed to improve muscular strength and general fitness; usually delivered in good humour - see *It's only pain - but recently also associated with bullying behaviour

Beat Retreat   Formal use of military drummers, originally to end an episode of fighting, or to mark the day's completion in the sense that citizens working outside a walled city by day were summoned inside for protection during the night. Now combined with the Naval *Sunset ceremony - the *Yacht's *bandies are particularly adept at this spectacular and moving piece of ceremonial

beat up *(RM)*   The process of intensive physical self-preparation prior to an attempt at passing the *Commando course

becket   Small loop of rope or nylon tape sewn into an item of clothing or safety equipment

bedroom boatrope   Yet another term for the male sexual organ

bedstead / double bedstead   Type 965 radar rotating aerial

beef screen   Originally the butcher's compartment in a large warship, but the term still describes a ready-use meat cold store in both *RM* barracks and HM Ships

beefer   One of the very few words in general usage which have entirely different meanings when used by Jack or Royal:
   (RM / RN)   A homosexual
   (FAA)   A flying instructor
This latter label has two possible origins - either **B for bastard** or: *"He's always beefing at me.."* Whatever the true explanation is, Royal Marines aircrew trained by the *Fleet Air Arm* must exercise very great caution when describing this experience to their green-bereted *oppos

beer baron   .   Someone who uses tins of beer (illegally) as a form of currency to give and receive favours

beer, *big eats, *bag off - and back on board   Jack's definition of a superlative *run-ashore

beer bosun   The messdeck rating responsible for maintaining the *beer locker. Can also be used for someone with an excessive fondness for *CSB

beer locker   A domestic refrigerator fitted with hasp and padlock, and installed in each messdeck. The keys are collected every evening at *pipe down. Jack's basic entitlement is three tins a day, but many sailors prefer not to drink at sea. The privilege of being able to invite family and friends down to the *messdeck while in port is a jealously-guarded one; it is also one of the few ways in which Jack can repay civilians who have taken him *up homers. The system is self-regulating in that abuse by one individual leads to collective punishment; the padlock is changed and its keys retained by the *Jaunty for a suitable period while the man is *picturised by his messmates. It is also a particular pleasure for Jack and Royal to invite their colleagues from the US Navy and Marine Corps on board for a *wet, since the supposedly *bigger and better* American ships are also totally dry

beer tokens *(RM)*   Pound coins

beetle crushers   Two versions:
1. Older term for members of the *Reggies Branch
2. *Jenny's nickname for her flat parade shoes, as worn for *Divisions

beetle watch   Jack's name for a cheap wristwatch of the era before digital models became commonplace. They were apparently powered by a small insect, which **beetled** around inside the case to work the hands, but then usually went *tits up just as soon as Jack was back at sea !

Beira bucket   A *pusser's galvanised bucket, both artistically and highly decorated, and played for as a trophy by ships mounting the **Beira patrol** between 1970 and 1974. This was a typically instinctive response to the threat of boredom; the sports involved were specified by the defending ship, and *jungle rules applied. The term is now used on occasion to describe any impromptu trophy played for by ships in company and detached from home waters

Belay !   General order to stop, or cease doing something. ***Belay the last *pipe !*** or ***Belay my last !*** is an instruction to ignore any previous message

Below !   Traditional warning cry when lowering or throwing something down - either between decks or over the side

bell end   The glans penis

Belle Isle *(RM)*   *Corps memorable date based on the 7 June 1761 action at the siege and assault on **Belle Isle** in Quiberon Bay. The laurel wreath of the Corps colours and badges commemorate the spirit and gallantry displayed by the two Marine battalions that fought throughout this fierce action

Bells, Smells and Yells   Jack's wonderful description of the island of *Malta GC which, in the days of the Mediterranean Fleet at least, seemed to consist mainly of churches, open drains, noisy children and goats. See also the *Ghut / Gut

bells in the head   Slightly mad

belt-fed *(RM)*   Adjective which increases any descriptive impact by an an order of magnitude, for instance: *"She *bangs like a **belt-fed** *Wombat.."*

belter   Something excellent, or a black-eye

BEM   Very unofficially - *Bunk Endurance Medal*

(the) **Bends**   Widely used general nickname for the many manifestations of *decompression sickness*. If a diver has been breathing compressed air at depth for more than a certain time, some of the extra dissolved nitrogen in his blood may form bubbles within the venous circulation. These return to the heart and are pumped out again; depending on their final destination these bubbles may cause obstruction in the:
   Lungs - known as the **chokes**
   Brain and spinal cord - called the **staggers**
   Skin - the **creeps**
   Joints - the **bends**, since the limbs are **bent** painfully

Benny   Current slang name for a *kelper* (Falkland Islander); the term is reputed to have been banned from use ashore by local military order in 1983. Jack soon got round that problem in his usual inimitable way, as shown by the following selection:
   Benny Arcade - Stanley fairground
   Bennydiction - local accent
   Bennyficial - Sir Rex Hunt !
   Bennyficiary - seafood processing plant
   Bennyfit - reaction to any suggestion of parochialism

Benny Hill - Mount Tumbledown
Bennylin - locally-mixed cough medicine
Bennytentiary - the cells in Stanley police station
See also *Stills and *Whens

bent   Jack's typical understatement for anything broken, or
something that has been severely damaged. A signal flag is also **bent** on
to its halyard before being hoisted. Also, because a rope is similarly
bent on to another one before being **spliced** to it, the phrase **bent on a
splice** refers to a sailor who is about to get married. Note also the
application of **bent** in the diving sense described under *Bends

bent shot   Homosexual - the term may be Glaswegian in origin

berseyquack *(RM)*   Alliteration of the word *berserk*, and hence a
very useful alternative to *banzai

bevvy   Glaswegian and Liverpudlian patter word for a drink,
widely adopted: *"Coming *ashore for a few bevvies, *Wings ?"*

Bible basher / puncher   Vicar; see alternatives under *amen wallah

Biblical code   Both the *Old* and the *New Testament* have a
traditional place in the Yeoman of Signal's ready-use library on the
bridge of HM Ships. There are times and circumstances when a Biblical
reference conveys more understanding and support (and even humour) in
a single line than any long and multi-part message could in several
paragraphs:
   *From **HM WARSHIP** to **CinC PLYMOUTH***:
ROMAN EMPEROR IN TOW BADLY DAMAGED PLEASE SEND TUGS

   *From **CinCPLYMOUTH** to **HM WARSHIP***:
REVELATIONS Chapter 3 Verse 11 [1]

Biff   Gentleman of non-European and distinctly African
origin; derived from the cartoon character of ***Biffo the Bear***. Another
explanation is a more chauvinistic one, namely that these letters stand
for *Bloody Ignorant (Flipping) Foreigner*. Most interestingly, *RM* usage
has this as a general term of abuse for anyone clumsy

biff   Two applications:
   1. Masturbate
   2. *(FAA)* Break wind: *"Ruddy Norah ! 'Oo biffed ?"*

Biffin's bridge   The female perineum, which Jack might define a
bit more succinctly as the shelf between her *playpen and the *gash
chute(2). Perhaps the term's origin lies in the fact that it is this
structure that he keeps **biffing** against. May also be written as
***Baffin's bridge**

---

1 Behold I come quickly : hold that fast which thou hast, that no man
   take thy crown

Big Dipper   A *Sea King helicopter when working as part of a *NATO* *dip gang with other (smaller) sonar-carrying helicopters

big eats   A large or special meal: *"The hospitality in Miami Beach was unbelievable; big eats every night with a different *grippo.."* See the entry *bag off for an additional applicaton

big girl's blouse *(RM)*   Wonderful term of abuse, originally employed for bulky and unfit new recruits breathing heavily, but now used more widely for anyone faint-hearted - or a chronic worrier

big reds *(FAA)*   Large red-handled pliers that are a standard and vital component of a *grubber's toolbox

big soft Nellie (esp. *RM*)   Enough said !

Biggles   Traditional nickname for the Flight Commander embarked in a warship; note that *Pilot is a term reserved for the Navigating Officer

bight   A loop of rope, which may tauten at any time, hence: *"Never stand with one foot in a bight.."*

bilge-free   Older term for someone full of booze, but just sober enough to pass scrutiny at the *brow when returning on board. Derived from the description of a correctly stowed and full cask as being *bung-up and bilge-free*

bilges   The lowest part of a ship, where a foul and noxious mixture of sea water and rain collected. The expression **bilge water** is used to describe something that tastes particularly unpleasant, or an opinion that is of little value; a **bilge rat** is an unpopular person, usually because of his unpleasant personal habits

Bill of Health   Declaration by a ship's Master that he has no contagious diseases on board and that his vessel has not arrived from a port where an epidemic of some kind is prevalent. This expression has now also come ashore in a non-maritime sense: *"I got the RAC to look at the car before I bought it, and they gave it a reasonably clean **bill of health**.."*

bill-poster's bucket   Jack's description of a busy lady of the night with well-used working parts

billet   Appointment or position within an organization: *"I asked *Drafty for a Married Accompanied **billet** in *Honkers. Guess what his reply was.."*

bimble *(RM)*   Anything slower than a *yomp, whether on skis or on foot (see illustration on page L - 177); the *Fleet Air Arm* also use this term for a relaxed piece of transit flying

bin   Get rid of, or abandon something. The word can be used in both direct and indirect senses, but is usually employed when referring to the abstract: *"We **binned** the project, but didn't *ditch the trials *kit - I used that for something else instead.."*

binge   The operation of rinsing out a storage cask to prepare it for new contents; modern methods of storage have rendered this word obsolete in the maritime sense, but the idea behind it has come ashore to describe the good rinsing out that results from a prolonged drinking session

Bingo fuel *(FAA)*   Minimum landing allowance; if your fuel state is down to **Bingo** levels and *Mother cannot be found, then the *reasons in writing may develop quite quickly into an *A 25

bird cage   A *WRNS accomodation block

birdbath *(RM)*   Method of maintaing personal hygiene in the field when water is in short supply. The participant stands in a half-filled washing-up bowl, soaps himself all over, and then uses the same water to rinse off

biscuit   Kneaded cakes of flour that were baked with the least quantity of water possible and then stored, as a bread substitute, on board. The advent of ship's bakeries made this staple feature of Jack's diet obsolete after WW1, but the expression *that really takes the biscuit* - in addition to the technique of **biscuit** baking itself - now has a wider meaning

Bish   Padre or chaplain; the *FAA* has **BISHTAX** as a (taxi) sortie to carry the padre between ships in a group. See *Amen wallah for other descriptive variants

bite   Spoof or deception played against someone, particularly when he or she has a strongly-held or cherished belief that cannot normally be the subject of humour in their conversation: *"*Scribes fancies himself for *Upper Yardie, although he's a right *pickle-jar* *rating. The boys got him on a cracking **bite** last week when he volunteered for *splash target coxswain..*" A pleasant way to defuse the situation when the person involved **bites hard** is to ask for your hook back ! See also *spoof

BITS   Beans In Tomato Sauce; see also *-ITS

bitter end   The inboard length of a ship's cable which, in the case of a ship's anchor cable, was secured to special strong points called **bitts**. If the cable was run out all the way it was at the **bitter end**, hence the popular expression for something at its limits

bivvy *(RM)*   Abbreviation of *bivouac shelter*; used as noun or verb: *"Just before dawn, we **bivvied-up** in a forest near the objective.."*

Black Angus   Near-legendary establishment with a highly dubious reputation, situated in San Juan, Puerto Rico

black as Jack's hat   *"It's dark outside !"*

black catter   A person who always tries to go one better, whatever your story or achievement. If you had a ***big black cat***, then he would have one too, only his would be bigger and blacker - (Note however that it is just possible he owns a panther..)

Black Day   *31st July 1970,* when the last *tot was drawn in the *Fleet around the globe; a rather touchy subject with the old and bold !

black drizzle   Diarrhoea

black ham   Collective noun for ladies of the night in Africa, especially in Mombasa; for Jack or Royal to seek their company in the pre-AIDS era was known as *going for a **slice of black ham***

black lighting *(SM)*   State of the control room lighting before returning to periscope depth at night

black maskers   Sticky masking tape of great durability and adhesive properties: *"If the Russians ever invent a ray that dissolves **black maskers**, then we might as well *wrap..."* Also an essential component (along with a large hammer) of the *RM repair kit

Black Mass   After-hours (and illegal) consumption of *neaters left over as *Queen's and then bottled

black outs   Black curtain material used in the *evolution of *darken ship. Also a nickname for the WW2 ***black knickers*** issued to *Wrens, although whether this was because they totally obscured the target (or because of their actual effect on Jack) is still unclear ! See also *passion killers

Handcarted

blackshod *(RM)* Operations in mountainous areas that are not actually Arctic in description, where and when *whiteshod* techniques would be appropriate

Black Stump Australian expression for somewhere very distant, now adopted by Jack and used in a similar way to *Nagasaki: "He's the biggest liar this side of the **Black Stump..**"

black watch *(SM)* The unofficial fifth watch of the normal four-watch system in a submarine, ie. those ratings who have been left *inboard for some official reason, but are still on the *boat's books

blank week When the Navy was paid fortnightly this was the week just before pay day, since it described the usual content of Jack's pockets. The associated **blank weekend** also forced a penniless Jack to remain on board

blanket stacker Dismissive nickname for a *Jack Dusty

blat   Two possible meanings:
  1. A new word for foreign currency where large numbers are involved, like Italian lire. These can then be grouped as required into **kiloblats** (thousands) or **megablats** (millions)
  2. Hit someone rather hard, or defeat him / them rather comprehensively (as an alternative to *frapped)

blazer   A smart dress jacket chosen (and supplied) by the Captain of HMS *BLAZER* for his gig crew in 1845, before the *bluejacket concept became standard as part of a laid-down uniform. It featured a short jacket with multi-coloured vertical stripes, a feature that lives on at Henley each year and is *still* associated with rowing and oarsmen !

blimp   A senior or rather stuffy *Pongo, from the famous cartoonist Low's expressive 1930's character *Colonel Blimp* - whose dimensions rather resembled those of the small non-rigid airships used by *RN Air Service* flyers in WW1. The Naval aviators gave their craft that title because a War Office manual stated that airships were of two kinds - (a)rigid and (b)limp !

blob   Several applications:
  1. Floating surface marker used in diving operations
  2. A skin boil. To **blob up** is to acquire a social disease
  3. **On the blob** refers to menstruation
  4. **A blob** is created on an *Uckers board by the process of **blobbing up**, or the creation of a pile of two or more of your own (or partner's) counters in order to block the opposition. A **triple blob** requires the throwing of two consecutive *double sixes to overcome, and so on. A *mixy **blob** that includes an opponent's counters as well has no obstructive value
  5. Older *RM* usage has **score a blob** in the same sense as *make a boob* or *drop a bollock*

block sweeps *(RM)*   A person employed on barrack cleaning duties: "No use asking me, mate - I'm just the *block sweeps*.."

Blockhouse *(SM)*   **Fort Blockhouse**, HMS *DOLPHIN*, Gosport - the spiritual home of British submarines and submariners for over fifty years. The excellent Submarine Museum and HMS *ALLIANCE* (a preserved A-Class *boat) are both open to the public and situated nearby

Bloggs *(FAA)*   Generic name for all student aircrew. This label is borrowed from the *Royal Air Force*, who even have an excellent cartoon character concerned with the adventures of this mythical chap

Bloke   Nickname accorded to the Commander or XO (*Executive Officer*) of a large warship or shore establishment; under this particular convention the Captain is *Father.   Note that in some ships *Father is actually a Commander in rank - or less. His XO then is the First Lieutenant, also known as the *Jimmy, or *Jimmy the One

blood   Several interesting usages here:

1. **blood bucket** - lifeboat; synonym for a blood wagon (ambulance)
2. **blood chit** - signed authorisation to fly as a passenger in a Service aircraft
3. **blood for breakfast** - warning of serious trouble looming
4. **blood red** - the colour of *distinction cloth inserted into the rank *lace of RN Medical Officers. For this reason the annual *RN Medical Club* dinner is always known as the **Blood Red Dinner**
5. **blood-stained** - a meeting or event where serious differences of opinion are anticipated, or have already taken place
6. **blood money** - older term (esp. *RM*) for a service gratuity or sum of prize money

blow *(SM)*   The process of **blowing** water-displacing **air** into a *boat's ballast and trim tanks in order to control or adjust her buoyancy. The old method of discharging sewage from a submarine was called **blowing shit** but this has now been replaced by the less noisy and slightly more refined process of *pumping poo

Blow Q ! (SM)   The rapid emptying of a ***Quick-acting*** trim tank at the fore ends of a submarine which can be flooded to allow rapid descent at a steep dive angle.   See also **Flood Q !* in this respect

blow the bilges down   Defaecate

blow the horns off a bull   Older description of great wind strength

blow through   Euphemism for sexual intercourse

Blow you, Jack !   Expression characterising official indifference to any real or imagined problem involving the *lower deck. Can also be used to portray a selfish attitude: *"**Blow you, Jack** - I'm *inboard.."*

blowback   An *Uckers move according to *Wafu rules that is made against an opponent waiting by the *shit chute to *suck back your pieces before they can get home. If this move is carried out around the corner it becomes a **bendy blowback**

blower   Telephone; this term originated with the early speaking-tube communication system between Bridge and Engine room

blowing the grampus   The process of waking a sleeping sailor who is supposed to be on watch by chucking bucket of cold water over him. The resulting effect was similar to that of a **grampus** (whale) blowing on the surface

blubber   Cry; the word originates from whaling days and the globules of fat (mimicking teardrops) that dripped down the carcass during the process of *flensing*

blue card man   Blue *station card of a special dutyman who is not required for routine watchkeeping, and therefore available for his special duties at any time. Conversely, a **blue card man** is also able to go ashore at any time providing those duties have been completed

Blue Circle radar   The first *SHARs were delivered without their **Blue Fox** radar sets; these were temporarily substituted for by a shaped lump of concrete inside the nose cone

Blue forces   Light **blue** is the colour of *NATO*, so one side in any *NATO* exercise always adopts this shade to oppose the *Orange forces of the *Warsaw Pact*. When friendly forces actually engage their own side in wartime due to some error or terrible misunderstanding, the incident is termed a **blue-on-blue**

Blue liners   Cigarettes of special manufacture which incorporate a thin **blue line** in the paper, and are still supplied as duty-free quota to entitled *RN* personnel. Seen by some authorities as incompatible with the ideals of preventive medicine, but regarded by others as both an important privilege and a vital component of Jack's morale. They are due to be phased out before the end of the decade. See also *DF's and *ticklers

Blue Peter   Two forms of usage:
   1. Blue-and-white flag *P* flown in a ship ready to sail
   2. White-blue-white ribbon of the *Long Service and Good Conduct* medal. See also *Pea-do in this application

blue-and-baggies *(FAA)*   Proper naval uniform, as opposed to the *green-and-baggies or *green-and-smellies which are both nicknames for flying suits (or *ovies)

blue-and smellies *(FAA)*   Aircrew nickname for maintainers

Bluebell   Metal polish; also the radio callsign of a mechanical or electrical engineer

bluejacket   Generic and descriptive term for Jack after 1858 when the first blue cloth double-breasted jacket was introduced as uniform. Before that Jack was simply a *tar, from the *tarpaulin clothing that he wore at sea

Bluenose   A warship that has operated inside the Arctic circle, and has a small paint job at the *sharp end to show this fact

Blues *(RM)*   No.1 (best) Service uniform, worn with the white Wolseley pattern helmet (see right hand figure on page **B** -28)

blue-veined steak   See *toggle

blue-water (navy)   Warships designed to sail the oceans of the world, not just in coastal waters like a *brown-water outfit

bluey   Free airmail letter form used in operational areas such as the Falklands / South Atlantic theatre

blunt end   The stern of a warship

blushing and farting   Someone who is severely embarrassed

boat   There is really only one kind of **boat** that goes to sea under the *White Ensign - a submarine, although strictly speaking, the old corvettes also had only a single continuous deck above the waterline, and therefore qualified for this description. Misuse of the term where *ship* is the correct description will *wind Jack up a treat, as well as displaying the speaker's ignorance of matters Naval. Ships can carry boats, but not vice versa. Note also that to *catch the boat up* implies the acquisition of a venereal disease, whereas to *push the boat out* means that the person described is being generous with hospitality, often in celebration. These two phrases are not usually connected ! Note also *liberty boat, from which the more general expression to **miss the boat** is derived

Boat people *(FAA)* Disparaging term adapted from the Vietnamese context to describe submariners

boatswain Commonly abbreviated and pronounced **bosun**; may be written as **bo'sun** or **bo's'n**. An officer, or more usually a *warrant officer, or *petty officer responsible for the efficient seamanship functions of the ship. Derived from the words *boat* and *suen* or *swain* - husband. Note also *coxswain *(cog suen)* and see also *buffer in contrast to this role

Bobby's helmet The glans penis

Bob's yer Auntie ! Occasional and amusing variation of the more common *Uncle* version, especially when describing the after-effects of a *bricking

bobstay The fraenum,a structure which tethers the penile foreskin, and which is often damaged by Jack as a result of excessive enthusiasm during a spot of *counterpane hurdling

body snatchers Older term for *crushers or *Reggies employed on *shore patrol duties

bog off *(FAA)* Phrase used to describe an aircraft disappearing over the horizon: *"Now, before you bog off into the wild blue yonder, make sure you all know *Mother's intentions.."*

bog standard Description of something that is a basic issue item, unadorned by any frills or subsequent modifications

bog trotter A native of Ireland

bogelscope *(FAA)* Radar *gadget carried in a *Bag for detecting and tracking *bogeys with

Bogey Traditional nickname for anyone with the surname Knight

bogey *(FAA)* Traditional descriptive label for an enemy aircraft; *bandit* is very much a Hollywood term

bograts *(FAA)* Older name for the *Middies and *Subbies serving as aircrew in a front-line squadron

bollocking (esp. *RM*) Very severe verbal rebuke or admonition, usually qualified by the adjectives *terrific* or *almighty*

Bombhead

bollocknaked   Spaghetti (*bolognese* !)

bollocky buff   Without any clothing; to be **in the bollocky buff** is to be in a naked state

bolter *(FAA)*   Older name for a touch-and-go carrier landing by an aircraft without its taking an arrester wire with the tail-hook; sometimes this was unintentional ! The term is now used when someone vacates a job or appointment very quickly: *"He's done a bolter.."*

bomb bosun *(FAA)*   The senior rating Armourer in a squadron; also a term for the Officer in charge of all explosive stores in a carrier

bomb-burst *(FAA)*   The result when a formation of aircraft encounters unexpected bad weather: *"Then the boys flew into a rapidly developing warm front. Total chaos - and a massive bomb-burst into practically every airfield in South-West England.."* This can also be used to describe the group action taken when some social pariah turns up in the *Wardroom

bomb shop *(SM)*   The torpedo or weapon storage compartment of a submarine

Bombay runner   The cockroach, also known as a *cockie

Bombay sweat   Older term for the result when a sailor was too drunk to leave his hammock, yet needed to *pump ship. The more modern version refers to the process of *swamping

bombed out   Depending on context this can mean drunk or, in a wider sense, weird or bizarre: *"That civvy scientist is bombed out of his box, we reckon !"* Royal also uses the phrase to describe mental aberration brought on by extreme tiredness

Bomber / *Bomber*
   1. A Polaris or Trident submarine; the American equivalent is a
      boomer
   2. Nickname for anyone with the surname Brown or Mills

Bomber Command circuit *(FAA)*   Label applied to a *Bloggs' efforts
when using excessive airspace around an airfield instead of keeping his
circuit line tight and precise. Also used when prosecuting a submarine
in a *Sea King and the *stick monkeys are not doing *jumps to the total
satisfaction of the *dip Boss

Bomber Queen *(SM)*   Diesel *boat crew's derisory nickname for
anyone serving in a *Polaris* submarine with air-conditioned comfort,
regular hygiene and generally well-ordered lives

bombhead *(FAA)*   Affectionate term for any member of the old *Naval
Air Mechanic (Ordnance)* branch, populated by big, strong *Ugh men who
seemed capable of bombing-up an aircraft by hand. See Tugg's
illustration on page B - 35 for a perfect summary !   The term is still
used for those *Weapons Electrical* ratings who specialize in aircraft
armament or ordnance (explosive) items, including ejection seats. They
wear red surcoats when acting as *roof rats

bone   Thirteen different applications !
   1. Give someone a hard time about something: *"That's the fourth time
      I've been **boned** about this morning's little incident.."*
   2. Be selected for some unpopular task or duty: *"Mickey's been **boned**
      off for fire sentry in the *middle, poor sod.."*
   3. Study a subject with particular interest, eg. for an exam: *"Spent
      the whole of my *make and mend yesterday **boning up** on *Sea King
      hydraulic systems.."*
   4. The white feather of water thrown up from the bow of a ship under
      way - at high speed a ship is said to have a **bone in her teeth**
   5. Older term meaning to scrounge or pilfer, after a legendary 18th
      century *bosun of that name
   6. Telephone - abbreviation of the rhyming slang ***telling bone***
   7. To have intercourse with a female, possibly an abbreviation of the
      slang word **trombone** or the deployment of one's **ham bone**
   8. Unintelligent, not very smart: *"The guy's **too bone** to realize that
      he's being *seen off something rotten.."*
   9. A **bone orchard** is a cemetery
   10. The Royal Naval Hospitals at Haslar (Portsmouth) and Stonehouse
      (Plymouth) are known in each area as **The Boneyard**
   11. A **bone dome** is an aircrew helmet
   12. **close to the bone** is a phrase implying reduced safety margins
      during an *evolution, or a dubious joke told in mixed company
   13. A really lazy individual is a **bone idle** *scrimshanker

bongles and dongles *(RM and SM)*   Special noise-generating devices
placed in the water by *SBS* personnel awaiting pick-up by submarine

bonk   Sudden and swerving change of course made by a *Seawolf* missile at Mach 2 as it acquires directional control and tracks the target; subsequent alterations to track are ***mini-bonks*** !

Bonsai trees   Broccoli spears, often served with *yellow peas

booby   Tropical seabird that was very easy to catch once it had settled, hence the term **booby-prize** for something that is really no prize (catch) at all

Boogaloo !   Sardonic dismissal of some claim made, or achievement boasted about; the component syllables can be emphasized heavily: *"So you've written a book about Naval slang, eh ? Well, matey, all I can say is **boo-ga-bloody-loo..**"*

boost / booster *(FAA)*   Another term for a catapult launch: "Given *a decent wind across the deck and a clear run, the old *Gannet could *launch herself quite nicely without the **booster**..*"

boot   Basically affectionate term for one's wife or steady girlfriend - **the old boot** - or (indicative of unhappiness): *"You're looking a bit **boot**."*   Also an indicator of handsomeness: *"He must be the ugliest man in the Corps - poor chap's got a face like a **busted boot**.."*

bootneck / bootie   A *Royal Marine*; the exact origin of this term is unknown, but the 19th century *RM* tunic had a leather tongue-fastening to hold its collar closed at the throat. Only became widespread after WW2 - perhaps as a variation of the US Marine Corps' *leatherneck

bopper *(FAA)*   Thunderflash, or *thundie

borne for social duties only   Said of somebody who is socially smooth but professionally not much use. Naval aviators are sometimes described as being **borne for gin and flying**

borrow   See also *acquire, but in a permanent and dishonest sense

Boss *(FAA and RM)*   Familiar, yet respectful form of address for a Squadron CO or Company Commander

bosun / bo's'n / bo's'un   See *boatswain

both oars in the water   Someone who has a mental problem or an odd obsession may be described as *not having both oars in the water*

both watches   *Muster of all the *hands at the start of a working day

bottle   Older Navy term for a reprimand or scolding: *"What 'e needs is a big dose from the foretopman's bottle.."* or: *"The Commander was handing out bottles all round.."* The word now describes personal courage and daring: *"Your first night parachute jump is a fairly significant test of bottle.."*

botty sex   *Brownhatter's aberration, neatly summarised, and adaptable further as *botty bosun, botty boy, botty bandit* etc.

boulder holder   Brassiere; if this item is a 46 inch D-cup extravaganza, it may also enlarge in description to become an **over-the-shoulder boulder holder**. *Tit hammock is an amusing alternative

bounce *(FAA)*   Attack another aircraft, usually from behind and above

bow and arrow run   Older term for a dangerous operational task carried out by an inadequately armed ship

bows under   Overwhelmed with work, from the old sailing term for a ship carrying too much sail for the conditions

box of ___   Collective noun in widespread usage: *"Who are those young chaps ? Has someone opened a new box of students ?"*

Boy Captain   The youngest Captain on the Navy *List, a feature in the career of many of those whose meteoric ascent will take them to the very highest ranks in the *Andrew

Boy Seamen   Young men aged 14 and upwards who used to be carried as operational members of a capital warship's crew; almost equivalent to today's (older) Junior Seamen

brace of shakes   Measurement of time based on the shivering of a sail that is coming up into wind; the figure of speech has come ashore to describe any very short interval

bracket   Get a first salvo of gunfire on one side of the target and a second salvo on the other; note also *straddle which refers to a single salvo with some of the rounds impacting on target

brag rags   Campaign medal ribbons on a uniform

brain fart   Any temporary mental aberration

bramah / brammers (esp. *RM*)   Something that is either brilliant or highly enjoyable: *"Parachuting into the sea ? It's a bramah.."*

Branch *(FAA)*   The term *Fleet Air Arm* was unofficial during WW2 and so it was referred to by the Admiralty as ***The Air Branch***. This name is now preserved as the *Royal Naval Reserve Air Branch*.   Note also The *Andrew and The *Trade (SM)

brass hat   Gold wire braiding on the cap of an officer of Commander's rank or higher. **Getting one's brass hat** refers to the actual promotion, whereas **an acting brass hat** implies only temporary elevation to the rank

brass monkeys   Cold. Abbreviation of the phrase *cold enough to freeze the balls off a brass monkey*; this referred to iron cannon balls contracting in very low temperatures, then falling through their brass storage tracks (**monkeys**) alongside the guns

brassed off   Quite literally, fed up with cleaning brasswork !

Bravo Zulu   Traditional letter group meaning: *"Manoeuvre Well Executed"* or, put more simply : *"Well done !"*   Often abbreviated: *"We got a *BZ from the *Flagship for that attack.."*

break out   Order to open up a stores container and prepare some item for its immediate issue or use: *"**Break out** the *medical comforts and stand by to issue a dozen *survivor's tots.."* See *barrico also

breaking strain of a warm Mars bar   Description of an individual with little or no willpower when it comes to resisting temptation. The words *chocolate bar* or *Crunchie* are sometimes substituted

brew   The container or urn from which a *wet of tea is dispensed: *"Let's stop and get a **brew** on.."*

brick / bricking   A number of variants to consider:
1. A naval (gunfire) shell is known as a **brick**
2. *(RM)* A half-section of four men mounted in a Land-Rover is also a **brick**
3. *Bricking* is a nickname for the surgical procedure of vasectomy

Bridge card   A folding card, published monthly, listing all *Royal Navy* ships, submarines and *Naval Air Command* squadrons, together with the names of their Commanding Officers, plus their seniority. The latter aspect is vital when determining the identity of a *canteen boat

brief *(FAA)*   The process of going over all relevant information prior to a sortie, adapted to more general use: *"What's the **brief** for that *cocker's P tonight ?"*

Brigham   The traditional nickname for anyone called Young, after one *Brigham Young Esq.*, founder of the Mormon church

brightwork   Brass or copper pipes and fittings that are cleaned during the *middle and morning *watches

bring up with a round turn   Correct someone sharply; another old sailing term from the cabledeck, where **a round turn** was always taken with the inner end of the anchor cable before this cable was paid out. As the ship dropped astern, the cable gradually tautened until the ship was finally **brought up with a round turn**

Bristol fashion   Everything neat, tidy and seamanlike in both appearance and function, based on the reputation of ships that used to trade out of Bristol. The full expression, which has come ashore to a wider usage, is *all shipshape and Bristol fashion*

broach   To break into a cask or bottle; **broaching-to** occurs when a vessel running before a sea is slewed around broadside

broad arrow   A mark indicating Government property, first used in the reign of Elizabeth I

broad pennant   The personal insignia of a Commodore when the senior officer afloat; note that this is not a *Flag in its true sense, which indicates the special authority of an Admiral, and also that the flag is swallow-tailed rather than square

broadside messing　　　Any system of feeding with long tables in the eating area and food brought from a central *galley

Brock's benefit (esp. *RM*)　　　Spectacular battle involving lots of high explosive, tracer and illuminating starshells: *"The attack on Mount Harriet was a real **Brock's benefit** once the Argies woke up.."*

broke　　　In addition to the financial meaning, the word also applies to an Officer who is forced to leave the Service; this stems from the *Court-Martial procedure of **breaking** that Officer's sword if guilt is proven on certain charges

broken brain *(RM)*　　　Someone who is not quite all there

bronzy time　　　Sunbathing; may also be bronzy-bronzy or bronzing

brothel creepers　　　Suede shoes with crepe or rubber soles

brow　　　Gangway used to link a ship to shore; on crossing over the brow in either direction, all *RN* and *RM* personnel pause, whether or not they are in uniform, to salute the *quarterdeck

brown
1. A colour traditionally associated with the Army, as in:
   brown clown - Army officer
   brown job　- anyone from the Army
2. A **brown hatter** can mean a homosexual, or (esp. *RM*) be a general term of denigration implying total uselessness or abject failure: *"Have you seen what the *Crabs did to *Lossie's *wardroom ? They've turned the place into a ruddy **brown hatter's paradise**.."* Or: *"Frankly, that policy meeting was a complete **brown hatter's tea party**.."* Note also that a **brown hatter's *scrambling net** is a string vest ! See page D - 87 for an absolute Tugg classic
3. Someone who spends a lot of time snivelling around his superiors may be described as a **brown noser**, or out for **brownie points**
4. **brown-water navy** - a coastal fleet as opposed to an ocean-going *blue-water one
5. Lumps of faecal matter floating in a harbour or anchorage are referred to as **brown trout** or **brown Admirals**, whereas **Admiralty brown** was *pusser's toilet paper until very recently
6. **brown envelopes** are special instructions handed out during Flag Officer's Inspections to test the flexibility and preparedness of the ship in a specific way

Brummie　　　Nickname for anyone originating from Birmingham

Brush the salt off his shoulders !　　　Older sardonic remark directed at someone telling exaggerated sea stories; the modern equivalent is: *"He's *swinging the lamp.."*

Canteen Cowboy

BSH   *British Standard Handfuls*, a sizing index for female breasts, otherwise known as *babies *bag rats

bubble
1. Tell tales or inform on someone; to **be bubbled** is to be found out. See also *tumbled
2. *(SM)* **The bubble** refers to the state of a *boat's trim, as displayed by a large spirit level clinometer in the *Control Room. To *lose the bubble is a term that has now reached General Service, and means that the person so described has lost trim control, thus implying a lack of understanding - or increasing confusion

bubbleheads / bubblies   Ship's divers working with compressed air which is expired into the water and rises in a cloud of bubbles to the surface. See also *pondlife

bubbly   *Grog - rum diluted with water, and certainly *Jack's champagne* in one sense, but not named **bubbly** for that reason ! This is a strict definition, but in general usage the term is employed for almost any form of rum, hence the request in a pub: *"I'll have a bubbly and black please.."* (rum and blackcurrant) or the statement: *"Only *Pussers' bubbly is the real thing.."*   When mixed *three and one with water in the rum tub, *neaters took on a foaming appearance, and it was in this state that it was issued to the **bubbly bosun** from each *messdeck who came to collect the *Tot in a rum *fanny when *Up Spirits ! was *piped.

Bucc   The *Buccaneer* low-level maritime strike aircraft, operated from carriers by the *FAA* between 1962 and 1978, and still rendering yeoman service in the hands of *RAF Strike Command* crews. May also be modified as *Buccanana* - a particularly lethal form of low-flying fruit

Buck / **buck**   Four meanings:
1. Nickname for anyone called Taylor or, inevitably, Rogers
2. **buck the system** - try to do things in an unorthodox or unofficial way
3. **Buck House** is a nickname for Buckingham Palace
4. **pass the buck** - see *slope shoulders

bucket of shit   Rather surprisingly, this is a frequent and affectionate form of greeting between Jack and an old *oppo: *"'Ello me old bucket of shit ! How's the family ?"*

bucket of sunshine / instant sunshine   Fairly standard euphemism for a nuclear weapon; *CND activists are known as the **Bucket of Sunshine Brigade**; see also *unscheduled sunrise

buckshee   Free; derived from the Arab word *baksheesh*

buff stoker   A baby stoker without any length-of-service badges

buff up   Clean and polish something, usually for *Rounds

buffalo   Occasional substitute used for *dubs, as in
Oh-five-buffalo meaning *Oh-five-double-oh* - or 0500 hrs

Buffer   Nickname for the Chief Boatswain's Mate - the Commander
or *Jimmy's right-hand man in respect of all work done around the ship
to maintain both appearance and fighting efficiency. Usually a stalwart
character of great experience and personality, he directs the **Buffer's
party**. Naval Air Stations will have an **airfield buffer** in an identical
role

Buffs !   Abbreviated exhortation to: *"Buck up, for (flip's) sake !"*

bug out *(RM)*   Tactical withdrawal, usually conducted in a big hurry

bug rake   A comb; the parting in a hair style is called a **bug run**

bugger-about list   The dark-blue equivalent of a *hit list* on
which individuals who have incurred the *Jimmy's displeasure may be
placed. Sometimes called a *shit-list* for this reason: *"The next man who
spills coffee on the chart table goes right to the top of my **bugger-
about list**."*   See also *lurk list

bugger's grips　　　　Tufts of facial hair specially preserved around the cheekbones as an affectation; these are sometimes also called *muff-diver's depth marks

Buggins' turn　　　　The process whereby a tri-Service job falls to the next incumbent in strict rotation, rather than being given to the best candidate

Bugis Street　　　　Eating-house locale in Singapore, sadly now demolished, but famous for its nocturnal population of transvestites. A crucial feature of the atmosphere was Jack and Royal's tolerant and rather civilized attitude to these *kytais. Many a *sea daddy brought his young charges here for educational purposes

bulkhead　　　　Jack's name for a wall; if somewhat inebriated he may well be involved in a spot of **bulkhead bouncing**! A **bulkhead crusher** is a *Harvey Wallbanger*

bulldog (esp. *RM*)　　　　Abrasive description of a female: *"'Oo was that **bulldog** I saw you wiv' down the disco ?"* Or, used in a different sense: *"That *party's got a *moosh like a **bulldog** chewin' a wasp.."*

bum　　A sextet of applications:
　　1. **bum bandit** - homosexual
　　2. **bum boat** - any vessel holding supplies or goods for sale in large open casks that look like **bombards** (mortars)
　　3. **bum fluff** - downy facial hair on someone yet to start shaving
　　4. **bum freezer** - hip-length reefer jacket, still used in Mess Undress
　　5. **bum plums** - prolapsed piles
　　6. **bum steer** - bad or incorrect advice

bumph　　　　Time-honoured description of the never-ending stream of printed forms, papers, hand-outs, instructions, orders, cancellations and amendments which arrive in any ship or establishment. The term indicates a wish that it was all printed on much softer and perforated paper

bunch of knitting　　　　Descriptive nickname for entangled ropes; sometimes also described as a **right bunch of bastards**

bundleman　　　　A married sailor, since he took his *dhobey home in a **bundle** for his wife to cope with; to **drop a bundle** implies an expensive *run-ashore

bundu　　General term for a remote or wild (jungle) area

Bungalow Bill (esp. *FAA*)　　　　Nickname for someone who, just like a **bungalow**, does not have all that much up top; *Kelvin is an alternative

Bungey / Bungy　　　　Nickname for anyone called Williams or (sometimes) Edwards

bunk up   *Turn in with a lady friend (Jack), or a chap (*Jenny !)

Bunker Hill *(RM)*   *Corps memorable date of 17 June 1775, and a battle of the American War of Independence in which Marines of the First and Second Battalions displayed conspicuous valour and unshaken steadiness when storming this area of high ground north of Boston

Bunny   Inevitable nickname for someone with the surname Warren

bunny food / bunny grub   Lettuce, or any green salad

bunting tosser   Communications branch rating or *(RM)* Signals branch member; see also *flag wagger

burberry / burbs   Traditional nickname for a blue Naval raincoat, since *Messrs. Burberrys* were among the original main suppliers: *"Some big *OD's *razzed me **burbs** !"* is a complaint that some presumptious colleague has *borrowed Jack's raincoat. The term has also been adapted into other phrases:
  shiny burbs - oilskins, or waterproof sailing clothing
   Wanchai burberry - oiled paper umbrella made in Hong Kong, and
      possessed of a highly pungent smell when put
      into use for the first time

burble   Ramble on in speech, without making anything clear: *"Listen *Bloggs, what on earth are you **burbling** about ?"*

burgoo   porridge

Burma road   Standard nickname for the main passageway running through the length of a ship. In some ships with city names, the **Burma road** will have the name (and associated street signs) of the main thoroughfare of that city

burmadoos   Bermuda shorts

burn   Time for a cigarette: *"Right lads, take five for a **quick burn**.."*

burning and turning   A helicopter with its engines running and the rotors engaged

burnt plum   The anal orifice

bush   A lady's pubic hair: *"A hand in the **bush** is worth more than two birds on the hand !"*

bush baptist   Jack's name for any funny church, of the type which appoints you as a pastor in return for $50 forwarded to a Box Number in Ohio. The *Church of Turkey is a European alternative

busking   Old Naval term for pirate vessels cruising along a coast looking for something to attack; now used for itinerant musicians who cruise along a queue of people, still in the hopes of finding some form of treasure !

buster *(FAA)*   Code word for full speed, or *as fast as you can* - note also *max chat

(the) butcher's bill   Casualty lists issued after a wartime action

button boy   The rating selected for his agility and steadiness to stand on the top *truck or button of the mast at a mast-manning display

Button your flap !   Older exhortation to: *"Shut up !"* derived from the special design of Jack's uniform trousers which had a **flap front** or *piss flap instead of fly buttons or a zip. The older design is still issued to *Yachties

buttons   As worn on the sleeve cuff of a Chief Petty Officer's uniform jacket; promotion to CPO is known as **getting your buttons**

buzz   Rumour; a **buzz merchant** is a rumour-monger, or someone who seems to have the **latest buzz** before anyone else. He will usually claim that his **buzzes** are *gen as in the drawing at page L - 167. Note also the lower grades of **strong buzz** or **good buzz** in this context. *"What's the buzz ?"* means: *"What's going on ?"* A *duff buzz or *gash buzz is one that turns out to be incorrect

buzz box   An intercom system

by the book   According to any laid-down Regulations

BZ   *Well done* - see ***Bravo Zulu** for a more complete explanation

Angels whisper

CHARLIE

cab *(FAA)*　Helicopter or aircraft

cabbage hat　Green beret

cabin　Any single room in a barrack block, *wardroom or Royal Marines Officer's mess *ashore. Senior officers will have a **day cabin** (sitting room) plus **night cabin** (bedroom) and always refer to them as such; a larger warship's commander may also have a **sea cabin** immediately adjacent to or beneath the bridge

caboose / caboosh　Combination of store, small office, workshop and hideaway

cack-handed　Clumsy; probably derived from the Greek word for bad

cackleberries　Hen's eggs

cackling your grease / fat　Talking out of turn, or failing to listen in a conversation

CAG *(FAA)*　A *Carrier Air Group* of embarked *SHAR and *Sea King squadrons

cag / *clag (esp. *FAA*)　Fog, or bad visibility in low cloud

cake and arse party　Jack's term for any state of total disorganization, often qualified with the adjective *real*. Note that this term is distinct from a *Wardroom *cocker's P which is a *cock and arse party

call for Hughie　To vomit

Call the hands ! Shrill *pipe made at the start of a working day in order to wake everyone up and get them *turned to

cam out *(RM)* Apply **camouflage cream** to one's face, or **cam nets** and other materials to a vehicle or tent

camel basher An Arab

Camship WW2 escort ship fitted with a catapult capable of *squirting a *Sea Hurricane* fighter off in order to deal with the menace of long-range Focke-Wulf *Condor* aircraft. The pilot then had to ditch alongside his ship, the initial letters of which stood for *Catapult Armed Merchantman*. Note the distinction between this and the *Macship; if anyone out there knows of the existence of a *Hurricane*, whatever its condition, will they please contact the author - or the curator of the *FAA Museum* at Yeovilton !

can man Civilian embarked in a ship as the *NAAFI **canteen manager** or *NAAFI damager

can of worms Failure: *"We did our best, but then politics turned the whole project into a giant **can of worms**.."*

can spanner Tin opener

Candidate *(RM)* Royal Marine who is working towards promotion as a NCO; the **Roll of Candidates** is maintained at *CENTURION*

can't fit that in (esp. *RM*) Gentle and rather pleasant way of expressing disapproval of something

can't make head nor tail of it ! Lovely expression used by the Yeoman of Signals when he was unable to make any sense out of a distant hoist of flag signals; this expression has come ashore into widespread usage

can't take a joke - shouldn't have joined !   Navy-wide expression of almost amused resignation at some of the crazy things that happen in the *Andrew; *(that's)* **life in a blue suit* is an alternative method of expressing the same sort of sentiment

canteen boat   Title awarded to whichever ship in a task group or squadron has the most junior CO, and therefore performs the most menial and least pleasurable tasks: *"Always first out and last in, then tied up miles from the *run-ashore.."* Derived from the old messdeck system whereby the youngest rating ran errands to the canteen for his messmates' tobacco and *nutty

canteen cowboy   A rating who fancies himself with the ladies (see also Tugg on page B - 43)

canteen messing   In the days before central messing each *messdeck's rations were prepared in the *galley, collected from there by the duty *cook of the mess*, and then consumed on the *messdeck. If the mess *cates wasn't too smart, the last few days of each month would see *herrings-in for every meal

canvas back   Someone who is always asleep. See also *golden gonker, *golden blanket / golden pillow award, *horizontal champion, *Unknown Warrior and *zeds merchant

CAP   Combat Air Patrol: *"We've got two *SHAR on CAP at a hundred miles, plus another pair at *Alert 5 on deck.."*

cap tally   Black cap ribbon carrying ship's name in gold lettering; note also the specific application of **different ships, different cap tallies*

Cape Horn fever   Older term for an imaginary disease

Captain General *(RM)*   *HRH The Prince Philip*, who has held this office since 1953. His insignia of rank are those of a *Field Marshal*

captain of the heads	Sarcastic title for the rating detailed off to clean the ship's *heads (latrines)

Captain's cloak	Nickname for the last of the *Articles of War

captain's tiger	A Commanding Officer's personal steward; the term is a legacy from the 19th century and the striped mess jackets worn by some Indian personal stewards of that era

car smash	Tomato sauce or tinned tomatoes; known as *train smash when bacon is incorporated. The *FAA* calls a champagne and brandy cocktail *Car Smash* because that's a frequent consequence of consuming too many

cardboard fo'c'sle	Jack's description of a *killick's progression to Petty Officer and his consequent moving out of *square rig; this is because the cap suddenly acquires a **cardboard fo'c'sle** as a peak

carpet crawler	A small child. See also *ankle biter / snapper, and *rug rat

carpeted	In trouble; **on the carpet** in the Captain's office for a spot of *picturising

carry away	Originally rigging that parted under strain or cannon fire and was **carried away** downwind or over the side. Now has a more general usage, often when someone loses emotional control

Carry on !	Order to resume duties following the completion of some other *evolution; the phrase may also be employed in a direct sense: *"After this two minute silence, **Carry on !** will be *piped at 1102.."*

Cash clothing	Naval Stores section where items of uniform or kit are held for sale rather than Loan or Issue; known also as *Slops, and very often closed for stocktaking (see also *Jack Dusty and associated Tugg cartoon)

cat o'nine tails	Instrument of punishment in the old Navy; if the rope tails were knotted, then it became a *thieves' cat. This device was stored in a red baize bag to conceal the blood drawn by it, hence the expression *the **cat's** out of the bag* which still means that retribution is imminent. Note also the association with the phrase *hardly room enough to swing a **cat**,* implying that the space being described is somewhat cramped

catch the boat up	See Preface and the entry for *boat. This is a very old Naval expression derived from the fact that Jack was not allowed ashore, even when sick, in the days of sail - for fear that he would desert. When the Naval hospitals at Portsmouth and Plymouth were built, they were positioned on creeks and could therefore be reached by water. The *sick boat* would circulate among the warships anchored offshore, take off those who were ill or injured, and then transport them *up either Haslar or Stonehouse creeks. The phrase *up the creek* has a more general meaning now, but it is originally related to the poor survival prospects facing a sailor taking this route to hospital care ashore ! **Catching the boat up**, or simply, **the boat**, now refers exclusively in the *RN* and *RM* to diseases of a social nature

Cates   Nickname for the **Caterer**; although this is now an official branch, the Officers' and the Chief's and PO's Messes still elect amateur caterers from amongst their members to look after wines, newspapers etc. and they use that title in an official sense.   The *Wardroom **Wine Caterer** is, traditionally, the *Medical Officer !*

C-balls   Nickname of the *CBGLO* or *Carrier-Borne Ground Liason Officer*, a *Pongo who used to serve in the older aircraft carriers to control and co-ordinate Ground Attack mission requirements ashore

..... WHOSE SPECIALIST SUBJECT IS BARON STRANGLING.

C-Troop   A group of not-so-young ladies who turn up regularly at the *RN Leadership's School*'s weekly dances

CD   *Clearance Diver* - a title now abolished, but still used as a collective noun for those diving on Navy business using gas mixtures, rather than the compressed air of Ship's Divers or *bubbleheads

CDA Mess   Special *Contagious Diseases Annexe* in large warships for men with venereal disease, often described incorrectly as

Contracted Disease Ashore. See *Rose Cottage for fuller explanation and note that these men also had their *tots stopped

CDF *Common Dog Factor* - the application of pure common sense (a quality not measurable by written examinations) in solving a problem. See also *pickle jar and *jampot lid

centrefold A two-dimensional object of Jack's fantasy and desire; actually to *trap one is classed as an ultimate achievement

(HMS) ***CENTURION*** The Royal Navy and Royal Marines' computerised Pay and Records establishment near Portsmouth, and referred to as a single word: *"Until CENTURION clear the payment, you can't have any money.."* Note that Pay Offices in ships and establishments have now become *Unit Personnel Offices*

centurion *(RM)* An officer who personally commands more than 100 men in a Unit, ie. the Commanding Officer and his Company Commanders

chacon Two forms of usage:
1. Wooden shipping container for logistic stores, developed in Chatham Dockyard - hence **Chatham container**
2. *(RM)* Personal rucsac packed for Arctic Warfare operations, and usually very heavy: *"The trouble with ski-ing downhill is that the ruddy **chacon** keeps *taking charge.."*

chain gang *(FAA)* *Roof rats dragging aircraft tie-down chains around the flight deck of a carrier, to the general discomfiture and sleeplessness of those *turned in below

chalk bosun Instructor Officer; see also *schoolie

chamfer up (pronounced with soft *c*) Tidy up and polish things for *Rounds. See also *tiddley up and *bougie up

chancre mechanic / chancre bosun Slang term for a *quack or *Dick Doc

Channel night Traditional *Sod's opera and final *Wardroom party night in a warship returning home to England. Derived from the older condition of **Channel fever**, the excitement which grips a ship's company when approaching home port after a long period at sea. The intensity of this fever still depends directly on the length of time spent away from the United Kingdom; also known as *Up Channel night

chap Pleasant conversational substitute for *One* when used in the first person singular; the phrase *One tends to become somewhat tired after cross-country ski-ing* then mutates into: *"A **chap** needs his *kip in a big way after spending all day on a pair of *pusser's planks.."*

Charlie-G *(RM)* The man-luggable (as opposed to man-portable) **Carl Gustav** anti-tank weapon which is now obsolescent

Chief GI

Charlie Noble   An H-shaped galley stove pipe seen in very much older warships, usually bound in brass and kept highly polished

Charlie time *(FAA)*   Planned time of arrival

chase the pisser   Messdeck card game involving the Queen of Spades

Chats / *Chats*   The historic Naval port and *RM* base of **Chatham**, and also a nickname for anyone called Harris

chatty   Grubby or unclean

check the ship for leaks   Polite way to indicate your intention to pass water. See also *pump ship and *spring a leak

cheer ship   Pleasant *evolution when Jack lines the rails and gives three cheers in unison. This might occur while steaming past the *Yacht when the *Lord High Admiral* is embarked, or when alongside and saying good-bye to a departing *Father

cheese down   The action of coiling down a rope, now used to describe the process of curling up with uncontrolled laughter, or in the sense of *coiling one down. A *tiddley coil of rope which finished off in the centre was known as a *Flemish coil*; the only other thing that Jack knew as *Flemish* was cheese - hence the connection

cheese 'ush *(SM)*   *Submarine Service* version of a cheese and onion quiche; the edge pastry of this creation is called its *guardrails

cheesy hammy eggy *topsides   Standard Naval fare consisting of cheese toast with a slice of ham incorporated, and an egg on top. The original version came from the China Station, but even in WW2 it was a gallant attempt to create something interesting out of *mousetrap, spam and powdered egg

chef's delight   Unsavoury habit of a chef who spits into his deep fat frier in order to test the oil's temperature

cherryberry *(RM)*   Member of the *Parachute Regiment*; their riposte refers to a *cabbage hat

chew   Three rather different meanings, depending on context:
  1. Fellatio; a homosexual indulging in this activity is a **chew bosun**
  2. **chewing someone out** *(RM)* indicates that someone has erred - and is being seriously *picturised for it
  3. To **chew the fat** as in discussing general topics at some length is an expression that has its origins in the steady and extensive mastication required to break down the tough rind of salt beef that had been pickled and stored in the brine barrels carried on board

chicken Chernobyl   Probably the hottest curry now available from your local Indian take-away, and a real *ring-stinger

chicken shit   American slang term used to indicate something of little real importance: *"I know it's all a bit **chicken shit**, but the *Boss wants this list complete and handed in by tomorrow.."*

Chief   Form of address to a *Chief Petty Officer*; note also that in the Merchant Navy **the Chief** refers to the *Chief Officer* (or in older times the First Mate) who is directly subordinate to the *Master* (Captain)

Chief GI   *Chief Gunnery Instructor*, a semi-legendary figure (especially at *Dartmouth) responsible for all matters of Ceremonial and parade-ground drill. Regarded with a mixture of awe and affection, but never forgotten once encountered, as on page **C - 56**. The *RM* equivalent at *Lympstone is the *First Drill

Chief Nightingale   The senior medical rating in a larger warship carrying medical staff

Chief Stoker's method   Hit something hard with a really big hammer ! Probably derived from the Chief Stoker's position in charge of the *fo'c'sle capstan party when working cable, and his tendency to strike the chain links with a *maul* (hammer) in order to get them running smoothly

Chief Stokers   Jack's nickname for the sea birds that are *always hanging around at the back end*

Chiefy   *Chief E* - the Senior Mechanical Engineering Officer or *SMEO*; note that his deputy is the Senior Engineer or *Senior

chin-strapped *(RM)*   To be down on one's **chin strap** with exhaustion or fatigue: *"After re-running the *thirty miler next day, me and Buck Taylor was totally **chin-strapped**.."*

Chinese wedding cake   A *duff made of *pusser's rice pudding with embedded currants and raisins

chinky   Two uses explained:
1. Chinese, especially when referring to food - **chinky nosh**
2. Diseased in the tropical sense (without intention of racial slur) as in: *"Worst case of **chinky** *toe-rot I've ever seen.."*

Chippy   Three applications shown:
1. The Shipwright artificer
2. Inevitably, anyone with the surname Carpenter
3. An orthopaedic surgeon

chit / chitty   A piece of paper, usually with some form of official permission or instruction written on it. *__Bar chits__ are used for most purchases in the *__Wardroom__

chockheads   An affectionate term that is best not used directly, unless seeking a serious *bite, for those *Fleet Air Arm* ratings who are members of the *Aircraft Handlers Branch* and who are also trained in fire-fighting techniques. A newer term is that of *wedge technician. See also page H - 146

chocolate fireguard / teapot   Another nice version of *He's about as much use as a..* See also *ashtray on a motorbike, *rubber dagger and *third nostril in this context

chocolate lager   Severe diarrhoea

Chogey   Chinese: *"When you get on board, ask the __Chogey cobbler__ to make you a pair of mess boots - half the price and twice the quality of anything you'd get ashore.."* __Chogey knicks__ are boxer shorts made in almost any material that you care to provide *Sew-sew with

__choke his luff!__   *"Shut him up!"*

chokey   Prison; see also *DQs and *slammer

chokker / chokka   Upset, fed up or totally exasperated, always applied in the emotional sense: *"Four months in Crossmaglen my son - and then you'll understand what chokker means.."* Derived from the old warship sailing term of *chock-a-block*, when two blocks rigged in a tackle have come together and no further movement is possible

chop   Signature, as in: *"Put your chop on this, please.."*

Chop chop !   "Hurry up !"

chop one off *(RM)*   Render a hand salute

chopped *(FAA)*   Withdrawn from flying training by formal executive action, after a series of warnings and a **chop ride**: *"Now *Bloggs, your mother's pet name for you is Boo-Boo isn't it ?   Well, Boo-Boo - you're chopped.."*

chopper-pukes   *Stovie term of derision for rotary-wing (helicopter) aircrew; *wobbleheads is an alternative

chrome dome   Abusive term for a slow-witted individual (whose head is as hard as **chrome**)

chuck one up *(RM)*   Render a salute

chuck up
1. Formal congratulations (esp. *RM*): *"The parade was a *bramah, and *First Drill got a big chuck up from the General.."*
2. Something smelly: *"After seven days and nights in a snowhole one does tend to chuck up just a touche.."*

chuckle gap   The area of bare skin on a ladies' thigh between her panties and stocking tops. See also *gobbler's gulch

chuff   Backside, or even tail-pipe: *"Then this Mirage came screeching past and BROADSWORD put a Sea Wolf right up his chuff.."* See also *jacksie, *six o'clock and *duck run

chuffed   Really pleased: *"When we won the *Argyll Bowl, the CO was mighty chuffed.."*   Another expression attempts to quantify this pleasure - **chuffed to ten**; note that the opposite is *dischuffed

chufflock   An intimate embrace

Chuffs and Puffs
1. Chiefs and Petty Officers
2. Special *meat pies, with a sausage embedded in the *clacker; these used to be sold by a pie shop just outside the Devonport Dockyard main gate

chummy ships   Two ships from the same home port between which there are strong bonds of friendship; can also be used to describe an organization which has a benevolent attitude to its employees: *"I really like flying 747's for Virgin Atlantic. The girls are smashing, certainly, but it's also a real **chummy outfit**."*

chunder   Australian version of *Technicolour yawn: *"Watch **under** !"*

chunter (esp. *RM*)   To mutter, mumble and grumble: *"The men don't seem to be **chuntering**, Sergeant Major - has there been a sudden outbreak of morale ?"*

church key *(RM)*   A device fitted with every kind of corkscrew, can and bottle opener

Church of Jock   Church of Scotland and Free Churches; note also the use of *Church of Turkey* in the same sense as *Bush Baptist

church pendant   One of the oldest signal flags still in use - a combination of British and Dutch naval colours dating from the Anglo-Dutch wars. It signified the temporary (but total) cessation of hostilities, so that both sides could conduct prayers and worship

CINC-NAG-HOME   Jack's name for *Her Indoors*, and a clever play on the more usual acronym of *C-in-C Nav(al) Home Command* !

CIP   A *Person* (guest) who is *Commercially Important*. When one of HM Ships pays a visit to some port in the *far flung, the usual pattern for invitations on board is *CIP*s for drinks and lunch; then VIPs (expatriate Brits especially) for an evening *Cockers P and the *Sunset ceremony

circuits and bumps *(FAA)*   Landing practice for pilots

circular file   Wastepaper basket

civvy / **civvies**   Civilian person / civilian clothes - or a group of civilian people; **civvy street** is the same as *outside

clacker Pastry crust on a pie, now used almost exclusively in admiration of the female form: *"Cor - look at the legs on that bit of clacker.."* (See page E - 101 in addition) A **clacker bosun** or **clacker mechanic** is a chef

clag / *cag Bad weather featuring low cloud or poor visibility

clamp / clampers A peculiar thick fog that sometimes affects the Lizard peninsula in Cornwall - and the *Royal Naval Air Station* at *Culdrose, which then beomes **clamped.** On the rare occasions that fog closed *Lossie, it used to be known as *Scotch mist* !

clanger A badly-timed remark that is sufficiently embarrassing to make the ship's bell **clang**

Clanky A *Mechanician specializing in ship or submarine propulsion systems; now there are no more Mechanicians as such, only Artificers or *Tiffs - but the nickname survives

Classified Material or information with political or military sensitivity: *"I'm sorry, but I can't tell you that - it's Classified.."* The degree of classification varies from *NAAFI RESTRICTED, via COSMIC TOP SECRET - to *EAT BEFORE READING*

clean into The process of changing from working *rig into clean or fresh clothing; presumably, Jack used to **clean into** his (filthy) coaling rig !

clean slate The helmsman's log slate of old, on which the course to be steered and distance made would be chalked - and then wiped clean at the start of the next *trick. The expression has come ashore to a wider use implying a fresh start, or when **wiping the slate clean** in cancellation or settlement of a debt

clear Nautical term with many general applications for tidying up, sorting out, freeing an obstruction, rounding a headland, emptying a space or completing Customs formalities. Note also the phrase **clear your yardarm** for the process of taking precautionary steps to ensure that no blame will attach if something goes wrong: *"As expected, the whole thing went to *rats, but he'd **cleared his yardarm** by getting someone else to authorise it.."* (See page **F** - 112)

Clear lower deck ! An order to cease work and gather together to hear the Commanding Officer speak, usually to make some important announcement

cleats (Big) ears

clewed up Clews are the cords from which a hammock is slung or suspended. To **clew up** with someone means to serve in the same ship, or join together for some adventure: *"After the reception, most of the boys **clewed up** in a pub down by the harbour.."* Note that this has an entirely different meaning to being *clued-up

climb to two feet and level off *(FAA)* *Turn in, or go to bed

clinch The operation of bringing two items together securely, sometimes fixing them with a **clinch** or **clench** - a specific type of nail in the case of wooden planking. The expressions to **clinch a deal** and **clench your teeth** both have this maritime and shipbuilding origin. See also *hard up in a clinch

clinkers The results of poor hygiene in the peri-anal region

clobbered Smashed up, or severely punished

clockwork mouse Submarine used to train surface ships in anti-submarine warfare techniques; also an older *FAA* term for an aircraft flown by a very experienced pilot which was used to train new *Batsmen in the art of controlling approaches to the deck

Cloggie Any Dutchman, but especially a member of the *Royal Netherlands Marine Korps* who train, exercise and deploy with Royal to Norway as part of *NATO*'s versatile *UK/NL Landing Force.* See also *Hertz van Rental and *Naafi van Driver

Close up ! The *piped order to proceed immediately to a place of duty: *"*Damage control and fire parties **close up** to the canteen *flat"*

closed-up A signal flag is **closed-up** when it is as high as its halyard will raise it

clouts   Underpants / knickers; see also *keks and *rompers

club run   A *run-ashore participated in by most of the *Wardroom, or by all the Commanding Officers of a Flotilla or Group Deployment

Clubs / Clubswinger   *Naval Physical Training Instructor*; see also (esp. *RM*) *springer

clued-up   Intelligent and smart; in possession of all the facts, or *all about

CND   The *Campaign (for) Nuclear Disarmament*; see also *Bucket of Sunshine Brigade. Jack feels that the **CND**'s somewhat unilateral and unconditional stance on removing the present strategic nuclear deterrent rather justifies his alternative explanation of *Criminal Neglect (of) Defence* !

coal-hole *(FAA)*   The darkened *looker's position in the all-weather *Sea Vixen* jet fighter (1959-69); his ejection seat was mounted lower in the fuselage than the pilot's, and did not have a clear canopy above it - only an opaque, frangible hatch and tiny window

coaming rash   The painful result of impacting one's shins on the raised edge of a hatch, hence also known as *hatch rash. Note also the specificapplication of *Moby rash

Coastie   Member of *Her Majesty's Coastguard*; their older nickname was *gobbie

cobbing   Obsolete *gunroom punishment of being beaten

cock / cock-up   Mistake: *"He made a **complete cock** of the first approach, so we had to do a *bolter and go around for a second try.."* Note also the *RM* usage of *self-adjusting **cock-up**

cock and arse party   Cocktail party; see also *cocker's P

cock one's dish   To break wind loudly while seated

cocked hat   Three entries made by *Vasco on a chart, and all supposed to be at the same point. Perfectly permissible error in older times when navigational techniques were not so precise; when these points were linked together they usually described a **cocked hat** - hence the more general expression: *"You could have knocked me into a **cocked hat**.."*

cocker's P   Cocktail party; the latter can also be written as *CTP*

cockie   Cockroach; see also *Bombay runner

Dabtoe

cocoa rats   Delusions and diarrhoea brought on by excessive intake of *kye. The solid blocks of unsweetened cocoa were brewed all night by the gangway staff to keep the cold out, and a typical victim would be a jetty sentry plied with too much of the stuff

COCKPIT *(FAA)*   Excellent quarterly Flight Safety magazine of the *Fleet Air Arm*; Tugg does the (highly amusing) illustrations

codswallop   Jack's term for a load of nonsense, another word that has come ashore to more general usage

coffee boat   Sum of money contributed to by all those in the **coffee** (or tea) **boat** for the purchase of *makings

coffin dreams *(SM)*   Occasional unpleasant nightmares experienced by nuclear submariners during long submerged patrols

coil one down   Defaecate

Coke-bottle shoulders   An anatomical feature possessed by those individuals who are unwilling to take responsibility in any matter - after the rounded shape of the classic *Coca-Cola* bottle. See also *sloping shoulders

cold fish   Efficient and zealous but apparently unemotional officer

cold move   Repositioning a warship in a dockyard or harbour without the use of her own engines

cold shot *(FAA)*   Steam catapult failure during an aircraft *launch from a carrier; the machine usually failed to get airborne and fell straight into the sea

collision mat   Enormous coir and fibre mat used to plug a hole in the hull in the event of a *graunch, secured by ropes fore and aft as well as vertically, and manned by Royal in the larger warships of old

Colours   Two regular forms of usage:
1. Ceremonial morning hoisting of the ensign
2. *(RM)* Abbreviated term of address for a Colour Sergeant

come alongside   To reach agreement with someone, especially during a discussion or argument. May also be used, aside from the obvious ship-handler's meaning, as an encouragement to someone having trouble understanding a concept during tuition or instruction: *"You don't think water discipline is necessary in the Arctic ?* **Come alongside***, my friend.."*

Come ashore, Jack ! *(RM)*   Advice to cease telling over-embroidered salty sea stories; see also *swinging the lamp

come-on *(RM)* Incident designed to lure Royal into an ambush or booby-trapped area in order to maximize his subsequent casualties

comic Any newspaper or publication that cannot really be given any serious credibility

comic cuts Jack's *Divisional documents and the written remarks contained therein; also an older nickname for Admiralty Intelligence reports !

Commcen Communications centre - the modern version of the Wireless Office of old

Commando *(RM)*
1. Battalion-sized Unit of Royal Marines. Royal has inherited this specialist forces role created in WW2. Currently there are 3 Units - 40,42 and 45 **Cdos** - linked into a brigade (3 **Cdo Bde** RM) along with Commando artillery, engineer, logistic and aviation assets; this formation is amphibious and also trained for Arctic operations. Enhanced by two *Parachute Regiment* battalions, it also did most of the fighting ashore in the Falklands during May and June 1982. See also *Cloggie for a note on *NATO* roles
2. **Commando course** A punishing test of speed, agility, endurance and stamina undertaken by all officers and men who wish to serve in, or with the Corps. Success carries the right to wear the *green beret, along with a *RN* or regimental cap badge in the case of Jack and *Perce. The actual Commando tests and timings have not changed in any way since WW2, but the build-up training period is much shorter
3. The **Commando Training Centre** - *CTCRM* - is at *Lympstone, Devon
4. *Come and do* this - then go and do that !

commencing cream Skin lubricant; see also *starters and *stoppers

commission
1. Warrant conferred on a *Royal Navy* or *Royal Marines* Officer by the *Lord High Admiral

2. The periods between refits when a warship is in active service, subsequently referred to as her *First Commission, Second Commission* and so on.
3. **commissioned ballast** *(FAA)* - Pilot's label for an an *Observer
4. **commissioned pie-thatcher** - a Catering Officer

commit aviation *(FAA)*   The sin of enjoying your flying

common dog   Common sense, a quality sometimes lacking in university graduates of otherwise high intellect. See also *CDF, *jampot lid and *pickle jar

companionway   Shipboard ladder; see also *accomodation ladder

compartment   Jack's equivalent of an office *on board, except that the *bulkheads may be curved to fit inside a warship's hull, and there is neither floor nor ceiling - only *deck and *deckhead !

complain   The block (of a rigging *block and tackle*) is said to be **complaining** if the centre sheave squeaks when it is in use

compo (esp. *RM*)   **Compo**site ration pack for troops ashore, of a legendary binding quality with regard to Royal's intestinal function

concrete cheeks   A condition produced by laughing so hard that your facial muscles seize up

concrete parachute   The military equivalent of a *nine bob note* - a homosexual

condensing snot   Snoring loudly; *percolating snot is a similar and possible alternative

congenital liar   An Officer's Appointer, or a weather forecaster

conning (the ship)   The business of directing a ship's steering, and nothing to do with confidence tricksters: *"Take the **con**.."* Or *(FAA)*: *"**Con** me back and over that other survivor in the water.."* Submarines have a **conning tower** for this purpose, called a *sail* on the other side of the *Pond

copper-bottomed   Copper sheathing plates fitted to the wooden hulls of old; they reduced attack by the *teredo worm* so that the wood lasted longer and - because barnacle and weed growth was less - made the ship go faster.   Hence the expression for something guaranteed to be worthwhile as having a **copper-bottomed guarantee**

Cordites   Standard nickname for any sporting team emanating from the old *Whale Island Gunnery School* in Portsmouth

corn / corned dog   Tinned corned beef

Corps Birthday   This Corps memorable date, 28th October 1664, was when the *Duke of York and Albany's Maritime Regiment of Foot* was first raised. The Duke was then *Lord High Admiral of Charles II's Navy, and later became James II; his *Admiral's Regiment* of fighting troops (who could also act as sailors) was the forerunner of today's Corps

Corps commish (commission) *(RM)*   Exact equivalent of the *RN* *Upper Yardman scheme; a bright Marine or Junior NCO can be selected for *Young Officer training and subsequently reach the highest ranks in the Corps. In the recent past one *King's Badgeman has made it to Major General's rank, a unique and proud distinction

Corps de Ballet *(RM)*   Wonderful *sod's opera routine that is the especial party piece of the *Lympstone *Seniors. The Exeter pantomime performed after *Crimbo by these stalwarts (dressed in ballerina costume and boots) produces tens of thousands of pounds for charity each year

Corps memorable date *(RM)*   A number of days in the Corps' 380-plus years of history are specially marked in Unit Routine Orders, as well as by various parades and dinners. These are the anniversaries of the *Corps Birthday, *Bunker Hill, *Gibraltar, *Belle Isle, *Trafalgar, *Gallipoli, *Zeebrugge, *Normandy, *Walcheren and the Falkland Islands, and recruits passing through *Lympstone have to learn them by heart. Can also be used in mild sarcasm: *"I don't believe it - Bill's actually buying a round ! Is this going down as a **Corps memorable date** ?"*

Corps-pissed *(RM)*   A *Royal Marine* obsessed with both Corps history and its current activities. The term is applied, almost in admiration, to serving and retired individuals alike. It has no real equivalent in the *RN* since *anchor-faced, a label which has similar overtones, can also imply inflexibility or lack of warmth. The Army's equivalent, which is exact, is *army-barmy*

cottage   Older slang term for a *messdeck, now only used in the phrase *Rose Cottage*

cough in your rompers   Break wind

counterpane hurdling   Possibly Jack's favourite indoor activity
(and Royal's as well !)

country pancake   A cowpat

Court Martial   Judicial trial before a court of military officers

coyote   Especial version of a *gronk. See *wolverine for a more
complete definition of this term

Cox'n / Coxswain (esp. *SM*)   The senior seaman rating on board,
a term now used pariculary in HM Submarines and minehunters/sweepers
where the **Coxswain** is the senior Chief Petty Officer, especially
qualified and selected for the appointment, and who is responsible for
discipline and *victualling. The word's origins lie in the roots *cog*
(a type of vessel) and *suen* or *swain* - husband

cow juice   Milk

Cowes rig   Amusing quasi-Victorian *split rig of white trousers,
winged collar and blue uniform jacket; used occasionally to enliven and
also smarten up a daytime *RPC or *Wardroom function

crabby   Dirty, filthy - perhaps derived from infestation with the
crab louse

Crabfats / Crabs / Crab Air   Original nickname for a member of
the *Royal Air Force* following that Service's formation, on April 1st
1918, by an enforced marriage between the *Royal Flying Corps* and the
**Royal Naval Air Sevice*. The colour of *RAF* uniforms is supposed to
have resulted from diversion of a huge but cancelled export order for
the Tsar's Imperial Guard following the previous year's Revolution in
Russia. This light-blue colour was identical to the greasy mercuric
oxide jelly (or *crabfat*) which was widely issued at the time for the
treatment of body lice - *crabs*. The descriptive term of *Crabfats* is
still widely used by senior Naval aviators, although now usually
abbreviated in common usage: "**Splot, please ensure that our *tame Crab
*puts in to grow a *full set.."* Or: *"What, Crab Air fly at weekends ?
You must be ruddy joking !"* Note also the term *Crimson Crabs

crabfat grey   *Pussers' **grey paint** between the wars was so thick
and sticky that it virtually had to be trowelled on by Jack when
*painting ship. In this case it was the similar consistency of the
paint to *crabfat (rather than its colour, as described in the
preceding entry cocerning the *RAF*) that remains synonymous with
Warship grey

crack   Similar meaning to *hack when referring to a problem,
but used in a more specific, active sense: *"Cracked 3 hours for the*

marathon last weekend.." To **crack on** means to continue, usually at an increased pace, whereas to **crack it** implies the completion of a task. Can also be used in the sense of **crack up*(2) and often heard as: *"You can't **crack me**, mate - I'm a rubber duck.."*

crack up
1. Fall about laughing, when used in a humorous context
2. Suffer a mental breakdown
3. Used in the past tense as a substitute for claimed or made out: *"Free-fall parachuting ain't all it's **cracked-up** to be .."*

crag rat *(RM)*   A *Mountain Leader* - the specialist climbers of the Corps

crappers   Drunk; *Harry **Crappers*** is a frequent form of usage

crash barrier *(FAA)*   Strong nylon net suspended across the flight deck to catch and stop an aircraft that had missed all the arrester wires with its tailhook when landing on; this evolution was termed a *barrier prang*. The British (again !) invention of the *angled deck* made this feature less important, but a crash barrier can still be **rigged* at a number of military air bases in the UK

crash draft   Sudden and totally unexpected appointment to a new ship or job, usually with very little notice to move

crash / crash out (esp. *RM*)   Fall asleep, especially when **crashing one's swede**. See also **gonk* and **zeds* in this context, but note also that to **crash out your smalls** means the same as to **dhobey* your **keks* !

cream in *(RM)*   To collide with something, fall over while ski-ing (see also **yeti* in this context) - or make a poor parachute landing

cream-crackered *(RM)*   Rhyming slang for *knackered*, meaning very tired or exhausted

creamer *(FAA)*   A really smooth landing

crease up   Double up with laughter at a funny sight or joke. See also *cheese down

creased   Face showing signs of severe tiredness or great pain: *"Spraining my ankle on landing really creased me.."*

Crimbo   Christmas. **Crimbo routine** at sea is very interesting; among many other traditional customs observed at sea, the most junior rating embarked borrows *Father's uniform and then does formal *Rounds of the ship !

crimp   A variety of applications:
  1. Old term for an agent commissioned to find the crew for a ship, often by drugging and kidnapping
  2. Use a special compression tool on a piece of detonator fuze
  3. To **crimp off a length** is to defaecate
  4. *(FAA)* To **crimp** is to pass into a deep sleep, whether from booze or tiredness: *"Don't bother talking to him - he's crimped out.."*

Crimson *Crabs *(FAA)*   The *RAF Red Arrows* formation aerobatic team

crippler   An unexpected set-back that must be coped with; to **slip a crippler** to a lady implies that she is going to get more than she bargained for during a *bunk up with Jack or Royal

critical *(SM)*   Term used to describe a nuclear boat's reactor after it has been started up by the process of *pulling rods*

crocadillapig   Any fierce-looking animal, of whatever size or type. If the beast is especially large and evil, the description may be enhanced by the adjectives *gynoferous or *gynormous. There some other variants, including the *lesser blotched hipporhinoflumboduck*, and the *rhinosnorarse* !

cross his bow   Annoy or insult someone more senior, usually unintentionally; it is both custom and good manners for a junior to give way to a more senior officer, thereby avoiding the collision (in the nautical sense) which could result from **crossing his bow**

Crossing the Line   Traditional, but completely unofficial ceremony enacted whenever a warship crosses the Equator. *His Oceanic Majesty, King Neptune,* together with his *Court,* come on board to initiate novices into the *Brotherhood of the Sea.* Splendid fun, with no distinction made between Officers and men in the normal sense as they are lathered, mock-shaved with a huge cut-throat razor, and then *thrown to the Bears* by being tipped backwards into a tank full of water

cross-dressing   A Writer in coveralls

Double-breasted matelot

cross-hatched *(FAA)*   Drunk, confused, or incapable. Derived from the magnetic indicators of the *Bucc instrument panel which became **cross-hatched** when the instrument went off-line, or failed

crow's nest   Senior WRNS rating's accomodation

crozzy   A crossword puzzle

crumb brush *(SM)*   Officer's steward

crumble   *"There's been a bit of a *crumble.."* means that someone has failed to do his or her job properly

crumpet   A particularly delicious-looking bit of *clacker: *"I'd crawl a mile over broken glass just to sniff the exhaust of the van that takes that bit of **crumpet**'s knickers to the laundry.."*

crusher   A member of the Regulating Branch (equivalent to the ship's police) - see *Reggies for a complete list

crystal cracker   Older nickname for a *Pinky, or a radio technician

CSB   Abbreviation of *Courage Sparkling Bitter,* a high-gravity and powerful keg beer especially brewed by *Messrs. John Courage* for Her Majesty's sea-going ships. Anyone suffering from the effects of over-indulgence in this excellent ale is said to have **CSB rash**

cuddy   A cabin situated aft for use either by the Captain or an important passenger

cuds *(RM)*   General term for the countryside, ie. the place where cows *chew their cuds*; can also be used to describe the area in which an operation is to be mounted or an exercise held

Culdrose   HMS *SEAHAWK,* the *Royal Naval Air Station* situated south of Helston in Cornwall. It is the biggest helicopter base in Europe, and parents the Squadrons and Flights of some 115 aircraft of various types. With over 3000 men and women on strength it is, in effect, the largest ship in the Royal Navy. The airfield's elevated position on the Lizard peninsula can lead to some very peculiar weather conditions varying from a thick and clinging *clamp to a forty mph fog; also known as **Cul-D**

cumshaw   Pidgin Chinese word for *Thank you !* adopted by Jack for anything that comes under the category of something acquired for nothing; see also *gizzit

cumulo-granite *(FAA)*   When conventional cloud comes down to the level of mountain tops, this feature should be avoided by aviators because it can really *spoil your whole day if flown into. Note also the term **cumulo-nasty** for a thundercloud

cushion creep *(FAA)*   The process of using the extra lift that is generated by a helicopter's rotor downwash close to the ground, in order to transition an overweight aircraft (or one at high altitude) into forward flight

cushy number   Rather envious description of a comfortable appointment or job

custard bosun   The Chief Cook - see page H -140

cut and run   Not cutting the anchor cable and running away, but the process of furling the sails on their yards and *stopping them there with light spunyarn; this could be cut with a knife so that the sails fell and drew almost immediately

cut his painter   Refers to death, since the **painter** here is a personal one and describes a sailor's link with life

cut of his jib   The shape of a person's nose in older times, since an efficient lookout could tell the nationality of another vessel purely by recognising the shape of its jibsail. This has now been adapted to comment on a person's style: *"He's a bit prickly sometimes, but overall I rather like the **cut of his jib**.."*

cuts very little ice   A wooden ship can make very little progress in pack ice, hence the modern usage to describe something that has made almost no impression at all on the speaker

cutlass   Short, heavy and curved naval sword used by Jack in hand-to-hand combat when boarding an enemy ship. Supposedly last used in anger when sailors from HMS *COSSACK* boarded the prison ship *Altmark* in Narvik Fjord, 1942. **Cutlass drill** is sometimes presented as a visually attractive item at the Royal Tournament

Cutter   Next size up from a *Whaler; it had light oars and a lugsail with a transom (flat) stern.   **Cutters** could also be towed by a pinnace if lots of *libertymen had to be ferried ashore

CW List   Older equivalent of what is now the *OAL, or *Officers' Appointments List*

DELTA

D *(FAA)* *Direction Officer*, specializing in Fighter Control and the **Direction** of fighter aircraft, in a tactical sense, at sea

dabber / dabtoe Denigratory term for a seaman rating (see also *AB) used by Royal, or by Jack when in a Specialist branch. Sometimes abbreviated to **Dabs** and see page **C** - 65 for Tugg's visualization

Daddy S Affectionate nickname for the *Supply and Secretariat* Commander in a ship or establishment; this title is more usually abbreviated to *Commander S*

Daddy's yacht An ignorant, slow-witted or otherwise useless sailor might well be addressed: *"Where the 'ell d'yew think yew are - yer bleedin' Daddy's yacht ?"*

dagger ( ) An officer who has specialized in *Aeronautical Engineering, Communication,* (aircraft) *Direction, Gunnery, Marine Engineering, Navigation* or *Torpedo and Antisubmarine Warfare,* and then passed the Advanced course in that subject: *"He's a dagger N.."* The term is derived from the way that these facts are recorded in the *Navy List, with a typeface symbol very like a **dagger** - but not to be confused with the *fighting knife* insignia used by the *Commandos

Damage Control The professional art of containing fire or water ingress to a ship in order to prevent its loss. Jack also uses the term to describe his *pash in the process of applying her make-up !

damager Manager, as in *NAAFI damager

dangle the Dunlops *(FAA)* Lower an aircraft's undercarriage prior to landing

dank   When used in the description of someone, this adjective pinpoints a rather anti-social and characterless individual. **Dank *hand** is a regular application, or **dank runner** when referring to *runs-ashore

daps   *Pusser's white plimsoles, or more recently - training shoes. Someone in a real hurry on official business is said to be moving just like *diarrhoea with daps on* - a nice alliteration, but rather unlikely !

Darby Traditional nickname associated with the surname Allen

dark and dirty   Rum and *Coca-Cola*; see also *light and dirty

darken ship   The defensive process of ensuring that no light whatsoever shows on the upperworks or hull

Darky Traditional nickname for someone called White or Whyte, but note also *Pinky

Dartmouth   Location of the *Britannia Royal Naval College* in Devon, with the College often referred to simply by this name. Jack would probably describe **Dartmouth** to you as the place where young Naval Officers are taught half-a-dozen different ways to say to their men: *"If you want me - I'll be in the *Wardroom.."*

DAUNTLESS   The former *WRNS training establishment near Reading. A *draft chit to this particular *stone frigate was Jack's pipedream until it closed in 1980; there is now a *DAUNTLESS* block at HMS *RALEIGH

Davy Jones' locker   The *duffy* (ghost) of *Jonah*, corrupted down the ages to mean the grave of the sea; note also *Old Grey Widow Maker

dawn strike   *Assault with a friendly weapon on waking up early; see also *morning glory

dayman Rating employed on duties requiring normal working hours, eg. a Writer, and therefore excused *watches; also used for someone in a ship which is day running from port. See *bag mealie in this respect

DCI *Defence Council Instruction*; these may be single service, or applied to all three services. A *DCI(RN)* is the successor to *AFOs

DD Entry in the ship's *muster book of older times to indicate that a sailor had died on board and been *Discharged Dead*. Jack might say, with typical grim humour: *"'E's gone *outside - DD.."*

Dead End Kids *(FAA)* Young wartime *RN Volunteer Reserve* Sub-lieutenants not considered for promotion to Lieutenant, ie. juniors without a future, but still employed in (dangerous) operational flying

dead horse See entry for *flog a dead horse

deadlight Hinged metal plate, usually of brass, located inboard of a *scuttle (a) to protect the glass during heavy weather and (b) to assist the evolution of *darken ship. See also *spoof !

dead Marine *(RM)* An empty wine bottle; the Duke of Clarence is supposed to have extricated himself nicely from possible offence to his hosts at a dinner party by suggesting that, just like a Marine: *"..that bottle has done his duty once and is now ready to do it again.."*

dead steam Water

deadlight Hinged metal flap which can be lowered and clamped over a *scuttle *sidelight in order to *darken ship. See also *spoof

Death Slide *(RM)* Laconic nickname for the aerial ropeway at *Lympstone down which all aspirants to a *green beret must descend

decimal bosun An Instructor Officer; see *schoolie for the complete list

Deck Landings *(FAA)* A *Wardroom game sometimes played after Mess Dinners in a carrier. A table surface is slicked with water or ice to simulate the wet deck, and then many napkins and elastic braces tied together to make an arrester cable. Participants pretend to be aircraft that are landing on, by hurling themselves headlong at this table - and then catching the arrester gear with their toes. A higher sea state can be simulated by moving the table legs up and down. Then, when the lights are turned out, *night flying* begins !

deck / deckhead The former is the equivalent of a floor, the latter of a ceiling. A **deckhead inspection** is carried out in the horizontal position from one's bunk. See also *Egyptian PT, *Mulley and *zeds for some alternatives

Deeks   The usual pronounciation of the acronym *DQs

deep one   Secretive or reserved individual, difficult to predict or divine: *"He's a really deep one, he is .."*

deep sea tot   Short measure - caused by the excessive rolling of a warship just as a *tot was being drawn

deep six   Beyond the lowest mark of the heaving line that used to be employed to sound out the depth of water beneath a ship: to invite someone to give something **the deep six** is like suggesting that it be subjected to a *float test

Deeps   *General Service ready-use nickname for a submariner. Often used for the very first time when a *draft chit for *SM* training comes in: *"Tell Deeps Smith to come to my office.."*

Defaulters   A formal muster and parade for hearing of charges of indiscipline; also the collective name for a group under punishment (sometimes pronounced as *undernourishment*)

defence watches   Eight hours on, eight off - around the clock. A very tiring routine for all involved, but essential for the fighting ability of a warship *closed up to a high state of readiness for action

definite maybe *(RM)*   Classic piece of non-commitment: *"Yes, I can give you a definite maybe on that one.."*   See also *positive perhaps

demo *(RM)*   Abbreviation of **demo**nstration: *"Just had a demo on that new S10 respirator - great bit of *kit, I reckon.."*

Detachment   The ship's embarked Royal Marines personnel; they live in an area of messdeck that is always called the *barracks

detailed off *(RM)*   Told to go and do something; see also *boned off and *jobbed

(the) **Devil and the deep blue sea / Devil to pay**   Both expressions have a naval origin, although the locations of the **Devil** appear to be different ! In the first instance it was the seam between deck and hull, meaning that there was only the thickness of the ship's hull planking *between the Devil and the deep blue sea*. The other **Devil** was the long plank running from stem to stern and immediately adjacent to the keel. The caulkers who had to keep this seam waterproof by ***paying** it with oakum (hemp fibres unpicked from condemned rope) and then sealing with hot pitch (tar) found the procedure very difficult, since this was the wettest and most inaccessible hull area of a careened vessel. The full original expression (which has now come ashore in a slightly different sense - to mean serious trouble) is *the Devil to *pay, and no pitch hot.*.

devil dodger   A Naval padre; see *amen wallah for a complete listing of the alternatives

DFs   *Duty Frees* - cigarettes supplied by the *Pusser. Note also *blue liners

dhobey   Original Hindi word now adopted for the business of washing clothes; may also be spelt as **dhobi** or **dhoby** in many variants:
  dhobey crusher - fiendish *Chogey laundry machine on board HM Ships which is apparently designed to rip the buttons off Jack's shirts and then fire them through his socks !
  dhobey dust - washing powder
  dhobey hitch - any *Wafu's knot which slips undone when it becomes wet; note also the **stoker's dhobey hitch** which is any totally unrecognisable knot
  dhobey itch - skin rash from imcomplete rinsing of clothes
  dhobey palace - laundromat / washeteria
  dhobey wallah - laundryman

diamond piece   The central, crucial and strategic component of a lady's knickers

dibs   Money

Dick Doc   Nickname for the most junior of three Medical Officers appointed to the old aircraft carriers; to a certain extent descriptive of his duties, because there was *Big Doc, Little Doc,* and *Dick Doc*

dicked   To be beaten comprehensively, especially in a sporting encounter. Being ****rubber dicked** implies that this **dicking** was achieved by unfair or illegal means; an ****eight piece dicking** is the highest grade of defeat possible at *Uckers

dickey   An interesting, multipurpose word:
  1. Weak or damaged: *"His heart's a bit **dickey**.."*
  2. A (false) white shirt, laced at the sides, but open at the

back for wear in tropical climates is a **dickey front**
3. **dickey bow** - a bow tie, usually one that is made-up commercially
4. **second dickey** - the deputy leader (from second **i/c**)
5. **dickey seat** - occasional seating arrangement in a vehicle or boat

dickhead   Idiot

diesel-electric drainpipe   A conventional (diesel-powered) submarine

dig out   Work hard or with great enthusiasm to achieve an aim: *"We wuz diggin' out blind to finish the job.."*   Can also be used as an invitation to help oneself: *"Need a *wet of coffee ? Dig out, mate.."* See also *fill your boots in this latter respect

digit   The finger, paraphased as ***Extractum digitum !*** for: *"Get your finger out !"*   The *FAA* in WW2 also had ***De-digitate !*** with exactly the same meaning

dim   Not very bright, hence: *"He's as **dim** as a NAAFI candle / Toc H lamp !"*

Ding dong !   "I don't believe it !"

Dinger   Nickname for the surname Bell

dingleberries   Prolapsed haemorrhoids (piles)

dining in / out   The tradition of inviting a new Commanding Officer or *HOD to **dine in** with the *Wardroom (or *RM* Officer's Mess) for the first time in his or her appointment.   Other officers may be **dined out** at the same function, as guests of the Mess; all members of the Mess are supposed to attend a **Dining-In Night**

Dink / Dinky Dai   Jack's generic nickname for an Australian, presumably to do with the words *dinkum* and *G'day*

dip   Multipurpose word with several distinct meanings:
1. Fail an examination or test: *"I **dipped** on the pass-out run.."*
2. Lose a rate or rank: *"She **dipped** her *killick's.."*   Or: *"He's been **dipped down** to Corporal again.."*
3. To **dip in** is to strike lucky: *"He's always **dippin' in**, the jammy git.."*
4. Lose out, or not receive a fair share: *"I'm always **dipping out**.."* See also *plums
5. Dive. *Monthly dippers* are the regular dives made by qualified personnel in order to remain current for pay; **dip money** is an item paid as a special supplement for dangerous or experimental diving. See also ***backy dips**
6. ***Dip Boss*** *(FAA)* is a term used by helicopters hunting submarines and refers to the on-scene tactical commander of the **dip gang** - who may well be a young *Sea King *looker.   Note also that the aircraft involved in this hunt will, at various stages, be **in**

the **dip** - hovering with their sonar equipment lowered into the water

7. To **dip one's wick** is to have sexual intercourse
8. **Dipping the ensign** is a warship's method of returning a salute
9. A signal flag which is **at the dip** is just below close-up and means that it is ready to be executed. Note that *at the full* indicates that it is to be executed immediately. Thus, if if an order is to be carried out smartly, after giving it one may add: "..*and that's at the full !*"

dirk   Seaman's clasp knife, also known as a *pusser's dirk. This is an instrument of great versatility because, as Jack himself would point out, it has to be capable of doing everything from splitting rock to spreading butter !

dirty dive / **dirty dash** *(FAA)*   Flying very low (and possibly illegally) beneath low cloud or bad weather in order to make the objective

dirty windows (a pair of)   Older *RM* term for two black eyes

discharge Shore   The process whereby, having committed a series of disciplinary offences and not taken heed of any official warnings, an individual is put ashore as a civilian, ie. kicked *outside

dischuffed   The direct opposite of *chuffed. Someone who is **mightily dischuffed** is rather angry and disillusioned; see also the term *gruntled

dismissed his ship / **the Service**   *Court-martial sentence on an Officer or a senior rate who is tried and found guilty, then put on half-pay while awaiting a new ship or appointment. To be **dismissed the Service** is equivalent to being *discharged Shore

dist   A basic abbreviation for the word *distribution* which in turn can be used as a verb as wellas a noun: *"Didn't you get the letter I **disted** on that subject ? You were definitely on the **Dist** (list).."*

DISTEX   A Disaster Control Exercise, as practised for near-real during *work-up at *Portland

distinction cloth   Coloured bands interleaved between the gold lacing of an officer's uniform sleeve. The older colours of white (*Supply and Secretariat*), green (*Electrical*) and purple (*Mechanical*) have been retained in the Merchant Navy. The blue of *Schoolies has disappeared totally. In the RN, only *blood red (*Medical*), dark red (*Dental*) and salmon-pink (*Medical Services*) are still in current usage, although the *Royal Naval Corps of Constructors*, when in uniform, sport a silver-grey colour, and the *RN Supply and Transport Service* have dark green

dit   Any written (or spoken) account of an incident or event in a sailor's life

Ditch   The English Channel

ditch   A trio of applications:
1. *(FAA)* Land an aircraft in the sea
2. Discard something (eg. *gash) over the side
3. Get rid of something (or someone) ashore: *"She **ditched** him just before *Crimbo.."*

ditty box   A lockable wooden container, often elaborately carved or embellished, in which a sailor kept his most prized or unusual possessions. See Tugg's cartoon on page **M** - 185. This item was originally issued as a *commodity box* for toilet gear etc. but then replaced around WW 2 by a small brown suitcase, which is no longer issued. The modern equivalent is a *messdeck locker which, thank goodness, may now contain a **ditty box**. HMS *RALEIGH*'s Daily Orders, referred to in the Preface, has a section called *The Ditty Box* which attempts, right from the start, to introduce a new generation of Jack to the delights of *JACKSPEAK* !

diversion kit *(FAA)*   Toothbrush, credit card, clean underpants, a small amount of folding money and a *franger - carried at all times in a flying suit pocket

Diving Stations *(SM)*   The state adopted prior to leaving surface; see also *"*Open up for diving !"*

Divisional system   Man-management scheme whereby the sum total of Jack's overall well-being, welfare, education and advancement is supervised and recorded by his junior **Divisional officers** or **DOs**; they report to *HoDs who, in turn, are responsible to the Captain for these matters. A good **DO** is very much at ease with his men, able to talk with them on a wide variety of subjects, and always accessible to them as a source of personal advice, help - and encouragement. See also *set of papers

Divisions   A formal parade held on special occasions, ranging from **Church Divisions** (every Sunday) all the way up to the *Lord High Admiral's Divisions held at *Dartmouth in the presence of *Her Majesty The Queen* (or her representative)

divvy   A **divi**dend or share; to **divvy up** means to pay up, or share out the spoils

dixie   Nickname for any large mess tin or cooking pot, but note also the *scab-lifter's special usage to describe an inflamed **appendix** prior to its removal in a *Boneyard

do the honours   Pour out the wine for your neighbour while seated at table

Doc   Traditional nickname for the Medical Branch *killick carried in frigate-sized warships, as distinct from the *Quack embarked for long deployments - or in wartime

docket   Naval name for a file cover and its contents, which together make up a *pack

dockyard goldfish   An alternative name for a *brown trout

dockyard jellyfish / oyster   A floating *green grolly that has been *flobbed up by someone with a productive cough.

dockyard matey   Traditional nickname for industrial personnel working in the (now privatized) HM Dockyards: *"How many **dockyard mateys** work in Devonport ? I should think about fifty per cent of them.."*

dockyard Olympics   The old process of refitting a warship whereby all the tradesmen lined up at the start of the day and then raced off to various places inside the ship. The first one to reach an area fitted his pipe, wire, duct or whatever - thus leading to a totally unco-ordinated jumble and a *snake's honeymoon ! At the other extreme was the **dockyard shuffle** describing a *dockyard matey's speed of progress when detailed to do a job close to knocking-off time

dockyard omelette / pizza The results of a *Technicolour yawn lying on the road; *pavement pizza* is a variant of this theme

dockyard tortoise A Cornish pasty

Doctor Fog *(FAA)* Met man; see also *Professor Fog, *weather guesser and *congenital liar

doddle Something easy

Dodger Traditional nickname for someone called Long

dodger Two forms of usage:
1. Canvas or fabric weather screen on an exposed part of the ship
2. A messdeck cleaner or sweeper is the **messdeck dodger**; note that Royal's term for this function ashore is *block sweeps

dodges and wheezes Ways of making life a little easier while still carrying out the allotted task; see also *wrinkles

dodgy deacon Vicar or cleric with homosexual tendencies; *pulpit poofter and *raving rev are recognised alternative forms

dog Diarrhoea and vomiting, especially when associated with a particular place, eg. Malta Dog; see also *bite !

dog and basket *(RM)* Nickname for the lion and crown beret badge of Royal Marines Officers and *Warrant Officers.

dog robbers A *RN* officer's *shore *rig for casual or relaxed occasions. Usually described as a sports jacket and slacks, with tie/cravat or polo-neck sweater, and generally a bit smarter than either *scruff rig or rat-catcher's rig

dog-shit day *(FAA)* Poor visibility in low scudding cloud and rain

dog watches Two (short) two-hour periods, inserted in the ship's routine to equalize the duty *roster. To say that someone has only been in *half a dog watch* implies that he or she has only been in the Navy for a comparatively short time. Probably derived from *dodge watches* since they were incomplete in one sense; other sources suggest that these were normal watches that had become *cur-tailed* !

Dogger Bank dragoons Jack's nickname for *RM* *Commandos during WW2

doggie Junior officer, usually under training, appointed as assistant to a senior Executive Officer or the Captain: *"I was *Wings' doggie for that first month - and a dog's life it was too.."* See also *gofer

Brownhatter

doggo (esp. *RM*)   Ugly, when referring to the opposite sex, and probably abbreviated from *doghouse* or *dog-like*. Can also be used to describe the process of being still and silent: *"We just lay* **doggo** *in the stream until the Argies got bored and cold - and stood up. Then Jumper Collins followed them back through their minefield and marked the route.."*

doing things around the edges   Older term implying peripheral involvement without any real contribution

dollar pick-up   Older *Singers term for a cheap taxi or *fast black

Dolly   Traditional nickname for the surname Gray or Grey

Dolphins *(SM)*   The gilt uniform brooch awarded to all ranks who have completed submarine training and passed the qualifying Boards; they are worn throughout a man's career in the Navy. Those associated with the *Submarine Service* ashore and awarded **honorary Dolphins** (not worn on uniform) may be required to **drink for their Dolphins** in the Chief's Mess. The brooch is placed in the bottom of a glass and covered with a mixture of spirits that must be *yam-senged until the **Dolphins** are trapped in the recipient's teeth ! The **Dolphin Code** refers to a group of numbers that correspond to messages which can be sent between aircraft and submarines, or between submarines themselves during exercises at sea; some are rather rude and funny:

Dolphin 113 : *"Oh dear ! The Staff are getting active again; which idiot gave the Admiral a shake ?"*

Dolphin 174 : *"I don't know how we are going to cope without you - but we are certainly willing to give it a try.."*

dolphins   A line of mooring posts

donk / donkey　　　Any petrol or diesel (especially a submarine's) engine. The term has been widely adopted in the aviation world: *"When the gearbox failed and both donks stopped, it suddenly became apparent that we were rather poorly placed.."* Or: *"The Heron aircraft has four piston donkeys bolted to its wings.."*

donk shop *(SM)*　　　Engine room

donkey walloper *(RM)*　　　Generic term for any cavalry officer; see also *Ruperts, *wah-wahs and *seagulls

Don't be afraid of the badges !　　　*"Speak up, lad - I won't bite your head off !"*

doofer　　　Like *doobrey*, a catch-all name that will do for anything Jack can't describe instantly or accurately. *Johnson is a *Fleet Air Arm* variant. The original **doofer** was the stump of a home-made *tickler which had been extinguished and carefully stowed inside Jack's hat as something that would **do for** later. The sudden order ***Off caps !*** at Divine Service would often produce a veritable snowstorm of **doofers** falling to the deck

dope on a rope *(FAA)*　　　An aircrewman

Doris　　　Standard nickname for a Naval Nurse

dose　　　When used on its own, this word implies the acquisition of venereal disease, but it can also be qualified in a more general way, eg. a **dose of 'flu** or a **dose of the *dog**. In the former context, see also *catch the boat up, *nap hand and *Rose Cottage

doss down　　　Go to sleep somewhere other than a bedroom or night *cabin; *(RM)* usually in a *green slug

double-breasted matelots　　　Members of the *Women's Royal Naval Service*, ie. *Wrens. Sometimes described also as **double bums** or **double bumps**; see page **C - 73** for Tugg's lovely interpretation

double-clews　　　Twice the number of *nettles **clewed** to a hammock meant a wider spread to the canvas as well as the ability to support a greater load. This is an example of Jack's humour from older times in that a fellow sailor who had *embarked / entered **double-clews*** had just got married !

double-dipper　　　*US Navy* term, occasionally heard in *RN* circles, for a retired officer re-employed as a civilian, thereby drawing both pension and salary

double-hatted　　　An officer with *RN* and *NATO* responsibilities; note also the even more responsible term of *triple-hatted

double-six   Crucial dice throw in *Uckers, also extending into real life: *"How the hell did he get the job ? Did he throw a **double-six** or something ?"*

doughbag *(RM)*   An overweight, slow-witted and generally useless individual

Down the hatch !   Drinking toast similar to ***Bottoms up !***

downbird *(FAA)*   Helicopter that has made a precautionary or emergency landing somewhere other than its intended destination, and which needs attention from the *grubbers of a **downbird team** before it can fly again

downstairs trot *(SM)*   Nickname for the *'tween-decks duty sentry in a submarine that is alongside

Do you (d'ye) hear there !   Preliminary announcement made over a *Tannoy or broadcast system to alert the ship's company just prior to an important *pipe

dozy (esp. *RM*)   Word used for a *doughbag: *"You **dozy** individual.."*

DQs   Her Majesty's *Royal Naval Detention Quarters* in the Portsmouth Naval Base. The term may also refer to any military prison staffed (or patronized) by Jack and Royal. See also *deeks

Drafty   Generic nickname for the various Desk Officers at HMS *CENTURION* who maintain the sea and shore *rosters for men in their specializations, and then issue **draft chits** ordering Jack when and where to move to next

dragon   Jack's occasional and charming description of his wife; see also *Field Marsha, *Generalissima and *CINC-NAG-HOME ! May also be used by Royal on sighting a *gronk during a *run-ashore: *"If I was St. George, I'd finish that **dragon** off rightaway.."*

drain out all over   Torrent of complaints, equivalent to *manking or *dripping all over someone

drain-sniffer   Any medical officer or rating involved in Public Health and Hygiene duties

dread / dreaded lurgie   Jack's term for whichever form of virulent influenza is circulating the ship or establishment at the time

dreadnought   Contraceptive sheath issued free on board to Jack *en route* to his *run-ashore. Also known as a *fearnought, but see also *wellies, *forget-me-nots and *frangers

dream sheet   The computerised *Drafting Preference Card* on which Jack and Royal state where they would like to serve in the future. The *Fleet Air Arm* also use this term to describe the daily *flypro

dress ship   Decorate a ship in harbour with signal bunting and lights for special occasions such as the *Lord High Admiral's Official Birthday, or for *Navy Days. The ship is **dressed overall** from the *jackstaff up to masthead and back down to the ensign staff

dressed up to the nines   Jack's lady when overdressed for a function

drift   Implied meaning: *"You get my **drift**, Sunshine ?"*

drill   Naval procedure: *"What's the **drill** for tonight's *Cockers P ?"*

drink   The sea; note also *oggin and *ogwash

drip   Multipurpose word to describe a moan or complaint. To present **a drip chit** implies the stating of a complaint in the official sense; **dripping all over** someone means complaining to him or her volubly, and at some length. *RM* usage also has **drip sesh** for any gathering where problems are discussed: *"Any **drips** ? See *Freshwater Tanky !"*

drive   Relaxed slang for ship command: *"Who's **driving** AMBUSCADE at the moment ?"* The plural form **Drives** is both a standard nickname and means of address for any *RM* vehicle driver

Droggy   Contraction of Hy**drog**rapher, a member of the service that is responsible for all the Admiralty's maritime charts

drongo (esp. *RM*)   Rather nice term of general abuse for a slovenly or ill-disciplined individual. The usual qualifying adjective is *complete*, hence: *"As far as I'm concerned, the man's a born-again *tosser and a **complete drongo**.."*

drop a bollock   Make an embarassing mistake; see also *blob(5)

drop a brown   WW2 expression concerning the effects of fear; the modern version is ***Adrenalin's brown !***

drop of all right   Expression of admiration for a drink (or an attractive lady !)

drop your guts / handbag   Break wind

drown the miller   An archaic expression for the process of diluting *grog by more than the statutory three parts water to one of rum. This might be done by a corrupt purser who sought to extend the ration further - and then pocket the difference

drumhead service *(RM)*   Short religious service taken in the field, or on *Corps and Unit memorable dates, when fallen comrades are remembered and mourned. Although a number of **side-drums** may feature as a centrepiece for such a service, the real origin is strictly Naval in that a **drumhead** was the top part of the capstan barrel of old - the section perforated with pigeon holes for inserting its capstan bars before *weighing anchor

drummer   A drum roll preceded most bugle calls in action - the nickname has passed on for *RM* buglers, but see also *Sticks. For some reason a **drummer's hook** is the *deck, so that to *hang something on a drummer's hook* means to drop it on the floor

dry as dust   Description of a Naval person who has not been to sea for a long time, like certain *Whitehall warriors and other forms of *barrack stanchion

dry idler   Jack's traditional nickname for anyone other than a seaman or stoker

dry run   A rehearsal without actions; see also *dummy run

DSM - SMR !   *Don't See Me - See My *Relief ! meaning: "I can't really be bothered to assist you with your problem, because I'm leaving this ruddy job in the very near future..'*

Dubs-40   *WD-40*, a waterproofing, preservative and generally indispensable spray fluid familiar to most motorists; also known as *pussers fix-all

dubs   *Double-O* suffix to a time, meaning on the hour: *"The meeting is due to start at oh-eight-dubs.."* (0800)

duck run   A lady's posterior - the bit that waggles as she walks. A chap with **duck's disease** is rather short, ie. his posterior is very close to the ground

duckboards   Latticed wooden floorboards found in showers and at the bottom of boats; presumably the term originates from their help in keeping Jack's feet dry - just like a **duck**! Certainly, the duck's overall waterproofness is a feature that is much admired and envied: *"The whole thing was as **watertight as a duck's arse**! 'Ow do I know that a **duck** is watertight? Well, 'ave you ever seen a **duck** sinking?"*

ducks   White tropical uniform, in the days before Terylene

duff   Multipurpose word:
1. A pudding, eg. **figgy duff, plum duff**
2. Useless: *"The radar's duff.."* or (esp. *RM*): *"We've been fed totally duff *gen again.."*
3. To **come one's duff** is vulgar slang for an orgasm, but see also *vinegar strokes and *Fratton
4. **ear duffs** are hearing protectors
5. To be **up the duff** is to be pregnant

dummy deck   Airfield runway area marked to look like an aircraft carrier's flight deck. Designed for pilot's landing practice, or the training of *chockheads; see also *ADDLS

dummy run   Complete rehearsal of a military *evolution, but without actually firing any of the weapons involved

dump   Another word with three completely different applications:
1. Defaecate
2. *(FAA)* **dumping the lever** means reducing a helicopter's collective pitch as quickly as possible
3. *(FAA)* Get rid of surplus fuel by **dumping it**

dung button   Anus; see also *burnt plum and *rusty bullet-hole

dung hampers   Underpants or *keks

dunk *(FAA)*   Two meanings:
1. Lower a sonar device into the sea from a helicopter
2. **The Dunker** is a helicopter underwater escape trainer in which all *FAA* aircrew undergo regular **Dunker drills**

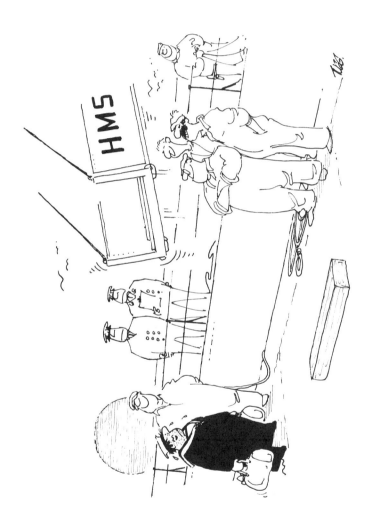

Adrift

duskers   The penultimate stage of a *FAA* pilot's *working-up to become night qualified in the *SHAR

Dusty Also two applications:
  1. Traditional nickname for the surname Rhodes and Miller
  2. A **Jack Dusty** is a *Supply and Secretariat* rating, abbreviated from the historic nickname *Jack o' the Dust* - a seaman of yesteryear who issued the flour provisions. Note also Tugg's absolute classic on p. **K** - 160

Dutch ovens   Breaking wind under a double duvet - origin obscure

duty hag   Jenny's own term, perhaps based on *Macbeth*, for the duty *WRNS rating in an establishment

dwang   Trouble: *"You, my son, are in **the dwang**.."*

ECHO

ear pounding Heavy verbal criticism

ease The process of paying out carefully on a rope, particularly if it it is under some tension. The expression *Easy does it !* stems directly from this

ease springs Polite alternative in conversation for the process of passing water. Two distinct explanations can be offered:
1. For Jack, *springs* are special mooring lines which come under tension as a ship moves fore and aft with the tide and current
2. *(RM)* The order *Ease springs !* is given following a weapon safety inspection after firing on a range

Easter egg *(RM)* Royal's nickname for a *Bandie wearing a red sash

Easy does it ! Handle something carefully, or more slowly - and with less vigour; see also *ease

eat a cow between two bread vans / eat a horse between two hammocks
Splendid piece of *RM* exaggeration indicating great hunger: *"I'm that bloody famished I could eat a cow between two bread vans, *no probs.."*
Another alternative concerns a **scabby donkey between two mattresses** !

eating irons Cutlery; see also *KFS and *gobbling rods

egg on legs A short, fat person

Egyptian An amusing trio retained from Jack's long experience of service at the far end of the Med:
1. **Egyptian flu** - a lady who is unwell because she's shortly going to be a mummy !

2. **Egyptian PT** *(RM)* - sleep; see *gonking or *zeds for some
   alternatives
3. **Egyptian *AFOs** - crudely printed pornography that caused
   as much laughter as sexual excitement: *"Stoq, - Oh
   pleise STOQ !" she crid in Exeters as his hand crapt
   slowley up her theigh..*

eight piece dicking   The most comprehensive form of defeat
possible at *Uckers in that your opponent has managed to get all eight
of his counters home before you've even managed to deliver one

electric ears   Headphones

electric hat *(FAA)*   A *Chockhead's hard hat and *electric ears

electric string   General term for any insulated cable

elephant's arsehole   A shiny brass hawsepipe installed aft on
the stern of towed array frigates, and used to stream the sonar cable

elephant's footprints *(SM)*   Spam fritters immersed in batter and
then fried before being served for breakfast

elephant's trunk *(SM)*   Canvas water chute rigged beneath a
submarine's *conning tower to collect any seawater entering while the
*boat is running *opened up in rough weather

elk's nest *(RM)*   Enormous hole left in the snow by Royal when he
*yetties on *planks, especially so when fully-laden with a *chacon

Elmer   General term for an American. In its fully expanded version,
the reference is to one *Elmer P. Chickenshit Junior - the Third*

embuggerance factor   Something random or unforseen that does not
exactly contribute to the execution of a plan or *evolution, but merely
delays and impedes it; may also be spelt *imbuggerance

empire builders   Any generously-cut shorts, but especially a pair of *pusser's white tropical ones

end for end   Reverse the position of something, or as Jack might put it a little more directly, *make it *arse about face*

endex   Abbreviation for **end of exercise**, but applied much more widely, for instance as a euphemism for death: *"Touch those terminals, mate - and it'll be **endex** for you.."*

equaliser   A hammer, used to great effect when employed in the *Chief Stoker's method

essence   A wonderful and easily emphasized word that indicates beauty: *"She's **essence** !"*   Or, perfection in form and function: *"It's an **essence** piece of *kit.."*   It may just be an abbreviation of *quintessence*, but it is especially common in *RM* usage. Visiting French *fusiliers marins* hearing this term must be extremely puzzled as to the connection with petrol !

Every man for himself !   Final order given when a warship is on fire or badly damaged and about to sink; it means that nothing more can be done by way of damage control and firefighting, and that there is no longer any need for Jack to await further orders

(in) **everyone's mess but nobody's watch**   Said of someone who is always around when there is fun to be had, but who disappears quickly when any hard work is in prospect

everything you know about that subject could be written on the outside of a gnat's bollock bag   *"You are not quite as clever as you think.."*   Note also that a **flea's tit** is the alternative geographical location

evolution   Any important seamanship task requiring co-ordinated action for its successful completion, especially in an emergency. The term is widely used in the *RN* for other procedures not directly related to the operation of a ship

-ex Suffix for exercise, tacked on to a number of words, eg.:
    *DISTEX - *Disaster Control Exercise*
    *Endex - the time that an exercise is declared complete
    *Gloppex - a *run-ashore or party where some serious
            drinking is planned or has taken place
     Navex *(FAA)* - navigation training sortie
    *Smashex - an exercise that simulates a submarine's loss

exag   Pronounced with a soft *g* and describing something that is really difficult to believe

exhibish   An alcohol-induced display of a lewd nature such as the *Zulu warrior ritual, but more especially the sort of live sex acts seen in clubs along the Reeperbahn in Hamburg

Exocet   Jack's wry and self-mocking humour applied to a cocktail barman's special mix: *"Just one - and you're wrecked.."*   Also used to describe his mother-in-law, because just like an **Exocet,** you can see her coming, the timing is always very awkward, there's very little you can do about it - and it tends to ruin your whole weekend

exped   Adventure training (expedition)

extenders   An extended long weekend, ie. Thursday to Monday, or Friday to Tuesday: *"Mitch ain't here Monday - he's on extenders.."* Some would have you believe this to be the normal *Wafu weekend !

extra   Additional musical item often played by the *Bandies towards the end of a formal dinner. A solo or duo piece featuring musical ability and/or great humour is presented, usually to the enormous approval of those who are dining

extra lights *(RM)*   The custom of paying a barman an additional sum of money when the bar is kept open after hours. All present are expected to make a contribution

extracting the Michael   Politer version of taking the *piss

eyeball it *(FAA and RM)*   Inspect something visually; take a long, close look at it with that simplest instrument of detection and inspection - the *Mark One eyeball*

eyelid inspection   Sleeping; see *gonking for a list of other versions

eyes in two watches   Description of an individual whose eyes appear to be moving independently of each other as a result of drunkeness, or tiredness - or both

(made his) **eyes water** *(RM)*   Laconic understatement applied to the effects of controlled military violence: *"A *Milan anti-tank missile arriving in an enemy *sangar doesn't half make the occupants' eyes water.."*

Clacker

FOXTROT

face aft and salute ! Order given to those on the upper deck during *Colours; also a tacit acknowledgement that whatever Jack's different opinions on some aspect of his ship's operation, he will ultimately obey orders: *"The *Boss tried to alter our *Ripple 3 crew *rosters, but *Wings wouldn't wear it - told him **to face aft and salute**.."*

face like a _____ There are some amusing variations to be heard on this theme when discussing *gronks:

> She 'ad a **face like** a bulldog chewin' a wasp, and teeth like *a row of condemned 'ouses..*

> Her **face** was **like** a walking *Hurt Certificate - with a mouth *like a torn pocket..*

> She had the **face** of a messdeck scrubber, and eyes **like** a *Dogger Bank cod..*

> *Her **face** ? Well, her *moosh was **like** a ruptured custard - an' the rest looked like a badly-packed kitbag..*

> *Not only was her **face like** a bag of smashed crabs, she was as rough as a badger's bum into the bargain..*

fagged out Tired, from the **fagging out** of an old rope's end. Hence also the term **fag end** for a frayed and stamped-on cigarette butt, and (presumably) the actual derivation of the word **fag**. Note also the original meaning of the term *doofer as a cigarette that has been half-smoked, extinguished, and then carefully stowed inside Jack's cap as something that will *do fer later..*

fair   Favourable, or unobstructed, hence the applications of a **fair course** to steer, the **fairway** of a channel or harbour - and the similar application in golf, a **fairlead** for a sail's sheet, and a **fair copy** for an error-free version of the original

fair wind   Especially favourable conditions, which may be direct - as when calculating the helpful effect of a following wind on an aircraft's progress, or oblique as in: *"The Admiral very much approves of this idea, so he's given the proposal a fair wind on its way up to the Minister.."*   Also used to ask for the cruet at table: *"Give the salt and pepper a fair wind in this direction please.."*

faith to plant acorns   Nice expression for someone with strong convictions, ie. he intends to **plant acorns** now which will grow into the oak trees from which his grandson's ship will be built !

familygram *(SM)*   40 word message that is sent weekly to each member of a *Bomber crew when on *Polaris* patrol; some of the words become a bit garbled in transmission, so Jack tends to call any form of computer-generated rubbish a **familygram** !

fancy waistcoats   Figure of speech that casts doubt over the accuracy of some statement

fang farrier   Dentist; see also *gnasher basher, *toothwright and *Top Gum

fanny   Oval or cylindrical mess *trap, originally used in the packing of tinned meat for general Naval issue. When it began in 1907, this technique was regarded with great suspicion by Jack, especially as a young girl named (Sweet) *Fanny Adams* had been murdered and dismembered around that time. The tins were re-used on the messdecks as utensils, but the coincidence resulted in *Fanny*'s name living on in a completely unintended way. The **messdeck fannies** used for *grog were also called *monkeys, about a half-gallon in size, and highly polished and decorated. Note that the word has nothing to do with the more general American term describing an intimate portion of the female anatomy, or the vaguely similar usage involving the posterior on this side of the *Pond

fanny mechanic   Gynaecologist; *quim quack is a recorded alternative

fanny rat   Chap who chases after ladies, often with considerable success; see also *lead on MacDick

fanny scratchers   Fingers

far flung   Anywhere away from the home waters of the United Kingdom, but especially east of Suez

fart in a spacesuit   Jack's phrase for something not only unwelcome and unpleasant, but which also has an enduring and persistent quality

fart in a thunderstorm *(RM)*   Indication of someone or something's general worth: *"His announcement had just about as much impact on the proceedings as a **fart in a thunderstorm**.."*

fart in a trance   Description of somebody who is a bit dreamy and unable to make decisions; has also been heard as: *"You look like a lost fart in a haunted milk bottle!"*

fartleberries   Yet another name for *bum plums or haemorrhoids

fast black   Official (black) saloon car *(RM)* although the older Singapore usage referred to the *dollar pick-up black Mercedes taxis (unlicensed) that would take Jack and Royal from *RNAS* Simbang to the *TERROR* Club, or to downtown *Singers and the delights of *Bugis Street

fast cruise *(SM)*   The process of exercising a submarine's crew in various emergency drills whilst **fast alongside** with the *lid shut

Fat Albert   RAF term, now adopted in the *Andrew, for the C-130 *Hercules* transport operated by *Truckies which performed prodigious feats of workload and endurance during (and after) the 1982 Falklands campaign. Jack grew to love ***Fat Albert*** and his *mailie drops at sea

fat, dumb and happy *(FAA)*   Failing to pay proper attention to the exacting business of flying: *"There I was, sitting **fat dumb and happy** in a forty-foot hover - when the Doppler threw a monster *wobbly.."*

fat knacker pie *(RM)*   Any food rich in calories, but especially puddings and sweets. May sometimes be heard as *naughty pie*, or even more simply as a **fat pill**

Father   Respectful (and affectionate) nickname for the Captain. See also the *Old Man - but never *Skipper*

Father Famine   Traditional nickname for the Supply Officer in charge of catering; note also Tugg's superb Rowlandson-like caricature on page P - 221

fathom   Standard measurement of depth or the length of ropes and cables. Derived from the Old English word for an embrace, it is approximately six feet - or the distance between the outstretched arms of a man

fearnought suit *(FAA)*   Thick jacket and trousers made of worsted felt, worn by fire-fighting crews: *"Listen lad, I was in a **fearnought suit** when you was still in a romper suit.."*

feat of arse *(RM)*   Rather mocking derivation that is the complete opposite of a **feat of arms**; an older play on words also has this phrase as a **feed of arse** for a *botty bandit

feet under the table   Expression meaning that Jack has made himself at home (while away from home) and is getting on very well. May also be used to describe good progress in the pursuit of some attractive lady

fell in three deep   Expression applied to some event that has been organized properly: *"When we got there a *tame Crab who'd flown *Tooms off *ARK in '77 **fell us in three deep** and marched us from one party to the next in what turned out to be a fantastic *landaway weekend.."*

fell off his perch   Description of some self-important or pompous individual's sudden come-uppance - and subsequently damaged reputation

(the) Ferchristsake wire *(FAA)*   The arrester cable nearest to the *sharp end of an aircraft carrier

ferret   Occasional rhyming slang for a beret

fetch up   End up somewhere after a *run ashore, or arrive suddenly on deck in an emergency, eg. after striking a submerged object: *"All of a sudden there was this *gynoferous crunching sound, and we all **fetched up** *topsides.."*

(a) few laughs and a few beers *(RM)*   *Very* unofficial translation of the Corps' motto *Per Mare Per Terram*

fid   A wooden spike, tapered for splicing rope; nowadays a handful or sheaf of papers, eg. a **fid of signals**

Fiddler's Green   An imaginary sailor's Heaven full of pubs, dance halls and enthusiastic ladies. When he *cut his painter and *shuffled off this mortal coil* (of rope that made up the painter !) Jack was said to have *gone aloft to **Fiddler's Green***

field gunner   A member of the *Devonport, Portsmouth* or *Fleet Air Arm* **field gun crews** who train all year for a competition held during the annual *Royal Tournament* at Earl's Court. The results are signalled world-wide to the *Fleet; the participants are famous for their speed, size and strength, and the way that these qualities are combined into a spectacular display of teamwork. See page **G - 131** !

Field Marsha   The military equivalent of *Her Indoors*; *Generalissima and *CINC-NAG-HOME* are alternatives

Field officer *(RM)*   Officer with the rank of *Major* - or above. When in *blues they wear tight-fitting overall trousers with boots and spurs

FIFO *(RM)*   Fit In - or *Foxtrot Oscar*: *"Look, mate - in this little outfit you've got to **FIFO** - see ?"* *SUSO has a similar meaning

Fifteen-two that bastard !   General challenge for anyone to do better, having just made a good play or stroke. Can also be used on non-sporting occasions; derived from the card game of *cribbage* where the sum of **fifteen** is unbeatable and results in **two points** scored. Sometimes misquoted as *fifteen-love* (as in tennis) but the meaning is identical

fifth five   Older term for Extended Service; the normal full-career commitment for Jack is twenty-two years. A **fifth five** took this to twenty-seven, but has now been replaced by the *Second Open Engagement* which is written as *2OE*

fifty up   Masturbation, hence the old tombola call: *"Five-oh, under the blanket - **fifty**.."*

figgy duff   Any stodgy or suet-based pudding

fighting gear   Table cutlery; see also *KFS and *gobbling rods

fighting knife *(RM)*   Correct name for the Commando dagger emblem

fighting order *(RM)*   Weapon, spare ammunition and magazines, water bottle, field dressing, poncho cape and mess tins, with all but the first item carried in special pouches or rolls attached to a close-fitting upper body harness

file 13   Wastepaper basket; see also *circular file

Fill yer boots !   *"Join in - help yourself !"*

Find, *Fix - and Strike   The operating philosophy of the *Fleet Air Arm*

finger trouble   Slang term (and excuse) for selecting a wrong switch, or using some piece of equipment incorrectly: *"Sorry, wrong number..finger trouble !"*

Fire-and-Lights   Older nickname for the *Master at Arms in a warship, because of his nightly responsibilities to arrange patrols 'tween decks and ensure that all fires were dowsed and all lights extinguished, for obvious reasons, inside the wooden hull

fire, flood, famine *(SM)*   Name for the Disaster Control exercises carried out during a *boat's *work-up

First Dog   The first of the two *Dog Watches:
    First Dog   1600 to 1800
    Last Dog   1800 to 2000

First Drill *(RM)*   The *Senior NCO at *Lympstone responsible for all Ceremonial, Drill and parade-related matters. Equivalent to the parade *Chief GI at *Dartmouth

first parade service *(RM)*   Any action that must be carried out at the start of a working day, eg. checking the engine, electrics, fuel and tyres of your vehicle. This phrase can also be used for anything else that usually begins a day in the office

first push *(FAA)*   The initial serials of a *flypro

first turn of the screw pays all debts   The newer version of *paying all debts with the topsail sheet,* ie. starting afresh in one's social or financial transactions just as soon as the ship leaves harbour

First Watch   2000 to 2359

fish-head *(RM / SM / FAA)*　　　Two meanings, depending on context:
　1. Identifying label for a *skimmer officer or rating in *General
　　Service: *"Unfortunately, I've then got to go and do some **fish-
　　heading** time in order to get my frigate *ticket.."*
　2. *Army / RAF* slang for anyone in a *Royal Navy* uniform !

Fishing Fleet　　　　　*Wardroom expression for those female
attendees, usually of an uncertain age, who turn up at ship's cocktail
parties. This term was around in the Med. between the wars

fish's tit (esp. *RM*)
　1. *"I couldn't give a **fish's tit**"* : *"I couldn't care less.."*
　2. *"That's like asking someone to suck on a **fish's tit**.."* -
　　demanding the impossible

fist　　　Effort, or attempt: *"I must say, that project was a real
swine, but he's made a damned good **fist** of it.."*

fitted *(RM)*　　　Hit a person: *"Nobby **fitted** him one.."*　　Can also be
used in a more passive sense: *"He got **fitted** up a *bramah while he was
home on leave.."*

five-finger salvo　　　A well-landed punch

five-finger spread　　　The result of having hand before mouth when
creating a *dockyard omelette

five lace-holes deep　　　*"..and if he pulls a little stunt like that
again it'll be *reasons in writing, and my boot **five lace-holes deep** up
his backside !"*

five-turd crap　　　An American import indicating a great sense of
pleasure and personal satisfaction at some achievment

fix　　　Enter an accurate position on a navigational chart; see also
*cocked hat and *Find, **fix** and Strike !

fizzog   Physiognomy - facial appearance and features as in: *"Get your rotten fizzog outa here !"*

Flag !   Reply to a challenging ship from a launch carrying a *Flag Officer; also a designated sentry's warning shout on sighting a car or launch *wearing an Admiral's Flag

Flags   Two distinct forms of usage:
1. Yeoman of Signals (sometimes also the nickname of a Ship's Communications Officer)
2. Nickname of an Admiral's **Flag Lieutenant**: *"The real perks of being FONAC's Flags is that you get to fly his *barge everywhere.."*

Flag Eight   Warning signal: *"Women on board !"*

flag flapper / wagger   Signalman; see also *bunting tosser

Flag officer / Flagship   An Admiral in charge of a large organization or group of ships, who flies an Admiral's flag when he is in command. The ship which wears this personal flag then becomes the **Flagship**; *getting one's Flag* means being appointed to the rank of Rear-Admiral. Note also the term *private ship

flake
1. Cradle lowered over a warship's side for re-caulking (older times) or re-painting
2. The process of laying out an anchor cable on deck in order to inspect it for weak links. Similarly, a rope can be **flaked down** into a neat and *tiddley coil

flakers   Dead tired, but especially so in *Harry flakers*

flame-out   Obvious *FAA* use, but also the crash stop of both engines in a *snorting diesel *boat due to poor handling in rough weather, or the collapse of an individual due to sheer fatigue

flanker (work a)   Achieve your aims by dubious or deceitful means

flannel   Elaborate story-telling, or a plethora of weak excuses: *"That man's got more flannel than a *pussers' blanket.."* Also the white shirt-like garment that Jack wears under his outer jumper. It has a square, blue-bordered neck

flannel bosun   Someone who pretends he knows all the answers; a politer term than *bullshit artist*. See also *black catter !

flaps down, and downwind *(FAA)*   Aviation term adapted to describe two or more sailors, in the old days when Jack's trousers were equipped with *piss-flaps and bell-bottoms, all *springing a leak in the *heads

flash
1. Smart, all dressed-up: *"He looked as **flash** as a rat with a gold tooth.."*
2. Signal another ship with a **flash-lamp,** now also applied to the process of passing a message in radio silence: *"**Flash** him that I intend to pass to his starboard side.."*

flash-up   As in boiler, so in temper: *"..and for Heaven's sake don't mention that chap John Nott - unless you want the *Old Man to flash-up a treat.."*

flat   Open space between decks, eg. the **Wardroom, tiller, canteen* or *Sickbay **flats**;* a sectioned-off area becomes a **lobby*

flat-cock sailor   An older nickname for a member of the *WRNS

flat-hatting *(FAA)*   Flying at high speed and low level (in a non-regulation manner); see also *wazzing

Fleet / fleet   Four variations of this word:
1. General term for the operational side of the *RN: "This decision will have to be promulgated throughout the **Fleet**.."*
2. To **fleet something** is to move a large / heavy object (or a group of men) in small, careful amounts
3. The area of ship's side that can be reached using a painter's stage
4. A creek or ditch - hence **Fleet Street** in London on the site of the old *Fleet Ditch*

Fleet Chief   This rank existed between 1972 and 1985 when it was replaced by the more tri-service title of *Warrant Officer. The only conversational relic of that era is the nickname of the *Warrant *Master-At-Arms* as in: *"That's about as likely as a **Fleet** Jossman's sea *draft.."*

flex Flexibility: *"Stacks of flex, boys - but nothing limp.."*

flid lid *(FAA)* Occasional version of *bone dome

flight level nosebleed *(FAA)* Helicopter crew description of any altitude in excess of about 5000 feet

flimsy A Naval Officer does not sight his *S.206 or sign to say he has read it; it is however common practice for *RM* Officers to be shown their confidential reports, whereas the *RN* Officer receives a thin and small piece of paper - aptly named a **flimsy** - which summarises the salient features of the main report

flipper to the front Punishment awarded in older messdeck games like *The Priest of the Parish* where the **flip** was carried out with a rolled-up towel or newspaper. The phrase is now used to describe a bright spark whose talents and performance single him (or her !) out from contemporaries

float test *Ditch something overboard. Also used as a euphemism for getting rid of something: *"Any dirty caps that are impounded by the Commander and which remain unclaimed after three months will be subjected to a float test.."* An alternative is: *"Give it to the splosh-maker !"*

floating gin palace A luxury cruise liner or motor yacht

flob To expectorate (spit) phlegm. The product may well become a *green grolly, or a *dockyard jellyfish / oyster if floating

flog a dead horse The process of paying off a month's advance wages at sea was known *working off a dead horse*; when this month was up, a straw effigy of the horse was hoisted aloft, and then allowed to drop into the sea. To **flog a dead horse** was to expect, in vain, that the crew would be willing to work any harder during that first month - since they had already been paid for it !

Clear your yardarm

flog the glass   The intervals between *watch changes used to be timed by an hour-glass, in the days before chronometers were carried on board. There was a fond belief among *watchkeepers that the sand would fall through more quickly if the globes of the hour-glass were shaken vigorously, or warmed under a coat as in *warm the bell. These terms are still used for someone who tries to shorten his *watch or *trick

flog the jockeys *(FAA)*   Operate a *Sea King's engines using the (overhead) manual throttles

flog yer log   Masturbate

flogged round the fleet   An old punishment, but only for the most serious crimes. The man thus sentenced was *lashed down to a grating in a small boat and then rowed to each ship in a port or harbour. That ship's company would then be *mustered on deck, to witness a dozen strokes of the *cat administered by one of their own *Bo'suns Mates, before the grisly process was repeated further on

Flood Q ! *(SM)*   Emergency *trim tank in a *submarine's bow area which can be filled rapidly, allowing the boat to dive steeply and away from an impending surface collision. The sea water that rushes in is sometimes described as *fifty friendly tons* !

flot can *(FAA)*   *Flotation canister device for use in emergency and* fitted on a helicopter's undercarriage sponsons

fluff your pinky   Break wind; see also Tugg's drawing

flunkey   Officer's steward; note also *crumb brush and *soup jockey

flutterbug   Older term for a helicopter

flutter-by   The massed flypast of helicopters which traditionally opens a *Naval Air Station*'s annual Air Day

FlyCo   *Flying Control* position in an aircraft carrier, where *Wings and *Little f reside during *Flying Stations

flying fish sailor   Jack's derogatory term for the fair weather sailors lucky enough to spend most of their sea time in the balmy waters of the Indian Ocean

flying plumber *(FAA)*   An *Air Engineering Officer* who is also qualified as a *Pirate

flying speed   The minimum speed required for an aircraft to get airborne and off the *deck, with a parallel in social life: "We're going round to the *Boss' house to get up some *flying speed* for *Taranto Night.."

Flying Stations   The state of operational readiness which a ship must be at for the *launch and *recovery of aircraft. *Piped as: "*Hands to *Flying Stations !" and repeated once.

flypro *(FAA)*   Standard abbreviation for a squadron's **flying programme**, and also known as the *dream sheet

FOD-plod *(FAA)*   *Evolution designed to prevent *Foreign Object Damage* to aircraft engines or equipment. A line of personnel is formed to walk slowly across an area and then *skirmish it to pick up any *gash lying on the *deck that might be sucked into a jet intake or drawn up into spinning rotor and propeller blades

foo-foo (dust) (may also be spelt *phoo-phoo*)   Any talcum powder used by Jack, sometimes violently scented. *Pusser's foo-foo *(RM)* is a foot and body powder issued in tropical zones to combat perspiration and the skin condition known as prickly heat. See also Tugg's cartoon

fore-and-aft rig   A *Petty Officer*'s blue suit, consisting of peaked cap, reefer jacket, and trousers creased **fore-and-aft**. See also *square rig

fore-endy *(SM)*   A sailor who works in the **fore-ends** of a *boat, as opposed to a *back-afty

forget-me-nots   Contraceptive sheaths; note also *frangers and *wellies

four fingers   Unofficial measure of a gill of spirit when issued in a straight glass. The classic *tot is therefore a double by normal standards - and about **four fingers high** off the bottom of the glass

Foxtrot Oscar !   The classic, phoneticically-expressed invitation to investigate *sex and travel*

frame a charge　　The process (undertaken before *Defaulters) of setting out the exact description of an offence and that part of the Naval Discipline or *(RM)* Army Acts so contravened. The phrase has no connection with the *civvy usage which implies a fabrication of evidence

framework of hospitality　　In the days of yesteryear, when rum was still issued to Jack, two *wetters* (wet lips) were equivalent to one *sippers*, two *sippers* were equal to one *gulpers*, and two *gulpers* equated to *sandy bottoms or *grounders* - the volume of a single *tot

franger　　Contraceptive sheath; see also *wellies, *freds and *forget-me-nots. For some rather obscure reason, a **franger** *sangar in the *RN* is a fried egg sandwich

frapped　　Three applications here:
1. *(RM)* Hit: *"We frapped the opposition good and hard.."* Note also that the French strategic nuclear deterrent is carried by the **Force de Frappe**
2. Cut someone down to size
3. Bound: *"That tarpaulin needs to be well frapped down to prevent it blowing away.."* Ropes and shrouds can also be **frapped** together in order to increase the tension force exerted

Fratton　　**Getting out at Fratton** is Jack's expression for *coitus interruptus* - the withdrawal method of contraception. This term is explained by the fact that on the railway line from London to Portsmouth, **Fratton** is the penultimate station before *Pompey !

-freak *(RM)*　　A total enthusiast who devotes time, energy and (usually) lots of money to his obsession:
　　kit-freak - always has the best and latest equipment
　　nutty-freak - heavily into chocolate and/or sweets
　　sports-freak - forever playing or training
　　mailie-freak - cannot wait for the daily distribution of mail

freckle　　Anus

Fred Quimby　　Artistic director of the *Tom and Jerry* cartoons until very recently. If a *T&J* cartoon is shown on video or at a Cinema Night, Jack will usually be heard shouting for **Good old Fred !**

fred / freddie　　Condom; see also *franger for some alternative names

free and easy　　Old sailing term, widely adopted elsewhere these days, for a ship whose sheets (sail control ropes) have been **eased** off, and is now running **free** before the wind

Free the *slide !　　*"Pass the butter !"*

freedom bird   Of *US* and Vietnam origin, but now widely used by Jack for any aeroplane taking him home, but especially from the Falklands

Fresh out !   The equivalent of *No chance !* in reply to a request for some stores item or perk

fresh out of ideas *(FAA)*   The consequences of a poorly-judged or badly-executed manoeuvre: *"Lift the collective lever too early at the bottom of an engine-off *auto and you'll end up too high, too slow - and **fresh out of ideas**.."*

freshen your hawse   Another old sailing term for a nip of rum or whisky taken when working long hours on deck in stormy weather

Freshwater Tanky   Navigator's yeoman responsible for the daily sounding of all freshwater storage tanks. In earlier times he was also part of the team that went to the Spirit Room to draw that day's rum allowance for the *Tot's distribution to the ship

Friday while   Older expression (esp. *RM*) for a long weekend leave

frisp   Acronym for something worse than a *Jockroach - an effing, revolting, ignorant, Scottish pig. Sometimes seen or heard as the (only just) politer version of risp

front up   Take an active role in leading a team, or take the lead when presenting some case or argument

(The) ***Frozen Chosen***   Royal's laconic description of the *Commando Unit that was *specially selected* for Arctic Warfare training - before the associated clothing and equipment were up to a reasonable standard !

fruit salad   Campaign and medal ribbons, especially the multi-coloured American displays. See also *brag rags

FUB   Acronym for the Fat, Useless (offspring of an unmarried mother)

Glory hole

F- 117

FUBAR   Another version of *SNAFU, in this case *Fouled-Up Beyond All Recognition*

fudging the issue   Faulty aims or reasoning processes in an argument or discussion

full chat *(FAA)*   Aircraft engine(s) developing full power; in contrast, *max chat usually refers to velocity

full power trial   Part of a warship's *work-up following a refit; adapted by Jack in a subtle sense: *"The *bricking went fairly well - I was able to run a **full power trial** just six days later.."*

full set   A beard, ie. the full set of moustache, sideburns and neatly-trimmed facial whiskers. Nothing less is permitted for Jack; Royal has the right to grow a *'tash, but not a **full set**

fungus face   A bearded individual; see above !

funnies   The particular pet subjects (or dislikes) of a senior officer: *"Watch out for Officers knowing their blood groups - it's one of the Admiral's particular **funnies** at the moment.."*

funny fags   Cannabis; see also *wacky baccy

furcle / furgle   *Grope and fumble with a female acquaintance

furious palm tree   A helicopter; the nickname was derived initially from the gently-waving motion of its rotor blades when the aircraft is *shut down and at rest. When *burning and turning it then becomes either a **furious** or a *rotating* **palm tree**. See also *paraffin pigeon and *kerosene budgie

GOLF

gadget   Radar set: *"I hold you on my gadget, *squawk 4543.."*

galley   Any area of food preparation (never a *kitchen*) but may also be qualified, as in **Main Galley** to mean a dining hall

Galley Gazette   Fictitious source for *buzzes, which are then quoted by rumour mongers. Similar to the *Japanese Journal of Useless Information* (another non-existent publication)

galley pepper   Jack's nickname in older times for the soot and ashes that would on occasion fall into the *victuals as they were being cooked; still used on a *banyan when sausages or steaks are being grilled over an open fire

galligaskins   Very old name for the wide breeches or petticoat trousers worn by Jack up until the early 1800's; the canvas material, impregnated with tar, was the only form of waterproofing then available for men lying across the yards aloft and handling wet sails

Gallipoli *(RM)*   Spring *Corps memorable date from 28 April 1915 when *RM Light Infantry* units of the Third Royal Marine Brigade and First Royal Navy Brigade took part in two weeks of very heavy fighting

game of soldiers *(RM)*   Exasperation with all things military. The phrase: *"Stuff this for a game of soldiers !"* means: *"I have become rather disillusioned, and also I am not entirely happy with your plans for the further conduct of this operation.."*

gangs *(RM)*   Lots of (something); **gangs of *redders** implies that the weather, or the object being described, is very hot. The word has a traceable origin in that a **gang** described the full set of standing rigging attached to the mast of a square-rigged sailing ship

gangway   A free path through a barrier or obstruction, but not a word to be confused with the *brow. The cry *Gangway !* on board means that an Officer or rating on some important mission needs to get past a group of men blocking a passageway or hatch. A **free gangway** is the usual state pertaining when a ship is alongside, or in a naval establishment operating normally; this can become a **closed gangway** for ceremonial or security reasons. The phrase: *"Gangway before I make a bastard !"* is a neat piece of *double entendre* inviting someone to get out of the way - or be knocked down fatally

gannet   A quartet of applicatons:
1. A sailor who is so hungry that he eats leftovers, or is always *going round the buoy for more to eat
2. *(RM)* Someone who eats quickly, and often
3. *(FAA)* HMS *GANNET* is situated at Prestwick Airport on the west coast of Scotland
4. *(FAA)* Former A/S and AEW aircraft, still flying for propfan research

gapped   Something left vacant for a short period, eg. an appointment within a ship or shore organization. In theory, a crucial job or position cannot be **gapped**; *RM*s have been referred to (very *very* discreetly) as **trained gaps**

gardening *(FAA)*   The process of aerial mine-laying during WW2; the aircraft involved were sowing *cucumbers* into the sea !

gardening leave   Nice slang term for a spell of leave spent at home between appointments, usually when the change-over arrangements do not dovetail perfectly. Can also imply trouble in that an Officer has been relieved of his command earlier than expected, perhaps because there has been a problem requiring investigation, or he has just been *court-martialled

gash   A widely-used word with three distinct meanings:
1. Anything surplus to requirement: *"You can have it - it's **gash**.."*
2. Anyone useless: *"Don't take him - he's a really **gash hand**.."*
3. Rubbish or refuse: *"*D'ye hear there - ****ditch no gash**.."*   Note that a **gash bucket** is a waste bin, while a **gash chute** is a pipe or ramp for *ditching **gash** at sea. Jack also adapts the latter term on occasion for the lower end of the large bowel
4. *"Any **gash** talent here ?"* as a question posed when entering a party or dance hall is an enquiry as to whether there are any nice young ladies present who are not inextricably committed to someone else

Gatling gob   Someone who talks far too much and far too often

gauntlet   A form of punishment in older times involving the whole crew. The man to be punished ran between the lines of his shipmates, each equipped with a knotted cord or *nettle, and was *lashed up by each of them as he passed. This could be done up to three times; for more serious crimes the perpetrator would be drawn past the lines more slowly, sitting in a sawn-down wooden cask. The more modern version of **running the gauntlet** describes someone having to face severe criticism

GBH of the earhole (esp. *RM*)   Condition suffered by someone being *picturised, or receiving a severe *bollocking

gear   Contraction of the French *de rigeur,* used in Liverpool originally as ***de gear***, meaning *first class* or of high quality. This became national usage at the time of the Beatles, with expressions such as: *"It's **gear** - fab !"*   The single word emitted with a loud belch at the dining table implies great enjoyment of the meal just consumed

gen Two different forms:
1. Genuine, truthful: *"The ship's going to Aussie next year - it's **gen** !"* Or: *"**Gen** *buzz - we're off Down Under !"* Note also that incorrect information is ***duff gen**
2. General information: *"What's the **gen** for tomorrow ?"*

General Service Two variations in usage:
1. Any non-specialist aspect of *RN* service. For instance, a *Fleet Air Arm* *Looker commanding a minehunter without aviation assets has returned temporarily to **General Service** (for his *fish-heading* time !)
2. The initials **GS** are often seen in the pattern number or stock description of some piece of *kit that is widely issued eg. a *Raincoat Man's Blue GS*

Generalissima The military equivalent of her indoors; see also the title of *Field Marsha and also of *CINC-NAG-HOME

gentlemen captains See also *tarpaulin captains and *all of one company in this reference to officers of a distant era who took command because of connections and privilege rather than proven ability at sea

george *(RM)* Euphemism for the act of defaecation: *"Now, before we get *yomping, has everyone had a **morning george** ?"* In older times it was also the standard nickname in the *FAA* for an automatic pilot

Gestapo Yet another soubriquet for *Regulating Branch personnel

get up to speed Two applications:
1. Absorb all the current or necessary information about a subject: *"I'm **up to speed** on that one.."* means: *"I've read all about that.."*
2. Getting **up to *flying speed** describes the first few *wets of a drinking session or *run-ashore

Get your hat ! Said to a rating who has just committed an offence, since he will need his hat to take off as an offender when he sees the *Bloke. ***Get both hats !*** is a jocular way of suggesting that the *dwang that Jack is in is very deep indeed this time

gets on my tits / gets right up my nose Jack's usual way of describing something or someone that annoys him; note *grudge fight

getting the logbook stamped *(FAA)* Recent sexual activity; see *back in date for explanation

getting yards Admiring and slightly jealous description of a sexual athlete. See also *stacks rating and the contrasting *plums

GIB *(FAA)* Acronym , amongst many others, for an *Observer - usually in a two-crew *stovepipe such as the *Toom. The letters stand for the *Guy In Back* as opposed to the *GIF* who sits in front of him !

Gibraltar *(RM)* Another *Corps memorable date, celebrated officially on 24 July (the date of its capture in 1704), but the place was under siege subsequently for so long that you could raise your glass to Royal and his *Cloggie comrades-in-arms of **Gibraltar** on almost any day of the year and not be corrected for it. **Gib** is the standard abbreviation, and **Gib gut** the local version of *Montezuma's Revenge / Aztec Two Step / Galtieri's Gallop* - all intestinal disorders that appear to be associated with Spanish-speaking involvement !

gimpy *(RM)* Two meanings, depending on the pronunciation used:
  1. Hard *g* - Unwell or not functioning correctly: *"He's got a bit of a gimpy leg.."*
  2. Soft *g* - Slang acronym for *GPMG,* or *General Purpose Machine Gun*

gin pennant Green and white triangular pennant flown to indicate an invitation on board for drinks. Smaller versions may be seen in some *Wardrooms; when an Officer wishes his colleagues to join him in celebration of some event he will fly this **gin pennant** on the bar

gingerbread Decorative carving and scrollwork on the stern of 15th to 18th century warships; this was often gilded, and has led to the modern expression of *knocking the **gilt off the gingerbread**

girl's time *(RM)* Self-disparaging description of any non-pensionable service completed before the age of 21; see also the term *man and boy

girt big knockers Large breasts

give the ferret a run Indulge in sexual intercourse; see also a rather different meaning for *ferret

gizzet / gizzit Contraction of *give us it,* ie. something attractive or useful which has been acquired for free: *"Where'd I get these pen and pencil sets ? They were gizzits from the brewery rep, and keep yer thievin' mitts off.."*

GL An Officer of the *General List,* from which all the future Admirals (except Medical and Dental) are appointed. The majority are Seaman Officers, but there are also a number of specializatons within this full-career list, viz. *Pirate, *Looker, *Pusser, *Grubber, *Steamie, *Droggy, *Schoolie, *dagger N etc. The other major groupings are the *Supplementary List *(SL)* and *Special Duty List *(SD)* Officers; a **GL transfer** is someone who has changed over from either of these. Note also the usual slang terms associated with these groupings - *GL smoothie* and *SL shag

glad rags The bright colours that Jack wears when going ashore

glimpers (esp. *RM*)   A quick and stimulating glimpse of thigh, *suzzies or any other items of (occupied) female underwear. The associated activity is **glimping**, but under certain circumstances it may well become *perving

glims *(FAA)*   Dim lights (originally tallow candles) now used to mark the edges of airfield taxiways; also an older Navy word for eyes as in: *"Dowse his glims !"* - give him a pair of black eyes

glitter   Marmalade or jam; see also *slide - butter. **Glitter** in WW2 was the shredded and metallized foil (*Window* in *RAF* parlance) dropped to confuse enemy radars

Globe and Bustard / Buster / Burster *(RM)*   Two rather confusing usages:
   1. The crest of the *Royal Marines*; the **Burster** is thought to have been the bursting grenade insignia of the old *RM Artillery* cap badge, corrupted by general usage to **Bustard** !
   2. The excellent bi-monthly Corps magazine - *The Globe and Laurel*

gloom room   A warship's Operations Room

glop   Any alcoholic beverage; someone who drinks to excess is a **glophead**. The fine wines of France may, in total ignorance, be dismissed as **Froggy glop**. This word can also be used as a verb: *"Since the *Avquack warned me off, I've not been gloppin' it as much.."*

glory hole   Originally, a name for the stokers' quarters. Now used for any cupboard or storage space (often discovered during *Rounds) which has become filled with unofficial items while at the same time hidden from view. For a perfect illustration, see page **F** - 117

glum bunny   Another version of not a happy Hector

glut box   Just one of Jack's descriptive labels for the vagina

go faster dust *(RM)*   An essential ingredient of Royal's cuisine in the field - curry powder

go round the buoy   Have a second helping, or repeat a training course having failed the examination first time

go through the hoop   Standard test of a correctly *lashed-up hammock; if it didn't go through it had to be undone and re-done !

gob-shite   A loudmouth who is always **gobbing-off**: *"He's so gobby, he could talk a glass eye to sleep !"*   See also *Gatling gob

gob-smacked   Totally speechless with surprise; **gob-flapped** is an older variant

Gobbie   Older name for a member of the *Coastguard*, now better known as *Coasties. The origin of this term is a little obscure, but until 1923 this Service was run by the Admiralty and manned by Naval pensioners. Whether these men tended to be *gobby* individuals (see *gob-shite above) or whether **Gobby** was a slang term for a pensioner remains uncertain !

gobbler's gulch   The gap between suspender belt and stocking top; see also *chuckle gap

gobbling rods *(RM)*   Eating utensils; see also *KFS, *eating irons and *fighting gear

God botherer / God walloper   Padre; see *amen wallah for a complete listing. A **God box** is a chapel or church

gofer / gopher   An assistant, who generally needs little brain power to carry out his task: *"Go fer this, and then go fer that.."* See also the term *doggie

goffer   Three very distinct meanings:
  1. *(RN and RM)* A big sea washing *inboard, which may have the disastrous consequences depicted elsewhere by Tugg
  2. To be **gofferred** can also mean being punched, hard
  3. *(RM)* Any non-alcoholic cold drink - a **goffer wallah** is the chap who sells them

gold-plated   Unecessarily luxurious, or packed with features of doubtful importance: *"They want 16 megabucks per copy for that new ground-attack helicopter - but the whole thing's a bit **gold-plated** if you ask me.."*

Golden blanket / pillow   Legendary prize for those individuals seemingly inseparable from their bunks. Sometimes called the **Golden *gonk award**. See also *Rip van Winkle and the *Unknown Warrior

golden bowler   Premature retirement on financially advantageous terms

golden eagle *(RM)*   The source of all pay and allowances. If Royal refers to a future time when *the **golden eagle** craps all over him*, he is only talking about his next pay day !

golden rivet   Non-existent final gift from a warship's builder, supposedly fixed somewhere into the keel in order to mark the end of her construction. Any invitation to enter a darkened *compartment down below in order to inspect this legendary feature should be treated with considerable caution

gollies   *Electronic Warfare (EW)* ratings

gongs   Campaign or valour medals; also *fruit salad and *brag rags

gonking   Sleeping; see also *Golden, *Zeds and *Egyptian (2)

goodbye-brains night   Social gathering where some serious drinking is intended - or one at which, in the subsequent descriptions, vast quantities of alcohol were consumed

Good game !   Cheerful expression used when conditions are absolutely miserable and the work either unremitting or non-existent

goofer *(FAA)*   Spectator watching aircraft operations in a carrier, standing in the **goofing gallery** or **Goofers**, a platform located high up on the island's superstructure. This verse from the *A25 song is a classic:

They gave me a Seafire to beat up the Fleet,
I duffed up the NELSON and RODNEY a treat,
But then I forgot the high mast on FORMID -
*And a seat in the **Goofers** was worth fifty quid..*

goon bag *(FAA)*   Aircrew immersion coverall suit, made of Egyptian cotton ventile material, with a single waterproof diagonal zipper plus rubber neck and wrist seals; also known as a **goon suit**

gopher   See *gofer

gorilla snot *(FAA)*   *Bailey's Irish Cream* and *sticky greens !

(it's) **got ears on it**   See *rabbit for more complete background; anything which has been *half-hitched, *proffed, *rabbited or *acquired as a gift can be described as **having ears on it**

gotcha   Equivalent to *pooh-trap, ie. a common mistake that is just waiting to be made

grab-a-granny night   Regular evenings at local dance halls when the more mature ladies attend, and Jack is usually assured of the action that he seeks. See also *C-Troop, *School of Dancing and the (*Wardroom) *Fishing Fleet

grabby   Archaic nickname for infantrymen used by *donkey-wallopers; Jack adopted this term for Royal in older times, but it is now obsolete

graft (esp. *RM*)   Hard work; often **sheer graft** or **pure graft**

grand slam   Losing control of all three sphincters when drunk

granny   Fussy, indecisive officer; see also *two-oh-six for an example of official usage

granny's footsteps *(SM)*   An irregular and ziz-zag course when dived

graunch   Sound made when a ship collides with something, or runs aground into the *putty

gravel belly   Royal, when operating as an infantryman ashore; the term used to be reserved exclusively for an Instructor in Small Arms

gravel grinder   A *Gunners' Mate* (older) or *Gunnery Instructor* (current) responsible for marching and parade ground drill. See also *tarmac tiff and *tick-tock tiff

graveyard watch   Midnight to 0400

grease   A trio of applications:
   1. Butter or margarine
   2. A **grease pit** is a ship's engine room and associated machinery spaces
   3. *Greasy spoon* is the generic name for any roadside *caff* where hygiene takes second place to almost everything else, and the *dog is the likely consequence resulting from any food ingested

greased weasel shit   An item which, according to legend, *slides easily off a shiny shovel.* Used now as a form of comparision for something that moves or accelerates quickly, or as a definition of smoothness when describing a smart talker and dresser such as a TV chat show host

green   Naive, innocent - or easily misled through inexperience: *"He must have been a bit **green** to believe the *Appointer like that.."*

green-and-baggies / smellies *(FAA)*   Flying overalls !

green beret   Symbol of an individual's having completed *Commando training with the Royal Marines, and also worn, when qualified, with varying cap badges by *RN, RAF* and *Army* personnel seconded to the *Royal Marines*. Sometimes referred to as a **green lid**. With one notable exception, there is no such thing as an ***honorary green beret***

green coat   To **wear the green coat** is to play dumb and stupid, or feign ignorance; origin uncertain at the time of writing !

Green Death   Jack's generic nickname for the 3rd Commando Brigade *RM*, a rather awed opinion enhanced by Royal's various activities ashore in the Falklands during 1982; may also be heard as **The Green Machine**

Green Endorsement *(FAA)*   Naval Aviation's version of an official *BZ, written in ***green ink*** in the paticipant's logbook, and awarded for some above-average or courageous and skilful management of an in-flight emergency

green grolly   A lump of phlegm or a nasal candlestick. May also be described as a **green gilbert,** and see also *dockyard jellyfish

Green Guide   A Naval publication listing the scale of punishments awardable for various offences

green parrot *(FAA)*   An aeroplane used as an Admiral's *barge

green rub   An unfair or raw deal: *"A *nap hand from that blonde he met in Fort Lauderdale ? Cor - talk about a **green rub** !"*

green slug   Military-issue sleeping bag which has a quilted outer surface and head cover: *"A dry **green slug** in the Arctic is an absolutely vital feature in the maintenance of a man's morale.."*

greenie   Nickname for a member of the Electrical branch, signified in a rating's rank by the letter *L*, or *WL* in the *Fleet Air Arm*; also subdivided into **heavy greenies** who get their hands dirty by working on electric motors and suchlike (but who are not really *grubbers), and the **light greenies** responsible for computer-based electrical control systems. The term originates from the **green** *distinction cloth of *Electrical Engineer* officers, a feature now sported only by the *Merchant Navy*. The distinction between **weapon greenies** and *pinkies in the *FAA* is sometimes very blurred

gremlin (esp. *FAA*)   A mischievous, elf-like creature who gets the blame for most defects and malfunctions in aircraft engines and machinery note also the term *Wrenlin*

grenade   Scotch egg

Grey Funnel line   Traditional in-house nickname for the sea-going part of the *Royal Navy*, and therefore a useful alternative to the *Andrew in that respect. Also the title of a super book by *Cyril Tawney* (published by Routledge, Kegan Paul) containing the words of many matelot ditties

grid   Face, or mouth: *"Get that down yer grid.."*

grimmy   See *gronk; the **Grimmy Trophy** is a rather chauvinistic item awarded by popular acclaim each time a warship leaves after a port visit - to the chap who *trapped the worst-looking lady and brought her on board for inspection

grip   Another potentially confusing trio:
1. (esp. *RM*) *"Get a grip !"* : *"Take charge of yourself !"*
   Or: *"It needed someone like him to grip the problem seriously ."*
2. A **pussers' grip** is a standard issue, light brown canvas travelling bag or holdall
3. *"He really grips my shit."* : *"I dislike him intensely.."*

gripped by the lower band   Equivalent to grabbing someone by the nether regions and thus exercising precise and total control over him: *"Grip them all by the lower band - hearts and minds will follow on soon after.."*

grippo   An acquaintance made (**gripped**) at a party or on a free treat / *run-ashore who then becomes the subject of further social transaction. No real distinction is made between male or female **grippos** in the simplest context; a *baron who has been *well strangled* could also be described as a *splendid* or *brilliant grippo*

Grocer   An Officer of the *Supply and Secretariat* Branch (or the *Grocery Dept): *"He started out at *Dartmouth as a Seaman Officer, but then his eyesight failed - so he *remustered as a Grocer.."*   See also *Pusser and *White Mafia

grog   Rum (*neaters) diluted *two and one that, until the *Black Day in 1970 was issued to ratings of *killick or Corporal and below. It was not issued to those marked in the *Victualling Book as *UA (under age) or T (for Temperance), the latter receiving an allowance of monies instead. When diluted in this way, the *bubbly would not keep for very long and so (in theory) could not be hoarded and consumed later, unlike *neaters which would last if re-bottled as *Queen's or *plushers and which then became the centrepiece of a *Black Mass. These illegal actions led to the occasional case of severe drunkeness in the *Chiefs and POs'* accommodation, and even death through gross over-indulgence. *Grog was named after Admiral Vernon - nicknamed **Old Grogram** after the grogram (**grog - rum**, geddit ?) boat cloak that he wore; he first ordered this dilution process to be carried out on the West Indies station in 1740. Note also:

grog blossom - an alcohol-induced flush to the cheeks
grog tub - any container in which drinks are mixed or diluted
grog money - substitution allowance paid to teetotallers

Groin Exchange / GX   The *Plymouth Sailing Club*, a traditional haunt of young Naval officers visiting or working in *Guzz

grolly   Something green, sticky, unpleasant - and usually associated with a productive cough or nasal discharge

gronk   A lady of less than perfect countenance or physique. Many messdecks have a rather chauvinistic **Gronk's board** on which past talent is displayed. Jack takes a rather practical and humanitarian line: *"Booze was invented so that **gronks** could have an even chance.."* See also *grimmie, *bagger, *coyote and associated alternatives

groping   The process of feeling a woman's body in an intimate way using a Braille technique

grot   A *snotties cabin or a room personalized by its owner: *"I'm just going up to the **grot** for some *Egyptian PT.."*

Field Gunner

groundbait Box of chocolates, or some other small *rabbit, given to a lady friend in pursuit of a greater prize

ground pounding *(FAA)* *Crab term used to describe the *SHAR when operating in a *Ground Attack* role; *mud moving is an alternative

group up *(SM)* Expression for a conventional submarine's main motor power configuration when aligned for high speed rather than endurance; also used by Jack to describe getting a move on generally

growler *(RM)* A pork pie; *NAAFI* landmine is a variant

grubber *(FAA)* Air engineering mechanic (or officer): *"The life of a Fleet Air Arm grubber is an appalling mix of blood, snot and lube oil.."* See also *plumber, *greenie, *pinky etc.

grudge fight Older 'tween decks system of sorting matters out when messmates *got on each other's tits. It was applied for officially and run in a boxing ring, under Queensberry Rules, by the 8springer. The event continued until one participant either declined or was unable to continue. Generally, this procedure sorted out problems very nicely all round !

grumpy (esp. *RM*) Adjective used in a nursery style to imply that someone is not very happy: *"As a result of that Promotion List signal the Adjutant was a rather grumpy frog for a while.."* He could also, in this context, have been described as a not very *happy Hector..

Grunter Occasional nickname for the *Bloke as a result of his frequent habit of merely grunting in reply to a question !

gruntled Pleased, similar to *chuffed in the sense that the person is not **disgruntled** or *dischuffed

guard and steerage Thirty minute lie-in allowed to non-watchkeepers (eg. duty men working after midnight the night before) instead of a *make-and- mend. Because the rest of the messdeck had *turned out and *turned to, it was sometimes an opportunity for a *nifty fifty, hence Jack's nickname for this concession of *guard and flog*

guardship *RN* warship performing some important escort duty, eg. accompanying the *Yacht, or anchored off during Cowes Week. Also used for the ship alongside in harbour whose duty it is to provide and man the **guard boat**, or a frigate or destroyer operating alone in a specific area, like the **West Indies guardship** - which is known as the *WIGS*

guesstimate Beautiful amalgamation of the words *guess* and *estimate* which works well in practice as something spontaneous (like a *guess*) rather than formal and considered (as in a written *estimate*): *"When will the job be finished ? Well, the current best guesstimate is early next week, but if the new parts don't arrive on time, we could be looking at delaying Easter leave.."*

guff   Two uses:
1. A load of rubbish; *"Don't talk such **guff**!"*
2. The *Journal of Royal Navy Medicine* (an excellent publication) is known more widely as ***The Guffer's Gazette***

gulpers   A long single swallow of an *oppo's *tot - either repaying some favour owed, or in clearance of a gambling debt. Note that two *sippers equal one **gulpers** in the *framework of hospitality

gunna-merchant   An individual who disappoints because he is always **gunna** do this or **gunna** do that - but somehow never does

gunner's daughter   The name of the gun to which *Boy seamen were married (tied) when receiving punishment

gunny bunny   *Field gunner's groupie

gunroom   The *Middies' or *Subbies' Mess at *BRNC* *Dartmouth, and similarly in the *Dartmouth Training Ship*. Most large ships of cruiser size upwards had a **gunroom** in which to park their *Snotties. It used to be a compartment on the lowest gun deck of a warship in the days of sail, but this has now been brought up to the main deck, although it is still separate from the *Wardroom

Guns   The Gunnery officer; see also *Torps

Guppy *(FAA)*   Nickname for the old AEW *Skyraider* aircraft

gusting   Jack's term for nearly, or about: *"How much do I think that will cost ? I'd say four thousand, probably - four thousand **gusting** four-and-a-half.."*

(the) Gut / Ghut   Nickname for Strait Street in Valetta, Malta - a narrow thoroughfare which wound downhill in the old city. Jack would buy *sticky greens for his *pash and cold Cisk or Hop Leaf (beer) for himself at the top on pay day; then, as his pockets grew emptier, he and Royal would descend to the lower levels for some sleazier entertainment fuelled by *Ambit and lemonade. Like *Bugis Street in Singapore, the locale has now been cleaned up

gut bucket   Someone with a large beer belly

Guzz / Guzzle   The naval base of Devonport, adjoining Plymouth. The two possible explanations for this nickname are:
1. GUZZ was the wartime signal letter group for the port's callsign
2. **guzzling** was what Jack did to excess on return from a long spell at sea in the *far flung
3. *"Cos it's allus rainin' when yer gets in, an' it's allus rainin' when yer **guzz out** again.."*

gynagorous   Huge

gynoferous   Frequent description of great size: *"Honest - it was this high ! The thing was a sodding great **gynoferous** *crocadillapig !"*

gyp   *Egyptian tummy* or *Gyppy tummy*; later on, **gyp** came to be used for any pain or aggravation: *"This business of changing *watches every week is beginning to give me the **gyp**.."*

gyro failure *(FAA)*   Nice way to describe the effect of too many *wets; in addition, if the individual affected is unable to stand up, his **gyros have toppled**

HOTEL

hack　A varied quartet, mostly *FAA*:
1. Achieve the standard required: *"You can **hack it**, *Wingsy baby !"*
2. Close down or shut off a piece of mechanical equipment: *"**Hack** the speed select levers, quick !"*
3. In the tactical sense, shoot down an enemy aircraft: *"The *CAP Sea Harriers **hacked** the Skyhawks as they came out from Falkland Sound.."*
4. An aircraft used for general flying purposes is known as the **station hack**
5. Journalist - sometimes (though not always !) a person who would benefit immensely from a quick **hack in the fork**

hackle　A process in rope-making where natural fibres are combed into straight lines by **hackle-boards**, blocks of wood or metal studded with steel prongs. This is the maritime origin for an animal *raising its hackles* when angry or frightened, and the hair stands up on the back of its neck

haircut run *(RM)*　Classic reason given to visit a local town on market day, when the pubs are open throughout the forenoon and afternoon

hairy-arsed　Traditional adjective describing the *matelot occupants of a *bear pit

half a *dog watch　A very short period of time, figuratively speaking: *"How kin 'e know, of all people ? The *sprog's only bin in half a dog watch.."*

half-blues　Smart *rig of white front and blue trousers

half-hitched   Stolen - from the process of putting a rope (in a **half-hitch**) around something in order to drag it away

half-masted   Colours at **half-mast** down the *jack as a sign of mourning - or trouser legs that are too short !

half-stripe   The addition of a half-thickness gold lace stripe to a Lieutenant's uniform sleeve, signifying promotion to Lieutenant Commander: *"I get my **half-stripe** next month.."* See also *two and a half

hammock   Classic sleeping method, and a piece of *kit still to be found in Naval *Stores, because with the insertion of metal rods as a frame, the canvas **hammock** now becomes a camp bed. A properly slung example can be seen in HMS *WARRIOR*, the warship museum that is part of the excellent *Portsmouth Maritime Heritage*, along with HMS *VICTORY* and the immediately adjacent *MARY ROSE*

hammy, cheesy, eggy topside   Classic Naval recipe of toasted ham and cheese with a fried egg resting on the summit; see *cheesy etc.

handcarted   Well *shot-away ! See the classic Tugg on page Q - 111

hands   Collective term applied to those (pairs of) **hands** available for seamanship duties and addressed as such in the *pipe *All hands on deck !* or **Call the hands !* Note also that an individual with pleasant social attributes is described as **a good hand,** or the *RN* and *RM* equivalent of *a good egg.* ***Hands to dance and skylark !*** was an older *pipe that meant a period of light-hearted fun, with no holds barred. The definition of a trained seaman - the *Able Rate* - is a man who can (lend a) **hand, reef** (a sail) **and steer** (a straight course)

hands on   To be in actual physical control of something, such as an aircraft: *"How much **hands on** time have you got ?"*

Handsomely !   Instruction to carry out an *evolution smoothly, carefully and evenly - as when lowering the *seaboat

Hang fire ! *"Wait just a moment !"* This term was also used in the wartime *FAA* (and subsequently) to describe a rocket projectile that had been fired but for some reason not been released

hang out of ___
  1. (When applied to the fairer sex) Cohabiting with someone
  2. *(RM)* A direct threat of violence to a faint-hearted *heap: *"Get your ruddy arse in gear, or I'll **hang out of you,** you *big girl's blouse.."*

hangar queen *(FAA)* An aircraft with a series of problems that spends more time on the ground (in a hangar) than in the air. The natural temptation to rob it for spare parts in order to keep others flying only prolongs its agony; also known as a **hangar Annie** or a Christmas tree

hanging mood Description of *Father's demeanour when severe punishments are being meted out at *Defaulters: *"The *Old Man must be in a real **hanging mood** - fourteen days pay for that ? Bloody 'ell !"*

Hannah *(RM)* Nickname associated with the surname Snell, after the famous female Marine *Hannah Snell* who enlisted and fought at Pondicherry in the 18th century. She later became the landlady of a pub called *The Widow in Masquerade* at Wapping

happy Hector *"Hey, Dusty - the *Fleet Jossman wants to see you, and he's not a very **happy Hector** this morning.."*

happy ship Any Naval organization with a good relationship between the *Upper and *Lower deck; the resulting shared sense of purpose and high morale are immediately apparent to a knowledgeable visitor. The Commanding Officer may then be the subject of praise: *"He certainly runs a **happy ship**.."*

harbour cotters *(SM)*   Fish steaks in batter, named after the **cotter** that is placed in a *boat's main vent actuator to prevent it opening up and accidentally flooding the ballast tanks while alongside in harbour

harbour hassle   The red tape, *bumph and shore routines that seem designed with the positive intention of preventing a warship or *boat from getting back to sea

hard   Beach or landing place; the sign *Admiral's Hard* on a wall opposite the *RM Barracks* at Stonehouse in Plymouth is not a cause for celebration as much as a statement of location

hard and blind   In a state of extreme sexual excitement

hard liers   Contraction of *Hard Lying Money* - a special allowance paid to Jack and Royal in certain ships or shore accommodation with sub-standard living conditions, eg. a small ship in dock without any shoreside electrical power or water supply

Hard shit!   *"Tough luck, *oppo.."* Note that *Tough titty !* expresses much the same sentiment

hard time   Close questioning or extra difficulty: *"I got a really hard time from the Command about that little incident, even though we probably saved the *civvy's life.."*

hard to fathom   Something that is difficult to understand clearly, an expression that has come ashore from the days of the *sounding line and associated problems of establishing depth in shoaling waters

hard up in a clinch   Jack's older figure of speech to describe a piece of misfortune that has befallen him, adding *and no knife to cut the stopping* if he cannot see a way out of his difficulties either

hardly out of the egg   Description of a very inexperienced individual

harness cask   A large open cask kept on deck in the days of sail, containing the salted *ready-use provisions that had been brought up from store below. Since Jack called all his meat provisions *salt horse, in thr belief that most of it had an equestrian origin, the **harness cask** was where the *horse without its harness* had been stabled !

Harry Freeman's   Jack's dated term for something that would now be called a *gizzit. **Harry Tate's** is also an older term, for anything amateur in the *RN;* the word *Harry* was a classic emphasis for something, eg. **Harry** *flakers, **Harry** *ratters or **Harry** *crappers (but not *Harry Krishna* !)

Haslar   A creek in Portsmouth Harbour where the famous naval hospital was built in 1746 and where Fort *Blockhouse is also situated. When **Haslar Hospital** was first constructed it was the largest brick building in Europe; its first Physician was the wholly admirable *James Lind* who proved that the consumption of fresh oranges and lemons was capable of curing the distressing maritime problem of *scurvy*. Later on, this source of Vitamin C was changed to lime juice, hence the terms *limey and *lime juicer used across the *Pond

hat flat-aback   Traditional description of Jack at his ease ashore in uniform, drink taken, and with his cap well back on his head

hat rack   Usually a homosexual, but the term can also be used to describe a very senior officer who is a figurehead without any redeeming physical or intellectual qualities beneath the gilded cap

hatch rash   Forehead or shin bruising that results from banging one's head on a closed (or closing) watertight hatch, or legs against the sill; see also *coaming rash

haul arse   American slang import meaning *to move quickly*

haze   The process of making life on board as uncomfortable as possible for a ship's crew, by forcing them to work extra watches doing menial tasks. This word still exists in America to describe fraternity initiation rites, but on this side of the *pond it has changed to **faze**: *"Smashing his car up didn't seem to **faze** him at all.."*

head sarnie   The Liverpool or Glasgow *kiss*, as opposed to a *knuckle sarnie: *"Does yer Mammy sew ? Well, get her to stitch this !"*

head down   Description of sleep: *"I'm going to get my **head down**.."*

head shed *(RM)*   Alternative for *puzzle palace when describing a Unit HQ

heads   The ship's latrines - originally a plank positioned over the leeward bow wave in the ship's **head**. Strictly speaking, the term should be singular rather than plural, but this convention is only observed *across the Pond

Custard Bosun

H - 140

heads up   Early warning of a problem which may soon develop and cause difficulty: *"Did anyone give you a **heads up** on that new system ?"*

heap *(RM)*   *Shambolic individual of poor personal appearance

(I) ***hear what you say, but*** -   A dreadful figure of speech being used more and more; it sounds conciliatory but in fact means: *"Your opinion is different to mine and so I won't take any notice of it !"*

Heart of Oak   The Royal Navy's traditional theme, derived from a patriotic song written by David Garrick to commemorate a number of British victories abraoad in the year 1759:
> ***Heart of Oak** are our ships,*
> *Jolly Tars are our men...*

The rhythm of this song was used by a warship's drummers when beating to *Quarters

Heartbreak Lane *(RM)*   Last leg of the *Endurance course at *Lympstone. Its name results from the fact that before entering it, the wet and muddy recruit has been running downhill for some four miles, with the camp buildings in sight for most of that time; suddenly he can only see hedges on either side, and the (now level) road appears to be climbing as well as heading *away* from the finish line

heave   A sextet of different applications:
1. **heave to** - stop in the water
2. **heaving line** - rope thrown from ship to ship, or from ship to shore, weighted with a *monkey's fist
3. **heaving tackle** - heavy ropework for lifting and shifting
4. **heaving his heart out** - being violently sick
5. **heaving** *(RM)* - smelly, filthy
6. (the old) **heave-ho** - good riddance to someone or something

heavy for'ard *(SM)*   *Fanny rat, or a chap with a particularly impressive issue of *wedding tackle

heavy mob *(SM)*   *Submarine Maintenance Group*

hedging and ditching *(FAA)*   The process of taking a lady friend for a walk near a *Naval Air Station*, with a view to a spot of *groping

helioproctosis   Condition in which someone appears to believe that the sun shines out of his or her backside; *proctoheliosis is a similar affliction

hen-pecked *(RM)*   A hangover induced by the excessive intake of Royal's favourite duty-free fluid - *Famous Grouse* Scotch whisky

hermit's box   The Captain's day and night *cabins, ie. the mechanism by which he can lead a completely separate existence in a warship if he needs (or wants) to

herrings in   Shortened form of *herrings in tomato sauce*. See also *-ITS, and hence *HITS*

Hertz van Rental   Mythical Dutch officer, along with his *oppo *Naafi van Driver, who can be asked for by Royal when getting a *bite out of his *Cloggie colleagues: *"'Oi, Pieter - 'ave you seen Cap'n Hertz van Rental ? 'E wants to ask you summat.."*

hexy blocks *(RM)*   Small cubes of solid hexamine fuel used, in the tinplate **hexy cooker** that they are issued in, to heat up the contents of Royal's *compo *rat pack in the field

high hover   State of great anxiety: *"Thank goodness that VVIP visit is over - everyone's been in a really **high hover** for the past few days.."*

Historics *(FAA)*   The *Fleet Air Arm*'s **Historic Flight** operating from *Yeovilton; a splendid sight as well as a glorious sound

Hit him with your handbag !   *"That was a really weak tackle !"*

hit the pit   Expression with similar meaning to *gonking or the process of *racking out

Hitler's Victuallers (*Hitler's Vittlers*)   *Cates and his staff

HMS / HMHS   Her Majesty's Ship / Her Majesty's Hospital Ship

HO   Abbreviation for *Hostilities Only*, ie. someone who served in the *RN* or *RM* for the duration of World War 2: *"I was in the Corps in my younger days - but only as an HO.."*

HoD   *Head of Department*; **HoDs 1100** means that a *Heads of Departments* meeting will be held an hour before noon

hog snarling   Qualifying description for *drunk*

hog wash / hoggin   The sea - usually heard in conversation as

the *'ogwash or 'oggin, or even the *og

hoist in   Understand something: *"Look Einstein, it's dead simple. If you ain't got no *ickies then you ain't gettin any *wets ! Can't you **hoist that in** fer Gawd's sake ?"*

holdover *(FAA)*   Delay between courses for students in the flying training pipeline; the young *Bloggses are sent to ships or Service establishments to do something varied or useful while waiting on their **holdovers**

(The) **Hole**   Nickname for the underground bunker of the *Fleet Operations Centre* at Northwood

holidays   Two similar applications:
 1. Bare patches on a newly-painted surface that have been missed by the paint brush
 2. Gaps in a line of men standing at *Procedure Alpha

Holy Joe   Yet another version of padre ! See *amen wallah for the complete list

holystones   Blocks of pumice used for scrubbing wooden decks; small ones were called *prayerbooks*, while bigger lumps were *Bibles*

home porting   The base port system for each class of ship; hence the derivation of *homers or *up homers, for a comfortable billet ashore with a family while in harbour or visiting abroad

homeward bounders   Large or crude stitching used by Jack to sew badges on, or make repairs while **homeward bound**, in anticipation that they would then be sewn on properly by the *dragon. The phrase is now also used in the *Boneyards to describe deep surgical suturing of lacerated skin

Honest, Chief - it just came off in me 'and.. Jack's traditional statement whenever anything breaks off or comes apart !

honey monster *(RM)* Two variants:
  1. Mechanical equipment for sewage handling or latrine (honeypot) emptying
  2. Any large, enthusiastic, but not very pretty lady with a particular weakness for *Royal Marines*

Honkers Hong Kong; also known as **Honky Fid**

honking A subtle trio:
  1. Glaswegian patter word (like *minging) for *handcarted or very drunk
  2. *(RM)* Smelling strongly
  3. Physically sick; **honking your ring up** is a severe episode of vomiting

hook Another triple:
  1. Nickname for an anchor; the *pick is an alternative
  2. (FAA) Aircraft **tailhook** for picking up an arrester wire on *recovery to the flight deck
  3. *"Can I have my **hook** back ?"* : *"You were on a big *bite there !"*

hooker Tubby little fishing vessel used for line fishing, but also a name for a ship nearing the end of her working days and looking her age. Both aspects of the name apply to the shore-based connotation of a prostitute working the streets and trying to **hook** clients despite looking somewhat tired and blown

Hooky Nickname for a *Leading Hand, so called because of the fouled anchor (or *hook) badge indicating his or her *rate; also a standard nickname for the surname Walker

horizontal champion Someone who sleeps a lot; see also *Rip van Winkle and the *Unknown Warrior

Horlicks   Politer alternative for *cock-up: *"Unfortunately, he then made a complete **Horlicks** of that as well.."*

hornpipe   A dance of Celtic origin, originally played on a wind instrument called a **hornpipe**; it was later adapted by Jack for two dancers instead of three, and with the music provided by a *squeeze-box

horoscope   An immediate future that is looking bleak: *"If you let me down just once more, you miserable little toad - you'll get your **horoscope** read - and no messing.."*

horrorscope   A really bad *set of papers or *comic cuts

horse *(FAA)*   Game played by aviators, using the numbers stamped on their aircrew watches, to discover who is buying the wine with dinner !

horse's neck   Brandy and ginger-ale mix, a traditional *Wardroom drink, often written as *2/3 HN*

hot *(FAA)*   A *Dip gang is **hot** when in contact with a *tube; note also the expression ***In hot***

hot bunking   Alternate use of bed / bunk space by sailors going on and coming off *watch, usually as a result of there not being enough safe sleeping accommodation for all the crew

hot press   Older term for a situation of such dire national need to *impress men for service in the Royal Navy that the *press gangs* were instructed to take any men that they could find - whatever protections or excuses they carried. See also the *Andrew

hot wash-up   A debrief and quick analysis held immediately after the completion of some event or exercise

hottie   A strong rumour or **hot** *buzz: *"I've heard various figures quoted for the next pay rise, but six per cent across the board seems to be the real **hottie** at the moment.."*

hour hog *(FAA)*   The *Pirate or *Looker who is getting more hours than anyone else in a Squadron's *stats sheets; he may also discover that he has become labelled **hog of the month**

housewife (esp. *RM*)   A cloth roll containing thread, needles, button all the sewing kit needed for the traditional task of *make and mend

howdah *(FAA)*   Obsolete nickname for the flightdeck-level control position of the old aircraft carriers; the duty *steamie sat in here and controlled the steam catapults at *launch

howling *(RM)*   Drunk; as with *minging, it can also refer to something that smells very strongly

Chockhead

hucked out   Somewhere that has been cleaned out for *Rounds

huffer *(FAA)*   Engine-starting generator trolley

humming *(RM)*   Stinking; also the secondary meanings for *minging, *howling and *honking

humungous   Enormous; see also *gynagorous, *gynoferous and *gynormous

Hurt Certificate   An official statement of a sailor's wounds that had been sustained in action against the enemy. This could be purchased by the *Pusser when that sailor retired from the sea - a crude form of lump sum pension. The modern *MOD Form 298 has no such monetary value, but is still called a *Hurt Certificate*. See Tugg's brilliant evocation of this in the latter half of this book

INDIA

icers *(RM)* Cold: *"Turn the heating up, will you ? It's really icers in here.."*

ickies Foreign currency of any kind, an all-purpose word that is the current usage of the older term *ackies. Although it has a general meaning as in: *"I'm going to get some ickies from the Cash Office.."* it can also be more specific: *"How many ickies do you get to the pound in this place ?"* Under these circumstances the **ickie** (whether it be a franc, dollar or cruzeiro) can be further subdivided into a hundred *klebbies. Note also **ickie store** - a bank

idlers Jack's contemptuous name for anyone not standing night *watches; see also *dry idlers for those **idlers** who are not stokers or seamen either !

If at first you don't succeed..
1. Hit it with a bigger hammer !
2. *(RM) In wi' the boot, an' then the heid !* (Glaswegian origin)

imbuggerance Alternate pronunciation for *embuggerance

immaculate *(RM)* Adjective reserved by Royal to indicate something of high quality or perfect appearance

Immortal Memory Traditional speech given by the guest of honour at *Trafalgar Night dinners throughout the Royal Navy, held on or around the anniversary of the *21st of October 1805*. The life and achievments of Lord *Nelson are recounted briefly, then some particular quality of his leadership highlighted as an example to those present; finally, a toast to *The Immortal Memory* is proposed and drunk

Impressment   The practice of taking a national subject, whatever his own feelings on the matter, into the armed services of his country in order to make good shortfalls in normal recruitment. This was a normal procedure for the army (particularly Cromwell's) as well as the navy, and the whole procedure of sending **press gangs** out into the country was underwritten by Parliament, which also passed the Quota Acts in 1795 requiring each district and town to provide a certain number of men for sea service - because the earlier Vagrancy Acts and their resulting steady supply of petty criminals and vagabonds could not meet the demand for seamen. See also *one of my Lord Mayor's men and *swimmer in this context, and note that the term **prest money**, a form of bounty or *conduct money* paid on enlistment still survives in the *Royal Marines* as the title of *Imprest Holder*, the Officer who responsible for all Cash and Accounts in a *Commando Unit or base. There are some further comments at *Andrew and *pressed

In and Out   Jokey nickname for the *Naval and Military Club* in Piccadilly, London; the title is derived from the embellishments of the gate pillars !

in dock   In hospital - as when a ship goes in for maintenance or repairs

In - hot ! *(FAA)*   Radio call made by aircraft carrying live ordnance on entering a weapons range. Quickly adapted to other pastimes: *"As soon as we got ashore, Bill was **in hot** on a couple of blondes by the swimming pool.."*

in the rattle   In big trouble and liable to appear before *Father at *Defaulters

in-lier *(RM)*   An Officer or *NCO* who lives *on board rather than *ashore. The *RN* equivalent is a *liver-in

in (the) **zone**   The *zone* referred to here is the ***promotion zone***, which in turn depends on an officer's seniority. This might be, for instance, three to nine years as a *two-and-a-half in order to be considered for elevation to a *brass hat. Going *overzone will mean a celebration of the *Passover; the behaviour of those *pregnant is sometimes a little contrived: *"Went to a real **in-zone** dinner party last night. I was the only guest junior to the host.."*

inboard   Two distinctly different meanings:
1. Home and dry, ie. inside or on board the ship: *"I'm **inboard**, haul up the ladder !"* is a gently cynical observation applied to those motivated purely by self-interest
2. *(SM)* Ashore or in the base, because a submarine's home is often a depot ship which has the *boat moored *outboard

inside wrecker (esp. *SM*)   A chef ! See *outside wrecker for explanation of this term

internal back splint   A *brownhatter's idea of fun

Irish   Long before Irish jokes became popular, Jack had his own:
Irish confetti - stone chippings or gravel
Irish hurricane - flat calm sea
Irish light ale - Guinness
Irish mail - bag of potatoes
Irish parliament - lots of talking, but no decisions
Irish pendant - poorly secured line or hanging fender
Irish pennants - loose threads on clothing
Irish pilot - an inshore guide who knows every rock and
 sand bar, but not the actual safe passage
Irish rise - demotion
Irish toothache - an erection or *stonker

Irish horse   A term that deserves a separate entry because it was Jack's nickname in the days of *salt horse (salted beef) for a lump of meat that was even more tough and stringy than usual. This term stemmed from the belief that the **Irish**, being so poor, worked their **horses** harder and longer than anyone else

iron chicken *(FAA)*   The (older) piston-engined *Whirlwind 7* helicopter

(the) **ish**   Derived from the word *Issue*:
1. A full scale of equipment: *"It's the **complete ish**.."*
2. Can also mean: *"That's all you're getting !"*
3. Adjective to describe a new piece of equipment or an item of clothing that is the height of fashion: *"He was in his new *trapping gear - designer jeans, Lacoste sweater, Porsche sunglasses - **the ish**.."*
4. Also as a single word for approximating a certain figure or level with *-ish* as a suffix: *"How much did that cost ? A thousand ?"* *"Mmm - **ish**.."*

It's only pain ! *(RM)*   Traditional and jocular encouragement at *Lympstone for recruits who are suffering while undergoing the rigours of *Commando training. Also painted on a signboard in *Heartbreak Lane to announce the 500 metres distant finish of the *Endurance course

-ITS   Suffix indicating *In Tomato Sauce*. The variants are:
B	-**ITS**	Beans
H	-**ITS**	Herrings
P	-**ITS**	Pilchards
T	-**ITS**	Tomatoes !

JULIET

Jack   Generic name for all *Royal Navy* sailors, derived from *Jack Tar*, the 18th and early 19th century *matelot with his glossy black hat, carefully dressed pigtail, and canvas breeches that, like the hairs on his head, were impregnated with high grade tar. See *tarpaulin for more detail on this aspect of clothing. The usual name associated with **Jack** these days is *Jolly Jack*, for the cheerful, willing, robust, randy, sharp and witty individual whose common sense, humour and insight have made a book like this possible ! Note also:

Jack Adams - older nickname for a stubborn fool
Jack *Dusty - a *Supply and Secretariat* rating
Jack-me-tickler - a sailor who thinks he knows it all: *"Don't come the Jack-me-tickler with me, you poxy little *scab-lifter"*
Jack of all trades - sailor who can turn his hand to anything, and almost had to, since unlike the *Army* who have infantry, cavalry and artillery, Jack has to provide all these features of military operations by himself !
Jack Strop - an argumentative sailor
Jack the Lad - someone who plays hard socially
Jack-with-Bumps - a *Wren
Jackproof - *nothing* is really **Jackproof**

See also *son of a gun for the historic definition of *Jack* !

jack it in *(RM)*   Give up

jack it up   Fix it; arrange for something to happen

jackanapes coat   The original name for a *monkey jacket* which was made of rough wool and worn by sailors on watch in cold weather. This has now become a *donkey jacket*

Jackie-boy *(FAA)*   Nickname for a pilot who is a bit too flashy: *"He's been something of a *Jackie-boy recently, but the *Trappers had his *number just as soon as they started work this week.."*

jacksie   Slang term for someone's posterior; see also *duck-run

jackstaff   Flagpole at the bow (or a masthead in some vessels) from which a nationality flag or **jack**, smaller than an *ensign*, is flown when in harbour. In *RN* warships this **jack** is more commonly known as the ***Union Jack***, whereas the (White) ensign staff is positioned aft. Note that it is incorrect, although common in *civvy street, to describe the *Union Flag* as the ***Union Jack*** - unless of course it is actually being worn on a warship's **jackstaff**!

jackstay   Two basic versions:
1. **Light jackstay** - manila rope rigged between two ships under way, along which a traveller block and suspended load can be hauled back and forth in a **jackstay transfer**
2. **Heavy jackstay** - as above, but a steel cable is used to carry greater loads such as fuelling pipes, and its tension is maintained by automatic winches

JAFO (FAA)   Newish acronym for *Just Another F(lipping) *Observer*, derived from an American TV series about some amazing helicopter that does impossible things; the *Lynx world quickly adopted this term, which in general usage then became *Jaffa*, as in *orange*. In turn, *Orange and *Zero were added to the descriptive library for *Lookers. The man who is responsible for *trapping *Lynx *Observers (and saying *"yes or no"* about their performance) then became, almost inevitably, the *man from Del Monte* !

Jago's Mansion   HMS *DRAKE*, the Devonport (Plymouth) Naval Shore Establishment

jahooblies The female breasts; see also *jamungas

jam bosun Another term for the Supply (or *Victualling) Officer

James the First The First Lieutenant; see *Jimmy and *Bloke. Also referred to as **James the Magnificent**. The entry for *Jimmy the One has a more complete explanation for the origin of this term

jammy Lucky: *"Howja fix that little *number, you jammy git ?"*

jampot officer See *pickle jar officer

jamungas (heavy emphasis on middle syllable) Enormous breasts

Jan / Janner Nickname for any sailor from the West Country, and by extension, anything that originates from Devon or Cornwall

Jaunty The *Master-At-Arms*, or senior *Regulator. This word is derived from the French description of *gentilhomme*, or *gentleman-at-arms*, and the name tends to go with a position rather than an individual, ie.: *"He's NORFOLK's new Jaunty.."* not: *"He's a Jaunty.."* See also *Joss and *Jossman

Jenny *Jenny Wren* - a member of the *Women's Royal Naval Service*

Jenny's side party *RN* warships visiting *Honkers get spruced up there by a formidably efficient team of Chinese women who are still led, after many years, by a charming lady called **Jenny**

Jesse The alternative nickname for a sailor named James

Jesus factor Something extra allowed for in a design to cover those imponderables which have not been (or cannot be) calculated by computer: *"Thirty thousand pounds all-up weight, including five hundred pounds of fuel as a Jesus factor.."*

Jesus nut The all-important feature which actually secures a helicopter's rotor blade system onto its driving shaft. Disconnection or failure of this item while in flight will result in the crew meeting the Man in person

jet jock *(FAA)* Member of the *stovie community

Jew's march-past The process of examining one's wallet to ascertain its contents, or the damage caused by last night's *run-ashore

jewing firm Older term for a group of sailors running a small tailoring and repair service on board a warship; now replaced by *Sew-sew

Jez *(FAA)* The *Jezebel* anti-submarine passive sonar system

jibber the kibber   Older slang term for luring a ship onto a rocky coast, usually by attaching a light to a horse with one of its legs hobbled to give the impression of a sailing vessel inshore of the intended victim

jibbering   *Cackling your grease, usually like a *three-badge parrot. See also *lipstall; the commonest usage is: *"You **jibbering** idiot !"*

Jig-a-jig Johnny ?   Traditional prostitute's request, now used almost as a euphemism for a brothel visit

Jimmy / Jimmy the One   The First Lieutenant of a warship; he is responsible for the general appearance and tidyness of the ship. In older times *jeminy* referred to *neatness* and *spruceness*, and the First Officer (beneath the Captain) who was responsible for this aspect became *Jeminy the First*, or as he is now, **Jimmy the One** !

jobbed   Told to go and do something - often an unpopular or unpleasant task

jobber   Rather like *doobrey, *doofer (or *Johnson), an all-purpose fill-in word employed when a more exact description fails the speaker

jock frock   A kilt; note also *Church of Jock

Jockanese   The English language when spoken with a thick Scots accent, and sometimes sounding like a foreign language for that very reason

jockroach   A persistent, obnoxious and annoying little Scotsman

Joe (esp. *FAA*)   Nickname for a rank-and-file member of a squadron: *"I'm just one of the Joes.."* or: *"The real trouble with our *Splot is that he can't forget he was once a Squadron Joe.."* A junior *RM* Officer was usually called the **Young Joe** in a ship. This leads onto the term **joed off**, or the process whereby a *Junior Officer (JO)* is *jobbed, usually at very short notice, to take over a duty: *"Charles went sick, so I got joed off as the *Jimmy's *gofer.."*

johnson *(FAA)*   Another all-purpose word in steadily increasing usage, similar to *doobrey and *doofer: *"Gimme that double-ended johnson will you ?"* In Baltic or Norwegian waters this item is supposed to become a **Johannsen** !

joining letter   Nice custom in the *RN* whereby a *DO, on receipt of *Drafty's intimation that a rating is due to join a warship at some time in the near future, writes him a pleasant and friendly letter outlining the duties and responsibilities that he will be expected to assume, together with a rough outline of the ship's planned programme

joke   Life in uniform generally, leading to the famous observation: *"Listen chum, if you can't take a joke, then you shouldn't have joined.."*

jolly
1. *Royal Marine*, a term later used by Rudyard Kipling in this fragment of verse from his *Barrackroom Ballads*:
   "Sez'e, I'm a Jolly - 'Er Majesty's Jolly -
   Soldier an' sailor too !"
   This nickname applied originally to the Trained Bands of the City of London who provided many recruits for the *Regiment of Sea Soldiers* that were forerunners of the modern Corps
2. A nice, pleasant trip that has no real underlying purpose.
3. A **jollyboat** is a vessel used for purely recreational purposes

joss
1. Luck of any sort; sheer luck or a total fluke becomes **pure joss**, whereas **bad joss** is bad luck: *"With my joss I'd fall into a bucket full of tits and come out sucking my thumb.."*
2. The **Joss** is short for the *Jossman or *Master-At-Arms*; see also *jaunty, and note *Fleet joss as well

Jossman   The most frequently used nickname for the *Master-At-Arms* in a warship; do not, unless you're rather bored and seeking a little excitement in your life, say to this man: *"Hello Chief !"* If he is a *Warrant Officer, then the older nickname (derived from the now superceded rank of *Fleet Master-At-Arms) still persists as *Fleet Jossman or *Fleet Jaunty

Jumbo   The largest foresail in a square-rigged ship, equivalent to a genoa in modern yachts; it is the percursor of the modern usage to describe something huge and elephantine

jump Enjoy conjugal relations with someone; also used by *FAA* *pingers, when chasing submarines, to describe the process of moving from one *dip position to the next

Jumper Nickname for the surnames Cross, Collins and Short

jungle bunny A lady of African or West Indian origin, or a *Royal Marine Commando* who is totally in his element when deployed operationally in the jungle

jungle drums (esp. *FAA*) The grapevine or bush telegraph for rumour and speculation: *"The **jungle drums** say that he's not doing particularly well in the new appointment.."*

jungle rules Any team game such as volleyball or football, when played without any real rules at all

Junglie Pilot or aircrewman belonging to a *Commando helicopter squadron supporting the *Royal Marines*, in contrast to someone appointed to a submarine-hunting *Pinger outfit. Note also the *Pinglie hybrid; he comes into existence when *Pingers move ashore for land operations, sometimes with unfortunate confusion resulting from a lack of map-reading experience !

junior Jack or Royal when under 17 years old; mature enough to fight in the Falklands but not, apparently, to serve Her Majesty in Northern Ireland. See also *Boy seaman

Juniors *(RM)* The Junior Command Course, compulsory for those *candidate Marines desirous of advancement to Corporal. Held at *Lympstone: *"I'm off up to CTC for my **Juniors** next week.."*

junket bosun   *Wardroom Steward

jury-rigged   A temporary and emergency (*de jour*) arrangement or *lash-up designed to get a vehicle, aircraft or ship back to base for repair, hence a **jury mast** or **jury rudder** that has been *jury-rigged*

KILO

kag / kaggage *(RM)*   Unwanted or useless equipment: *"Don't bother with that lot - leave it behind. It's all just so much **kag**.."*

kaki   Short for **kaki-poos**, ie. shit: *"Tried to drop me in the **kaki** did he ? Right, just you watch me *stitch him up !"*   There is a possible relationship with the *Army* word (and colour) **khaki** here

kecks *(RM)*   Underpants; see also *shreddies. In Liverpool **kecks** is a slang word for *trousers*

keel hauling / keel dragging   17th century naval punishment where a weighted- down culprit was hoisted up to one yardarm, with a rope tied around his body that ran down beneath the hull and up to the yardarm opposite. He was then dropped into the water and dragged against the barnacle-covered hull, smacked against the keel, and then pulled up to the surface again, half-drowned. For additional effect, a cannon - the *rogue's gun - was also fired just over his head ! Hence the modern expression: *"If the *Old man finds out he'll probably **keel haul** you !"* It may be that the phrase *great hardship* originated in this way, since someone who was **keel hauled** had to *under go a great, hard ship*..

Kelvin *(FAA)*   A not very bright *Bloggs: *"In fact, we judge this man to be something of a **Kelvin** - pretty close to Absolute Zero.."*

kerosene budgie   Another name for a helicopter; see *paraffin pigeon for a fuller listing

KFS *(RM)*   *Knife, Fork and Spoon*; see also *eating irons and *gobbling rods

kick it into touch   Solve a problem by getting rid of it

Jack Dusty

killick   Older word for a small stern anchor, now used for any
*Leading Hand because of the single fouled anchor sleeve badge of a
*Leading *rate

'kin 'ell !   Expletive abbreviated; should be listed under *F* !

King's badge / squad *(RM)*   Royal cipher awarded by *King George V*'s
1918 Order to the best Marine passing out of training from *The King's
Squad*; this device is worn on the upper left sleeve of his uniform
throughout a man's career, even if he subsequently becomes
commissioned as an Officer - as many **King's badgemen** have done

King's (or Queen's) **shilling**   Traditional bounty paid in older
times on enlistment into the Sovereign's service, and a development of
the original *prest* described under *Impressed. An unscrupulous
recruiter might buy some unsuspecting chap a mug of ale, place the coin
in his beer and wait for it to be consumed; the wretch was then deemed
to have struck a bargain having swallowed the **King's Shilling**. Some
pewter drinking vessels still have a glass bottom to guard against this
possibility ! The term is still used when referring to a person's date
of entry into the Corps or the Navy

kip
1. Sleep
2. Protective sheet of dark-green and waterproof material from which
   a *basha or *bivvy can be constructed. Derived from the stores
   item - *Kit Individual Protection* - and also known as a **kip sheet**

kit   Also two meanings:
1. Equipment, in the general or specific sense: *"It's **good kit**."*
   means that something works well, or perhaps: *"It's a special
   piece of kit that works underwater.."* could be applied to
   almost anything designed to function in that demanding
   environment
2. Underwear, especially of the feminine kind, referred to in a
   low growl: *"Get yer **kit** off, darlin'.."* See also *lagging in
   this particular sense

kit muster   Formal inspection of a rating's full issue of clothing and personal equipment, often as a punishment for a persistently slack or untidy individual; also a euphemistic term for vomiting, presumably because the stomach contents have also been laid out for inspection !

kitty / Kitty
1. Pooling of cash for some joint purchase: *"Anyone for another beer - there's still a fiver in the kitty.."*
2. Nickname for the surname Wells (from the nursery rhyme: *"Ding-dong-dell, Kitty's in the well.."*

klebbies   Local (foreign) currency. One *ickie - of whatever description - equals a hundred **klebbies**, a term also used to describe small change in a sailor's pocket; as the ship leaves port those **klebbies** are rendered almost useless and become *shrapnel instead

klicks (esp. *RM*)   Kilometres

knack-all *(RM)*   Nothing; a version of *naff-all*, or stronger

knacker
1. A useless individual, particularly if he is an overweight **fat knacker**. Note also the special use of this latter phrase when referring to any food with a very high calorie value as **fat knacker pie**
2. Testicle: *"After the *bricking my starboard knacker didn't half give me some *gyp.."*
3. To be **knackered** means to be very tired or *chin-strapped; an inanimate object may also be **knacked** - either broken or seized
4. **knacker crackers** are the thighs of a large *party
5. **knacker lacquer** is hair spray, because if you were crazy enough to spray it on your *parts, the **knacker lacquer** would add *lustre to your cluster*

knee-jerk response   Criticism of some quick-response decision made by a higher authority that has not been thought through properly

knee trembler (sometimes **KT**)   The process of *giving the ferret a run while leaning against a wall

knicker python   The penis; in its complete form the phrase refers to a *one-eyed knicker python* or *trouser snake

knob jockey / knobber   A *brownhatter, but the terms are also used in an asexual but abusive and derogatory sense

knock down   The process of disassembling something, derived from the ship's cooper of yesteryear who could **knock down** a cask when empty into its component hoops and staves for more compact storage. Also used in sailing for a yacht that has been **knocked over** onto her beam ends by a violent squall

knock it on the head Give up; abandon an attempt to do something

knock the gilt off the gingerbread Spoil the telling of a joke with an early punchline. This modern usage is derived from a much older one; **gingerbread** was the decorative carpentry and scrollwork round the stern of a warship, often highly gilded or painted. The firing of a broadside, or the impact of enemy shot, rather spoiled this adornment by **knocking the gilt off the gingerbread**

Knocker Common nickname for anyone with the surname White or Whyte

knocking shop Brothel; see also *bag shanty

know the ropes Jack, when properly trained and experienced, knew both the location and function of *every* component of a ship's general rigging; the phrase has now come ashore with a wider meaning that can be applied to anyone with special or practical experience

knuckle A trio of applications:
1. Hit somebody with a fist, or smack him with a **knuckle sarnie**
2. A **knuckle bosun** is the nickname for an aggressive individual who is always getting into fights; *punchy is a suitable adjective !
3. To **knuckle under** means getting down to work and finishing a task; this stems from the 19th century custom of touching the left fist to the forehead in salute and acknowledgement of a superior's orders

kouffed (it) Died; amalgam of *coughed it* and *croaked*

kronks *(RM)* Basic unit of *Noggie currency , but can also be used for any *Skywegian *krone* (crowns)

kye / ky (sometimes **ki**) Hot cocoa drink made from grated or crumbled blocks of unsweetened chocolate

kytai / kyte   Male transvestite in Singapore, often of Eurasian origin and stunning appearance. Jack's rule of thumb was that the ugly ones were usually *real* women !   See also *Bugis Street; they are also found now in *Gib

LIMA

laced
1. Gold **lacing braid** and curl sewn onto the lower sleeves of an Officer's reefer jacket to indicate rank, eg. *Uniform for sale, 40 in. chest, 34 in. waist and laced to Lieutenant Commander..*
2. Extra alcohol added to an otherwise innocuous *wet in order to get the victim drunk

lagging
1. Insulating material wrapped around boilers and steam pipes
2. A lady's clothing, particularly her underwear: *"C'mon darlin' - get your lagging off.."* See also *kit in this sense

laid up   Taken out of service for repair or refitting; in the human sense this means being **laid up** in the *Boneyard

lamp
1. Hit someone: *"Ginge jumped up and lamped him.."* Derived perhaps from the older expression *trim his lamps* as in (2)
2. **Lamps** are also eyes; **lamp covers** are sunglasses

landaway *(FAA)*   Navigational training exercise which involves a day (or weekend) trip to some pleasant destination

landman / landsman   In theory, this was a man who had volunteered for sea service in a British warship, but was without any formal naval training. He was paid on a lower scale than an ordinary seaman, although his actual volunteering might have attracted a large cash bounty of *prest* money ! In practice, however, the term soon came to be used for any *pressed *lubber

landmine   Loaded bun in a *pusser's *bag rat

larbolins   Older term for sailors in the port (**larboard**) watch; the opposite (starboard) watch men were *starbolins

lash-up   Expression derived originally from the process of running the *gauntlet, but now adapted in at least three different forms of usage:
  1. Temporary, improvised or home-made construction (esp. *RM*): "*Even though it was a *right **lash-up**, the thing worked fairly well..*" See also *jury-rigged in this context
  2. Provide generous hospitality: "*After we *dicked the Army at Twickenham, the whole team got **lashed-up stinking** in the Long Bar..*"
  3. Traditional early morning call for Jack to get up and *secure his hammock and bedding: "***Lash up** and stow !*"

Last Dog   The second of the two *Dog Watches:
  First Dog   1600 to 1800
  Last Dog   1800 to 2000
This is Jack's favourite watch at sea, because in a normal *watch system he will not have to *turn to again until the 0800 *forenoon watch of the next day, leading to the expression **Last dog and all night in** that anticipates an undisturbed night's sleep

last in, first out   Normal etiquette concerning the carriage of senior officers in boats, but note also the procedure detailed in *accomodation ladder

last shot   Final chance of promotion before passing out of the *zone; if this turns out to be a miss, then ceremonies for the *Feast of the *Passover* will be appropriate

laughing gear   Mouth: "*Get your **laughing gear** round this lot..*"

laughing kitbags *(RM)*   Something hugely amusing: "*Then this *Pongo Major went and split his trousers right in the middle of the parade - the boys were **laughing kitbags**..*"

Gen buzz

launch *(FAA)* Active, and also passive description for aircraft taking-off from a ship or *Naval Air Station*: "*801 Squadron* **launched** *at 0450, an hour before first light, for the attack on Stanley airfield..*" Or: "*The *Lynx was *ranged and* **launched** *immediately to investigate this new surface contact..*" Note that the term *take-off* is rarely used in Naval parlance, and neither is *landing* when *recovery is actually the process described. However, just to confuse the issue, aircraft will **land on** (board) during the latter *evolution and their crews might well describe this as *being recovered* !

Law of the Navy The seniority system as laid out in the *Navy List. An Officer appearing higher in the List is the more senior; in a task group this single fact will determine which warship then becomes the *canteen boat

lay-apart store Place where items of *kit not required for immediate use are placed; can very easily turn into something of a *glory hole unless subjected to regular *Rounds

Layer Older name for the senior member of a Naval gun's crew, sometimes responsible to a *turret captain, but who was also responsible for the difficult task of setting that gun's *elevation*, in conjunction with the *Trainer - who looked after the *azimuth*

lawful occasions Ships going about their **lawful occasions** are vessels plying their trade in a legal fashion; if doing so under a British flag, they are entitled to the protection of the *Royal Navy*

lazy lane *(FAA)* Short cut from the runway into a Squadron's dispersal

lazy lob Partial erection; see *lob

lazy shot A steel or concrete weight put over the side of a sea boat on a *shot line to assist diving operations

(like a) **lead fart** Description of something that has not been well received; see also *fart in a spacesuit !

Leading Hand / Rate   The third rung on the Naval promotion ladder, equivalent to a *Corporal* in *Army/RAF* terms. Possession of the **Leading *Rate** indicates elevation from the *Able Rate, and is denoted by the wearing of a *killick badge, hence the general nickname for the rank. The shortened form **Leading** is acceptable when addressing or referring directly to a **Leading Hand**: *"Leading - will you open a new file *docket, please.."* or: *"Leading Smith is the *phot who took that amazing picture.."*

lead on MacDick   Phrase describing someone lacking discrimination or judgement in his sexual activities, and who appears to be careless of the possible consequences: *"Ever since the Falklands he's been a complete lead on MacDick *merchant.."* Such a person may also be described as *using his dick as a compass*

leatherneck *(RM)*   Traditional nickname for *US Marine Corps* personnel, and probably the origin in WW2 for the term *bootneck. Relationships between the two Corps are traditionally close, as might be expected between two organizations that fought against each other in the Wars of American Independence ! See also *Bunker Hill and any honest account of why *The White House* is that colour; the best overall *Candidate passing out from his *Juniors at *Lympstone each year is awarded the **Leatherneck Trophy** donated by the *USMC*. Note also the *USMC* connection behind the *Tunney Cup

lecky   General abbreviation for an electrician

ledger bosun   Another name for *Scribes - a Writer or Pay Clerk

left footer   Roman Catholic; someone who digs with the wrong (left) foot

left wing   Unorthodox behaviour that offends sensibility: *"Jock got all his type ratings with one airline, then immediately switched to a rival outfit - a bit left wing if you ask me.."*

legoland / moon city   General name for any new barracks or rebuilt shore facility like HMS *RALEIGH* where modern techniques have been employed in both design and construction

legless   Drunk

leg it   Run (away) - can also be used when there are no *wheels available, and the only means of getting somewhere is to **leg it**, ie. walk ! Royal's ideal running shoes would be a pair of *Nike Leggits*

leg over   To **have your leg over** is to indulge in sexual intercourse, but in a horizontal rather than the vertical *knee trembling mode; the phrase **legover and chips** can describe a successful *run-ashore. See also *beer, big eats, bag-off and back on board in this particular social context

length of service   There are some superb visual images for Jack to call on in order to describe time in the *mob, as confirmed by the following selection:

- *He was in when Long John Silver only had an egg on his shoulder..*

- *Listen lad, I was in Baghdad when you was still in yer Dad's bag..*

- *Jim's been in that long he had a *survivor's tot from the MARY ROSE*

- *Shiner *signed on when Nelson was a *middy / Cunningham was still a cadet..*

- *I was on the Main Gate when you were still on Cow & Gate..*

- *Young George ? He was learning to fly when Pontius was the Senior Pilot..*

- *When God said "Let there be light..", Jan was the duty *greenie..*

- *I've had more sea-miles than you've had *pusser's peas..*

- *Bill took the *King's Shilling when *VICTORY was still part of Epping Forest..*

- **Colours must have been in that ruddy store when the Dead Sea first reported sick..*

- *Clive and Mike joined the *Fleet Air Arm on the day they were scraping Icarus off the main runway..*

- *When I joned the *Andrew there were no official numbers, because we all knew each other..*

- *Reckon' 'e was a regular in the team when Jesus was playin' full-back fer Israel..*

- *Nelson ? Never knew 'im - but his father was a right hard case..*

let the end go   Failure to pull on a rope, and actually releasing it, thereby letting the ship and/or team down. Used nowadays to describe someone who has given up without making any proper effort, or has slackened off to a state of inefficiency during *RDP

liberty boat / libertymen   Small vessel used to transfer libertymen ashore and vice versa. The *pipe *Libertymen to clean !* orders those so privileged to cease work and *clean into their *shore rig. *Libertymen fall in !* orders them to muster at the *brow prior to boarding the **liberty boat** which, in a shore facility, might well be a *pusser's bus. The expression to *miss the boat is now popular parlance for failing to grasp an opportunity, but its origins lie in missing the **liberty boat** - which wasn't coming back

licence to breathe Jack's rather rueful and older nickname for his *station card

lid *(SM)* *Conning tower hatch - *"Shut the lower **lid**!"* means: *"Close and secure the inner *conning tower hatch.."*

(He) lies like a pusser's menu / flat fish / hairy egg / *Appointer / Met man / cheap watch *"I don't think that he is telling the truth!"*

Lieutenant An Officer's rank to be found in most of the world's navies, including the *Royal Navy* which also has the lower grade of **Sub-Lieutenant** in addition (or **Lieutenant j.g.** for *Junior Grade* in the *US Navy*). Its origins lie in the French words *lieu* and *tenant*, the *place-holder* for the Master or Commanding Officer. Both the Spanish speaking and Italian navies omit the prefix, hence *Tenente* and *Teniente* as their versions of this rank

life in a blue suit Resigned acceptance of the vicissitudes of life in the *Andrew: *"Sold your house - and then had the *draft cancelled ? Dear, oh dear - that's **life in a blue suit** I'm afraid, my friend.."* Submariners often extend this joke with the subtle little alteration to **life in a pink frock** !

light and dirty Light rum (Bacardi) and *Coca Cola*

lightning conductors Gold stripes running down the trouser seams of a Captain's or *Flag Officer's Mess Dress uniform

limers A soft drink (traditionally prepared from sachets of powder) and issued in tropical zones, or during very hot weather. Now made from ordinary squash or cordials, but the name has persisted, even if orange or lemon is the flavour concerned

limey / lime juicer Sir James Lind, the first Physician at *Haslar Hospital wrote a treatise in 1753 that showed lemon juice to be effective in treating the sailor's scourge of *scurvy*, an affliction caused wholly by a deficiency in Vitamin C. It was not until 1795, over forty years and thousands of deaths later, that the formal prescription of lemon juice as an anti-scorbutic was instituted by *Their Lordships of the Admiralty*, and then only because of the persistence of Sir Gilbert Blane, one of Lind' successors. Lemons had to be bought in the Mediterranean; **limes** grew in the British West Indies colonies, so **lime juice** was soon substituted as a daily issue, and scurvy ceased to be a problem in the *Royal Navy*. Jack's counterpart in the United States of America nicknamed him *Limey* as a consequence, and his ships as *lime juicers*; this name has persisted on the other side of the *Pond for all things British, usually prefixed by the word *Goddamned* !

line shoot *(FAA)*   A tall story, or exaggeration in the recounting of some event that is worthy of recording in a Squadron **line book**

lined up   Charged with an offence under the *Naval Discipline Act*

lip lock   Prolonged kissing; see also *swapping spit: "..an' then *she slaps this bloody great **lip lock** on me !"*

lipstall *(FAA)*   What happens when your brain moves quicker than your mouth; see also *burble

liquorice legs   Shiny black gaiters worn by the Officer in charge of a formal Guard, and by *Guns

List   The *Navy List*, an official document published annually by *Her Majesty's Stationery Office*. The term is also used twice yearly when referring to the latest batch of promotions (or alterations to the List !) signalled from the *MoD: "No good news for me on this **List** unfortunately. Just one more *shot, then the Feast of the *Passover.."*

lit up   Older term for drunk, hence the furore about the radio commentator who described a Spithead review one evening: *"The Fleet's all lit up.."*

Little f *(FAA)*   Official nickname for *Lieutenant Commander (Flying)* in an aircraft carrier or *RN* Air Station. He acts as deputy for *Commander (Air)* who is also known as *Wings (rather than *Big f* !)

liver-in   Officer or rating who lives on board during the week, even if he has a home elsewhere; the *RM* equivalent is an *in-lier

living high off the hog   This expression appears to originate from the occasional welcome relief of pork substituting for the usual *salt horse (beef) in a sailor's monotonous diet at sea

loafing stations   Older term for a shore establishment where Jack did very little apart from **loafing** while awaiting his *draft chit for a ship

loan clothing   Special uniform items issued only to those required to perform a specialist task or job

lob in *(FAA)*   Land an aircraft somewhere, usually en route to somewhere else: *"On the way back from Guernsey we **lobbed in** to Exeter and picked up the Senior Pilot.."*

lob on   To **have a lob on** means to have an erection; a state of partial arousal is described as a *lazy lob. This meaning is recorded as being in use in the 18th century

lobby   A small compartment opening onto a *flat, eg. the *QM's lobby* which is used when alongside

loblolly boy   Older term for a young lad who assisted the Ship's Surgeon, as described in the novel *Silas Marner* by Tobias Smollett. Still senior to a *pox doctor's clerk ! *Loblolly* was the nickname given to a thin, watery gruel served in the Sick Berth

LOBS !   Alarm call in older training establishments meaning: *"Look Out, Boys - Seniors !"*

lobscouse   A dish served in sailing ship days, especially in those vessels working out of Liverpool, consisting of minced salt beef, stewed vegetables and broken ship's *biscuit in layers. The term *Scouse originates from this recipe

lobsters   Jack's archaic nickname for the *RM Light Infantry* of old, because of their scarlet tunics; the *RM Artillery* (blue) were called *unboiled lobsters* by the same token !

local   Local promotion; see also *acting

Lofty   Traditional nickname for anyone tall, or with the surname Lofthouse

logbook stamped *(FAA)*   Aircrew method of describing successful social activity: *"Went up to *Smoke for the weekend and got my logbook stamped.."* See also *back in date

logged   The formal recording of a reprimand issued to an Officer by the Captain of his ship, in the sense that the event has been recorded as a matter of significance in the Ship's Log. It is torn up when that Officer moves on to a new appointment: *"I got logged for letting off a *thundie in a *Crab mess, yet the bloody *Wafus do that sort of thing all the time.."*

loggerheads   Hollow spheres of iron at each end of a shaft; these were heated in a fire, then plunged into a tar bucket in order to melt the pitch for *paying into the seam of a hull's planking. The spheres were obviously never in contact, hence the expression of *at loggerheads with each other* which has come ashore to describe those who are in a state of permanent and serious disagreement ! See also *Devil and associated entries

Loggies *(RM)*   Members of the *Commando Logistic Regiment RM,* an organization that contains five different cap badges on its *green berets, and which proved itself most convincingly during the land battles of the Falklands campaign. At one stage, the 650 *Commando **Loggies** ashore were successfully re-stocking combat supplies forward for a Division of over 7000 men; this amazing teeth-to-tail ratio of more than 10:1 is unlikely to be equalled in any future difficulty

long burst (esp. *FAA*)   A lengthy conversation that is mostly one-way

long call   Expression heard at the *Wardroom dinner table to indicate that something needs to be passed up from further down: *"Long call for the water, please.."*

long course   Play on words derived from the official titles of the *Dagger courses for officers undergoing specialization training: *"He got sent into a local Government establishment for the long course in mailbag sewing.."*

Long John   Sailor who is always quoting Naval history and traditions

long ship   Older term for ship noted for her poor rations or victuals, now used to describe a *Wardroom displaying poor hospitality, ie. no-one offers to get you a drink

long shot   A cannonball, or a shell fired at extreme range and with little real chance of scoring a hit - but considered worth a try in the circumstances prevailing at the time. The phrase has now come ashore to a wider usage

long Tom
1. Paintbrush on the end of a long pole
2. *(RM)* Long wheelbase *Land Rover* vehicle

Look at the state of that !   Traditional cry of semi-amazement when confronted by a person in outrageous clothing, or someone very much the worse the wear for drink: *"So this is the famous King's Road, eh ? Nothing much to see here after all...ruddy Norah ! Will you* **look at the state of that** *!"*

Look for the rules !   Excuse to lift the edge of an *Uckers board, thereby causing the counters to slide, and thus effectively ending the game; the size and degree of inebriation of your opponents should be considered very carefully before employing this tactic

looks like a ___   See *face like a ____

Looker *(FAA)*   Traditional nickname for an *Observer: *"Are you a *Pirate or a Looker ?"*   See also *zero, *talking Navbag, *Pound for pound, *Orange, *JAFO, *commissioned ballast and *winch weight

looney / loopy juice   Any form of strong alcohol

Lord High Admiral   An honorary and singular title at present reserved for the Sovereign; thus, the current most senior officer in the *Royal Navy* is a woman - *Her Majesty the Queen*. This title used to be one of the nine great Offices of State, but between 1688 and 1964 it was often vacant (*in commission*); there were however some sinecure appointments, including the Duke of Clarence (later *King William IV*) who rather annoyed everyone by exercising his right and power to take the Fleet to sea ! The **Lord High Admiral** was also vested with the title of *Captain-General in order to grant the authority of military command; note that this office rests at present with the **Lord High Admiral**'s Consort, *HRH The Prince Philip*

lose the bubble (esp. *SM*)   The *bubble concerned is in the clinometer spirit level of a *boat which is used to adjust trim; if this bubble disappears from sight then there is a danger of trim control being lost

Lossie *(FAA)*   The former *RN Air Station* of HMS *FULMAR*, now under *Crab ownership, but until recently also the spiritual home of the *Bucc. Locals still refer to the *Wardroom* rather than the Officer's Mess ! Aircraft that are *In hot to the Tain ranges roll in past the *Glenmoranjie* distillery, which explains why that particular fluid is still the *FAA*'s favourite whisky

lost the number of his mess   Euphemism for someone who has died in action, or from an accident ashore while serving in a ship

lovats *(RM)*   The No.2 Service Dress of the *Royal Marines*; this is **lovat green** in colour. See also *Blues

Lover's Leap   Nickname for the first train leaving London for Portsmouth early on Monday morning. Ironically, some of the occupants may have already got out at *Fratton the night before !

low hover   An anxiety state; see also *Wall of Death

low stratus   Clouds of steam put out by an unattended boiling kettle

Lower deck   Collective term for all non-commissioned members of the *Royal Navy*, ie. everyone not actually commissioned as an Officer in the *Upper deck (or *Upper scupper !) For *lower deck lawyer* see *messdeck lawyer

lubber   An unimpressive person; a **landlubber** is such an individual when encountered ashore

lumpy jumper   Civilian female, in contrast to a *Jenny Wren; also used to describe a WRNS *wooly pully

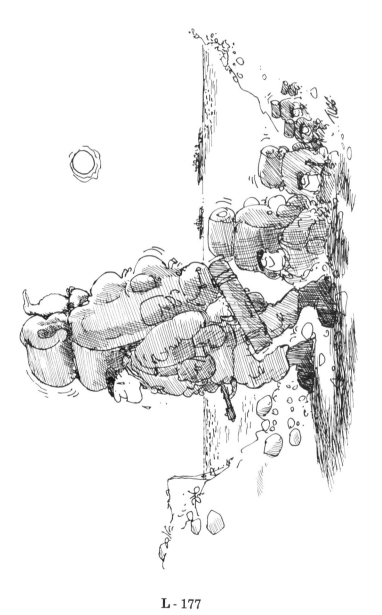

Bimble

L - 177

lumbered   Rather like *lurk, but more in the sense that there was no-one else available or suitable: *"One volunteer required with a keen sense of duty - and a University degree. Guess who then got lumbered.."*

lumped   Hit some portion of your anatomy against something hard: *"Watch me elbow, *Doc, fer Gawd's sake - I lumped it against that bleedin' hatch cover when I slipped just now.."*

lurk   Similar to *boning off or *joeing off an Officer or rating for a particular duty: *"I got lurked to look after the Captain's maiden aunt at the *Cockers P.."*   Most *XOs and *Jimmys will maintain a private **lurk list**; see also *lumbered and *bugger-about list

Lympstone   The *Commando Training Centre, Royal Marines* (also known as *CTCRM* or *CTC*) situated on the eastern bank of the Exe estuary; the spiritual home of all *Commandos and those who wear the *green beret, and in addition, the base for all *NCO, Command, Weapon* and other related *Specialist* training in the *Corps. See also *Royal, *nod, *Endurance course, *Smartie tube, *Peter's Pool, *Heartbreak Lane, *Tarzan course, *speed march, *nine miler, *thirty miler, *First Drill, *Juniors, *Seniors, *King's Badge / Squad and - *It's only pain !

Lynx   The main frigate-borne ship's helicopter now that the *Wasp has been phased out (1988); an all-weather, two crew and twin-engined aircraft that is capable of high speeds, great agility, and the carriage of missiles, depth charges or torpedoes

MIKE

Macship WW2 vessel - the initial three letters stand for *Merchantman Aircraft Carrier* - which were an additional feature to the *Camships in Britain's response to the the threat of German long-range *shitehawks(2) operating against Allied convoys crossing the North Atlantic. They were built with flat decks over a tanker or grain-carrying hull. After fighter-carrying escort carriers appeared on the scene, they then began to operate *Stringbags in the anti-submarine role; for a brilliant evocation of these ships and that era, read Lord Kilbracken's book (see Bibliography section)

made up General term for promotion that can be heard in the *Wardroom (with the subsidiary meaning of *selection* for this) as well as on the *lower deck in its proper sense: "*Splot got **made up** in in the *List yesterday, but the CO didn't even get a *mench.." as* compared with: *"My B13 is in and I see the *Old Man next week to get **made up**.."*

Madhouse Nickname for the *Ministry of Defence* in London; derived from the more official abbreviation of **MoD**, but in addition, an accurate description of some of the frenetic activity to be encountered inside that enormous building

Mae West Still the unofficial but frequently-used name, after all these years, for an aircrew inflatable buoyancy aid. The large pectoral curves induced to one's outline on operating this lifejacket are reminiscent of the splendid *jahooblies possessed by Ms **Mae West** during her cinematic heyday in the 1930s

magic binos Older term for radar, a device which enabled the user to see in fog or bad weather. Now used for the NVG (*Night Vision Goggles*) which can be attached to a pilot's flying helmet instead of the visor, allowing safe tactical flying in total darkness

magic writing *(FAA)*   Flight information presented in glowing letters on the HUD (Head-Up Display) of a *SHAR

mahogany bomber *(FAA)*   Term borrowed by Navyators from the *Crabfats for a desk in the *Madhouse: *"My last trip in a Hunter is programmed in for this afternoon - then I'm off to *drive a **mahogany bomber** in Whitehall for a pair of years.."*

mailies   General term for any post, hence **maily-*freak** for someone who is in a state of turmoil awaiting the *pipe: *"Mail is now ready for collection.."* A **maily** in the singular sense is an envelope, but note *bluey as well

main galley   Equivalent of a central dining hall in a ship or establishment, but see also *galley

majority *(RM)*   The process of being *selected for promotion to **Major**, which, because of differences in comparative rank, is equivalent to acquiring a *brass hat - as for a *Lt. Col.* in the Army, or a *Commander RN / Wing Cdr. RAF*: *"He got his **majority** early because of that, and then went straight back out to Northern Ireland.."* The Officer in command of a ship's *Royal Marines* *Detachment is traditionally nicknamed **The Major**, and the most junior *RM* officer is **The Soldier** or *Joe

make   A quartet of applications:
   1. **make a signal**   - transmit a message
   2. **make and mend**   - period in a ship's daily routine set aside
            for the repair and maintenance of Jack's
            personal clothing and kit. Nowadays used
            to describe an afternoon off
   3. *Make it so !*   - formal response from the Officer of the
            Watch in order to initiate some piece of
            ceremonial: *"*Sunset, sir.."   "**Make it so** !"*
   4. **make your number** - introduce yourself to the Captain or *HOD on
            arrival in a new appointment, in a similar
            manner to a warship signalling her pendant
            number when joining the Fleet

makee-learnee   Pidgin Chinese for someone who is a novice

makings
   1. The ingredients for a *wet of tea or coffee, ie. powder, sugar
      and milk
   2. Tobacco and cigarette papers for making *ticklers

Malta GC   Former strategic base of the Mediterranean Fleet; the scene of much stoic heroism despite strong Axis bombardment during WW2, for which the island was collectively awarded the *George Cross*. Although no longer a *NATO* asset, and following a period of strained diplomatic relations, *RN* ships are now visiting with increasing frequency, thereby reinforcing strong historical links and introducing a new generation of Jack and Royal to such features as:

Malta *dog - a severe form of diarrhoea and vomiting

Maltese breaststroke - reversal of the normal swimming stroke into a scooping action: *"Gimme your money.."*

Maltese gharry horse - an animal with particularly muscular hind-quarters, hence: *"She had a backside / face just like a **Maltese gharry horse**.."*

Maltese lace - any garment with holes in it

Maltese pound - containing thirteen ounces

See also the term *my brother in Gozo

man and boy　　　　Proud statement that usually accompanies any description of length of service: *"I was in the *Andrew twenty-nine years **man and boy**.."* Note that Royal will refer to his service as a *Junior in a different way when making an identical claim: *"I did twenty-nine years in the Corps, including three years *girl's time.."* See also the interesting comparisons under *length of service

man fat　　　　Another term for seminal fluid; the others are *population paste and *baby gravy

man from Del Monte *(FAA)*　　　　The *Lynx *Observers *Trapper; see *JAFO for a more detailed explanation

man up *(FAA)*　　　　The crew process of boarding, strapping-in and then completing all the pre-flight checks of an aircraft before *launch

mandraulic　　　　Mechanical apparatus worked by muscular power alone; the modern version of *Armstrong patent. See also *handraulic

mankey　　　　Something dirty or filthy

manking　　　　Complaining in a whining or repetitive manner: *"Don't come in here and start **manking** all over me about transport.."*

Marines　　　　There are constant references to Royal, his history and terminology throughout this book, but it is as well to remember that many nations have **Marine Corps** of soldiers who are especially trained and adapted to the problems of war at sea - including the Argentines ! See also *Cloggie. Royal's origins lie with the 1664 Order in Council that raised 1200 men for the *Lord Admiral's Regiment of Sea Soldiers* (see also *Jollies); this number fluctuated until 1755 when the force was re-organized into a permanent feature serving in warships in order to maintain discipline, provide sentries, and play in the ship's band. Later on, artillery functions were added, so that one gun turret's crew of most large *Royal Navy* warships were all **Royal Marines** rather than seamen. The distinction between *RM Artillery* and *RM Infantry* was abolished in 1923. Later on, *Commando tasks were added; after WW2 this latter role was adopted specifically by the *Corps, with *Army* personnel supporting the artillery, engineer and general logistic functions.

The relationships between the *United States **Marine** Corps* and *The Corps of **Royal Marines*** are extraordinarily close, both in terms of current liason and past development, as well as their expertise in the amphibious warfare role. During the Wars of American Independence they actually fought against each other ! Although the *USMC* is technically junior (formed in 1775) it is numerically over twenty times the size of its British counterpart; on both sides of the Atlantic Ocean the reputations of both Corps are mutually respected as unsurpassed in an unbroken history of fighting spirit and devotion to duty in the service of their respective countries

mark   Originally the *fathom markings on a sounding line; this has led to the shoreside terms of ***mark*** *my words* and *made his **mark*** from the old naval methods of determining depth under a warship's keel

marry-up   Work two lines as one, or bring things into line: *"The ship sailed long before we could **marry-up** all the paperwork for those new stores.."*

Master-At-Arms   A senior *Regulator, and the equivalent of a ship's *Police Sergeant*; see also *Jaunty and *Jossman

matelots   Royal's collective term for Jack (pronounced *mat-lows*); the **matelot's shuffle** can be observed whenever Jack gets on the dance floor with his *pash - one step left, one to the right, a quick wiggle

- and then the same all over again, at a pace that is often independent of the beat. A **matelot's gorge** was a big meal of steak, egg and chips on getting home from sea, perhaps leading to the term *Guz ?!

mattress mamba   Yet another term for a penis, as a herpetological equivalent of a *knicker python, or a *one-eyed trouser snake

maulers   Hands

max chat *(FAA)*   Flying at full power and high speed (usually at low level): *"The *Boss called *buster, but I was already at **max chat** and going like a bloody train.."*

max out *(FAA)*   Become overloaded mentally: *"Flying low level I can handle the *nav and *poling OK, but give me the radios as well and I just **max out**.."*

mayfly *(FAA)*   Number of aircraft available for the tasking and completion of a planned *flypro

measured his length (esp. *RM*)   Fell flat on the ground after tripping

Mech / Mechanician   An engineering branch structure of senior *rates drawn from the non-artificer stream which sadly became defunct in 1983. These splendid men were rather scornful of *Tiffs, because this latter category had achieved their qualification in an easy way compared with their own hard graft and wide experience at sea

medical comforts   Special items of food and drink (eg. soup, chocolate, brandy) held for issue only in cases of medical need

meltdown   Physical state of a telephone being used by someone who is extremely angry: *"You should have heard the *bollocking that the *Boss got from *Wings ! The phone almost went into **meltdown**.."*

Mench *(RM)*   Abbreviation for the operationally-awarded honour of being **Mentioned in Despatches**

mental dwarf / pygmy   Common term of abuse

merchant   Frequent suffix in many descriptions; see *gunna-merchant, *whinge-merchant and similar labels for an individual rich in those qualities

Merlin   The *Sea King replacement; also the engine of the *Seafire* fighter aircraft (FAA derivative of the *Spitfire*) and the ship's name of the wartime *Naval Air Station* of Donibristle, near Rosyth

Mess number
1. *Wardroom account number for signing bar chits etc.
2. Conversational way of pointing out a mistake, so that the chap who has it wrong should buy everyone a drink: *"The *rig of the*

*day is No.4s my friend - what's your **Mess number** ?"*
3. *(FAA)* By long tradition, an Officer's outstanding **Mess bill** is
   settled by **Mess funds** if he is killed whilst flying on duty.
   This account is not formally closed until midnight, so the
   rest of the Squadron can drink on that **number** in a wake for
   their dead colleague
4. *"He's lost the **number of his Mess**.."* is an older *lower-deck
   term to describe a sailor who has *kouffed it

messdeck
1. Jack's home in a warship or shore establishment
2. **Messdeck justice** is the informal dispensation of punishment to
   someone who persistently trangresses either the written (or
   unwritten) rules. For instance, on the rare occasions when a
   sailor or marine is reluctant to comply with the normal
   standards of daily hygiene, a **messdeck scrubbing** may be
   visited upon him
3. A **messdeck lawyer** is a *Jack-me-tickler who is always arguing
   the toss or quoting regulations and rules
4. The **messdeck *dodger** is a rating employed on cleaning duties
   there
5. When *buzzes travel around a ship they do so via the **messdeck**
   (bush) **telegraph** system

messman   A civilian contracted by the Wardroom Committee to
undertake all supplies and catering, reputedly the richest man in the
ship and the envy of all !

metal moth   Rust: *"This car has been *wellied by the **metal moth**.."*

met man   See *weather guesser or *Professor/*Doctor Fog

Mexican hat dance   Highly excitable state displayed by a
senior officer towards someone lower in the chain of command: *"When I
got up to *Flyco the Captain was doing the **Mexican hat dance** all over
Wings.." See also *wall of death and *high hover

Mick
1. Any Irishman
2. **Take the mick** - to taunt or make fun of someone
3. Older slang for a hammock or **hammick**

Mickey Duck   A cartoon film; the term is an amalgamation of
Mickey Mouse and Donald **Duck**. Two **Mickey Ducks** and a *shitkicker has
nothing to do with the drinks list of a cocktail bar, but merely
indicates that two cartoons are preceding the Western in that night's
cinema programme ! There may however be a demand for *Fred Quimby

Mickey Mouse killick   A young *Leading Hand who hasn't even got
his first (Good Conduct) *badge to go with the *hook. The prefix can
also be applied in a similar vein to badgeless POs and inexperienced
(technical) Chiefs

Ditty box

middle   The **middle watch,** and least favoured of all, since it runs from midnight until 0400

Middy / Middies   Midshipman / a group of Midshipmen. See also *Dartmouth and *Snotty

Milan *(RM)*   Portable anti-tank missile of European manufacture, used with great success by Royal in the Falklands to demolish enemy defensive *sangars. In this context see also *eyes water !

milestone   Different pattern of water in a heavy sea that makes the whole ship slam and shudder: *"Ouch, there goes another **milestone** on the way home.."*

mincer   Another term for a *brownhatter

mind over matter *(RM)*   *"It's quite simple, really - I don't **mind**, and you don't **matter**.."*

mindfart   Alternative to *brain fart as an excuse for having trouble with the operation of a bank of switches

minesweeping   The process of going around the half-empty glasses at a party and pouring their contents into your own glass in order to extend proceedings after the bar has shut

mineswiping   Nickname for the crucial business of mine clearance, as performed in the Gulf during 1987-89 by Jack in a fleet of glassfibre-reinforced plastic **mineswipers**

Ming china   Affectionate description of an older warship: *"He took that lovely old piece of **Ming china** down to the South Atlantic and brought her through the whole conflict without so much as a scratch.."*

minging (pronounced with a hard *g*)
  1. *(RM)* Adopted Glaswegian slang word meaning drunk: *"Jus' two beers an' the boy was **mingin'**.."*
  2. *(RM)* Depending on the context, it can also mean smelling strongly: *"Three weeks ashore in the Falklands an' we wuz all **minging** pretty bad.."*

mismuster   Arrangement made for those who missed their noon *tot to draw it later on in the day. Now used for any issue process: *"Lima Company will draw Arctic clothing from Main Stores at 0800 today; **mismusters** 1600.."*

mixy blob   Weakened and easily surmountable barrier to forward progress around the board in an *Uckers game; also a label for someone of mixed parentage

MOA *(RM)*   A **Marine Officer's Attendant,** or *(Army)* a batman

mob (esp. *RM*)   Royal's conversational equivalent of the
*Andrew, but this term is occasionally used by Jack as well: *"How long
you got to go in the mob then ?"*   This has absolutely nothing to do
with swarthy Italian gentlemen, and neither has *heavy mob

mobile Navbag *(FAA)*   Another disparaging term for an *Observer

Moby rash   The damage inflicted on oneself by crashing
or coming off one of the *Mobylette* mopeds that can be hired by Jack
when visiting Bermuda

Mod plod   A member of the *Ministry of Defence* constabulary. See
also the term *plastic policeman

modo   Totally useless person with a hint of physical deformity,
possibly derived from *Quasimodo* - the *RM* equivalent is a *spaz

molar mangler   Dentist; see *fang farrier for a complete list

Mombers   The Kenyan naval port of Mombasa; see also *black ham

money for old rope   Expression of maritime origin that has come
ashore. *Old rope* was condemned as both dangerous and useless; anyone
that could sell this was getting good money for something worthless

monkey in a ball of wool   Jack's older figure of speech for a face
framed by a *full set of whiskers: *"'Ey *Skers - yer *moosh looks like
a monkey in a ball of wool.."*

monkey jacket   Shorter length *bum-freezer jacket of Mess Undress

monkey on a stick *(FAA)*   The *Lookers are fighting back at last !
Nickname for a pilot, with the alternative of *trained monkey

monkey's fist   Elaborate knot tied around a small weight which can then be thrown for some distance at the end of a *heaving line

monkey's orphan   Sailing warship era term for a young sailor too inexperienced to send *aloft

Moon City   See also *legoland; the term is applied to any group of buildings with a modern or futuristic appearance

moosh   Face, also used as a form of address: *"'Oi, Moosh - whereja think you're slidin' off to ?"*

More yet !   Classic drill order given when adjusting the straightness of line in a parade formation; many other applications in daily life

morning glory   An erection on awakening; in the right circumstances this might lead on to a *dawn strike

Morning Prayers   The Commanding Officer's first meeting of the day, when ship's business and the future programme are discussed

Moses   Nickname for the youngest man (**Baby Moses**) of a ship's company

most dangerous thing in the world *(RM)*   Prior to 1982, this was defined as Jolly Jack with a rifle; now, post-Falklands, the **most dangerous thing in the world** is an *Officer with a map*

mothball fleet   Ships lying alongside or at anchor which are in a deliberate state of preservation. Although inactive, they can be made ready for sea again in times of national emergency

Mother *(FAA)*   Radio and conversational description of an aircraft's parent ship or carrier: *"*Pigeons to Mother - 270 degrees at 65 miles.."*

motion lotion *(FAA)*   Aviation kerosene

motor mouth   Someone who talks too much; see also *Gatling gob

mousetrap   *Pusser's basic cheddar cheese

mozzie   Any flying and biting insect

Mrs B's   **Mrs Beeton's**; see entry at *B's for example

MRU   The acronym for *Much Regret Unable* - the polite declining of an invitation which has now almost become a word in its own right: *"26 *WMPs for drinks before lunch on Sunday, sir - and only four MRUs.."*

muck or nettles *(RM)* No real choice between two unpleasant possibilities: *"You can go right or left, but not straight up. Take your pick, it's either **muck or nettles**.."*

mud moving *(FAA)* *SHAR attacking a weapons range; *ground pounding is an alternative term

mudguard A Deputy Head of Department - since it is a DHod's job to take all the mud and muck thrown up by his *Wheel !

muff diver Someone partial to oral intercourse on a female; in this respect the tufts of facial hair known as *bugger's grips* can also be described as **muff diver's depth marks,** and the wearer asked about their calibration

mufti Formal civilian clothing: *"Should I wear uniform for this interview, or is it **mufti** ?"*

mulct Older term for stoppage of pay, usually as a fine consequent to formal punishment; see also *Northeaster

mulley A quick *kip, so named after the Secretary of State for Defence who, while seated next to his Sovereign, dozed off during the (noisy) *1977 Silver Jubilee Royal Review of the RAF*

muppet Acronym applied to someone in the *Andrew who is of poor aptitude or competence: *"You, my son, are a complete **muppet** - the most useless person Pusser ever trained.."* The term is also used for members of the *mineswiping fraternity

murder face A very ugly individual

muscle bosun An individual who practises the art of body building or who trains hard at weight lifting. Most *springers and *Field Gunners are **muscle bosuns**

mushroom troop *(RM)* Complaining description used by those who feel that they are not being told enough about what is happening: *"We're the classic ruddy **mushroom troop** - fed on shit and kept in the dark.."*

musical veg Baked beans and/or peas

muster
1. The formal inspection of issued equipment which has been laid out in a neat and regulation manner is a **kit muster**. If the standard is satisfactory, then the lay-out is deemed to have **passed muster**
2. Can also be used as an order to group together at another location, as in the *pipe: *"All *hands **muster** on deck.."*
3. To **muster one's kit** also, depending on context, means to vomit !

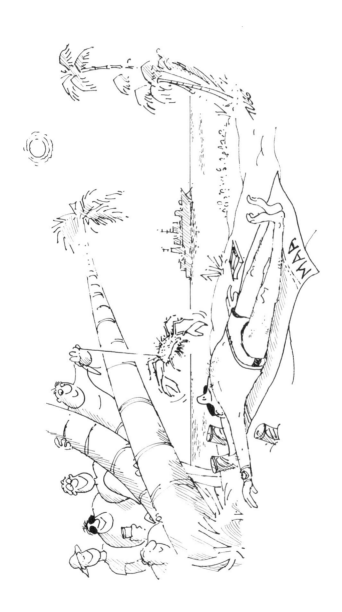

Banyan

My brother in Gozo !   Traditional Naval disclaimer, a conversational device adapted from Jack's experiences ashore in Malta to shift the blame onto someone else: *"It wasn't me - it was my **brother in Gozo.."***

my Navy   *"Smoke in front of the general public while wearing your uniform ?   Not in **my Navy**, you don't !"*

NOVEMBER

192 − 200

n   Algebraic expression that can frequently be heard in use to describe a degree or quantity: *"The *Boss was **n** pissed-off to hear that his suggestion had been rejected by the *Puzzle Palace.."* Another version would have him *pissed-off to the **nth** degree*

NAAFI   Acronym for the *Navy, Army and Air Force Institutes*
1. The **NAAFI damager** is the civilian canteen manager or *can man who is carried in most HM Ships
2. Used to further good effect in describing a low-quality individual: *"He's a bit of a **NAAFI rating** in fact - No Ambition And Flip-all Interest in what's going on.."*
3. See also the security *classification of **NAAFI RESTRICTED** !
4. Note also the mythical **Major Naafi van Driver** along with his colleague Captain *Hertz van Rental; either name can be used by Royal when seeking a *bite from his *Cloggie friends
5. **NAAFI landmine** - a pork pie or *growler
6. **NAAFI wad** - older term for a slice of cake

NAC 89 *(FAA)*   Formal record of training and progress throughout a *Fleet Air Arm* pilot's career; the aviation equivalent of a *S.206 which may contain gems such as: *"When this pilot lifts into the hover he initiates a sequence of events over which he appears to have very little subsequent control.."*

Nagasaki   Japanese city which has assumed a place in Naval legend equivalent to Timbuktu in a wider parlance. A rating who is physically well-endowed with regard to his *wedding tackle may be described as being *rigged like a **Nagasaki donkey;** anything larger or faster than life can also become the largest or fastest (whatever) **this side of Nagasaki** !

nagging machine Another of Jack's nicknames for the missus. However, he is also wise enough to observe sometimes that ***nagging*** *is just endless repetition of the uncomfortable truth..*

nap hand Older term for a *dose of *gonz and siff* acquired during *all-nighters or a *run-ashore. Syphilis, thankfully, is very rarely seen these days, so the phrase now refers to a mixed infection, such as the *boat along with a herpes virus - or pubic crab lice

native leave Special leave granted to local boys when a ship visits a port near their home towns

NATO standard The equivalent of: *"One milk, two sugars.."* in reply to the question: *"How do you like your coffee ?"* ***"NATO standard,*** *negative two !"* would be a reply indicating that no sugar was needed

nause (esp. *RM*) Difficulty with authorities, especially civilian ones, and usually when trying to obtain permission to do something: *"Flightplan into the London Special Rules Zone ? Not worth all the* ***nause,*** *my friend.."* Or: *"The boys seem to have been quite well-behaved during their *run-ashore in Trondheim - some* ***nause*** *over a missing traffic sign, but nothing too serious.."*

nautical nausea Seasickness

Naval stores Any *pusser's item: *"They are called* ***Naval stores*** *because they are meant to be* ***stored.*** *If *Pusser wanted them to be given out then he would have called them issues.."* See also *Slops

navalised Something that has been made *Jackproof, usually by the process of taking a civilian item of equipment, doubling its weight, attaching a hook and some navigation lights, painting it grey, then increasing the cost ten-fold - and announcing availability in the New Year (without specifying which one !)

Navy cake   Older *brownhatter's term for a sailor with homosexual tendencies; the modern version is *seafood*

Navy Days   Bank Holiday weekends specially selected in the major port areas when Jack and his ships and submarines are thrown open to the public. Various additional exhibitions and flying / marching / handling displays ensure value for money, with all proceeds going to local and national Naval charities

(The) **Navy List**   A crucial document, published annually as a matter of public record, in which the order of seniority and the qualifications of every Officer in the *Royal Navy* and *Royal Marines* are recorded. (*WRNS* and *QARNNS* Officers' details also appear) - see also the *List

Navy News   Excellent monthly colour newspaper of the *RN* which regularly wins prizes for both style and content. Widely (and also nationally) distributed, it is read by Admirals and *ABs alike. This periodical also features Tugg's regular cartoon strips about the life and times of **JACK** - some past gems have been reproduced in this book

neaters   Undiluted rum; this was only issued to *POs and *CPOs, and lasted longer than *grog. See also *Black Mass and *Up Spirits !

neck oil *(RM)*   Beer; something that you get down your neck for internal lubrication

negatory / negative   An answer confirming a negative state rather than the word *no*: "*Any wine left in the bottle ?*" "*Sorry, mate - that's a definite negatory..*"

Neil-Robertson   A form of restraining stretcher that is winchable up a ship's side, or into a helicopter

Nelson's blood   Rum

nerve gas   See *CSB

Neptune's sheep   Jack's older name for *white horses* at sea

nettles   The cords that make up a hammock's clews; a single, knotted length was used by each member of the crew to *lash-up a shipmate who had been sentenced to run the *gauntlet. In one sense therefore he was being stung by their criticism of his behaviour, which gives rise to at least one modern application of the word **nettled**. If the plant's name only came into usage in the last century then it is also possible that this label stemmed from old Jackspeak as well

Never cut towards your oppo !   Jack would say, as he did just that !

new wine in an old bottle   The process of upgrading an older warship by the installation of new weapon systems into her at a periodic refit

newted *(RM)*   Drunk; single word summary for someone who is as *pissed as a newt*. See also *handcarted, *legless and *shot away

nibblers   Personnel working in a shore establishment who arrive at work late and go home early, muttering about travelling time; this is a creeping habit that occasionally requires some spot checks at the main gate !

nice (quiet) **little number**   An easy shore job, or any employment requiring minimal effort to succeed; becomes a *quiet number* as well if there is no supervision into the bargain !

nicknames   Most of these standard and traditional pairings appear alphabetically in the text, but they are also listed here for completeness:
   Bagsy Baker; *Bandy* Evans; *Baz* (for anyone called *Barry*); *Bogey* Knight; *Bomber* Brown; *Brigham* Young; *Brum(my)*(anyone from Birmingham); *Buck* Taylor; *Bungy* Edwards (or Williams); *Bunny* Warren; *Buster* Brown; *Chalky* White; *Chats* Harris; *Chippy* Carpenter; *Chirpy* Finch; *Daisy* May; *Darby* Allen; *Dicky* Bird; *Dinger* Bell; *Dodger* Long; *Dolly* Gray; *Doughy* Baker; *Duke* Earle; *Dusty* Miller (or Rhodes); *Dutchy* Holland; *Edna* May; *Flash* Gordon; *Geordie* (anyone from Newcastle); *Ginge(r)* Jones; *Happy* Day; *Harry* Freeman; *Hooky* (or *Johnny*) Walker; *Jan* or *Janner* (anyone from the Westcountry); *Jesse* James; *Jimmy* Green (or James); *Jock* (any Scotsman); *Jumper* Collins (or Cross or Short); *Kitty* Wells; *Knocker* White / Whyte; *Nobby* Clark(e) or Hewitt / Hewett; *Nosey* Parker; *Nosmo* King; *Nutty* Edwards; *Oggie* (any Cornishman); *Paddy* (any Irishman);*Pansy* Potter; *Pedlar* Palmer; *Pincher* Martin; *Pony* Moore; *Pusser* Hill; *Rattler* Morgan; *Rusty* Steele; *Soapy* Watson; *Scouse(r)* (any Liverpudlian); *Shady* Lane; *Sharky* Ward; *Shiner* Light (or Wright); *Slinger* Woods; *Smoky* Cole; *Smudge(r)* Smith; *Snowy* White or Winter/bottom; *Spider* Webb; *Spike* Kelly; *Spud* Murphy; *Swampy* Marsh; *Sweeney* Todd; *Tab* Hunter; *Taff* (any Welshman); *Tank* Sherman; *Tansy* Lea or Lee; *Timber* Wood(s); *Tug* or *Tugg* Wilson; *Whacker* Payne; *Wiggy* Bennett; *Windy* Gale; *Yorky* (any Yorkshireman);
Note also the nicknames which are alliterative, as in:
   Andy Anderson; *Harry* Harrison; *Jacko* Jackson; *Johnnie* or *Johnno* Johnson; *Robby* Robinson and *Sully* Sullivan
as well as those which merely imitate, such as:
   Lester Piggott, *Scobie* Breasley; *Bobby* Charlton; *Ronnie* Biggs; *Ginger* Rogers; *Sherlock* Holmes; *Chopper* Harris; *Legs* Diamond; *Nick* Carter; *Aggie* Weston; *Danny* Kaye; *Connie* Francis; *Fezz* Parker; *Perry* Mason and even *Sandy* Shaw !
plus the labels that describe the complete opposite of a person's physical appearance such as *Tiny* for anyone enormous in the vertical plane, and *Slim* for the chap whose circumference needs reduction

Bootneck

nifty fifty   Slang term for masturbation

Nigerian lager   Guinness

night bar   *Wardroom facility of a small cupboard stocked with beer, spirits and mixers for those Mess members returning *on board after the main bar has closed, but desiring a *wet before *turning in

night fighter   Any coloured person

night of the Long Knives   The *Medical Services Officers'* annual dinner !

nine o'clockers   Traditional snack taken between the main evening meal and *turning in. Usually consists of a sandwich or bag of crisps, along with a *wet of tea or *kye

Nines   **Number nines** - extra work and *musters as a punishment

nine miler *(RM)*   One of the *Commando tests that must be passed in order to obtain a *green lid. This involves a squad *speed marching, in fighting order and with rifle, over a nine-mile road distance in under ninety minutes (eighty-one for Royal's Officers !)

nipper   A short length of rope used to bind an anchor cable to an endless *messenger cable* that ran from the capstan around a series of pulleys. As the thick anchor cable came up and inboard through the hawse holes, it was hove to the *messenger* with a secure (but quickly-releasable) **nipper.** The boy seaman responsible for this procedure (also called a **nipper**) then walked back with it towards the hatch leading down to the cable locker, cast off the light lashing at just the right moment, and then ran forwards again to repeat the process. There would always be half-a-dozen **nippers** in place as the anchor was being *weighed, and the boys had to be quick, dexterous and agile - hence the modern usage ashore

Nisum   Abbreviation for *Naval Intelligence Summary,* and used to describe essential background information on any matter affecting Naval men: *"I've just had a quick **Nisum** on those new rules for Lodging Allowance.."*

no can do !   Pidgin English form that is in frequent usage to decline some request

no Dopples *(FAA)*   *Pinger description of a flat calm sea which does not give a good return for the Doppler inputs of a *Sea King's flight control systems; this may be extended into social transactions: *"How did you get on with that bird you *trapped last night ?"* *"**No Dopples** sadly - complete *waste of rations.."*

No No !   Response of a motor launch carrying anyone for whom no specific reply exists when it is challenged by a ship, ie. no marks of respect need to be paid

No probs / No sweat (esp. *RM* / *FAA*)   Frequent response to a request for help, or in discussion of some task; either phrase indicates an instinctive willingness to overcome whatever difficulties lie ahead.   Even if used somewhat ill-advisedly, it is still a much better attitude to take than the one which leads to: *"Sorry - can't be done.."*

No treating rule   A *Wardroom custom whereby junior officers do not buy senior officers their drinks, thereby preventing a well-heeled junior from gaining advantage over his less wealthy contemporaries. To your superior you would say: *"May I *write for you, sir ?"* If the response is positive it will also be accompanied by a *Mess number: *"Yes - and thank you. A pint of *CSB on Number 6 please.."*

nod / noddy *(RM)*   Royal's equivalent of a *nozzer at *Lympstone. Said to be derived from the issue woollen cap comforter which the recruits wear so badly as to look like **Noddy's hat**

Nog / Noggie *(RM)*   A Norwegian, or anything belonging to that splendid country; see also *Skywegian

HRH The Prince of Wales took command of HMS Bronington on February 9th, 1976.

noggin   Small drink: *"Anyone like a **noggin** ? I'm *writing.."*

nonch (esp. *RM*)   Abbreviation of ***nonchalant*** and often used in a sense of admiration: *"Baz cut away from the main parachute, deployed his reserve canopy, and then landed almost in the circle - **dead nonch**, like it was all a *demo.."*

nooners
1. When the sun passes over the *yardarm at midday, time for the first alcoholic drink of the day
2. Can also be a euphemism for popping home at lunchtime in order to *give the ferret a run

north-easter   See entry for *Not entitled !*

nose bag   Reference to eating: *"I'm off to get my **nose bag** on.."*

not best pleased   Polite description of a senior officer's annoyance at some occurrence

Not entitled !   Official response to Jack when, in older times, he stepped up to the pay table and had so many *mulcts against his name that his pay account was not in credit. The initial letters of **NE** can also be found on the compass rose, hence the additional term of *northeaster: *"Cor - all I got was ruddy soap coupons - a regular bleedin' *north-easter.."*

not three bad   Frequent figure of speech used as an alternative to the expression *not too bad*

notice for steam   Specific feature of a warship's *sailing orders when alongside, which can then be used in other contexts: *"No-one seemed to know when the wretched bus was due to turn up, so we all stayed at pretty short **notice for steam**.."*

nozzer   New entry trainee seaman, said to be named after an instructor at HMS *GANGES* in Shotley around 1910 who was possessed of a particularly large nose. See *RALEIGH* also and note the *RM* equivalent of *Noddy

nub end   A *doofer (in its strictest definition sense) of a cigarette that was on the borderline of being worth saving

number   A personal number for identification and records; Officers were not supposed to have numbers, but in practice this statement has blurred with the computerized pay system operating from HMS *CENTURION*. Note also *nice little number as a pleasant job and the phrase *had his number* in a targetting sense, as seen in the example for *Jackie-boy. Note also the term *make your number, in the sense that a ship's **number** is the internationally-recognised signal group that identifies her precisely and uniquely

number crunching   Any paperwork or planning that involves staff tables - lists of men, equipment and vehicles: *"Trying to fit a *Commando Group and all its *kag into a North Sea ferry demands flexible **number crunching** of the very highest order.."* RN usage refers to any kind of data processing task using a computer

(his) **number got hoisted**   Older expression similar to *lost the number of his mess, but more appropriate to death in action

Number One
1. The First Lieutenant. Scc also *James the First / the *Jimmy
2. **Number Ones** refer to Jack's best blue uniform, with gold wire badges
3. There is also a **Number One punishment** on the scale (**Number One** via *Nine to **Number Fifteen**) authorised by the *Naval Discipline Act*, but fortunately this is little used since it refers to death by execution

Nummer Wun   The Senior Crown Agent in Hong Kong

nutter   An individual lacking in wisdom and judgement, the description further embellished by the adjectives *total* or *complete*. There are some charming additional phrases to be heard in this context:
- *The lights are on, but there's nobody home..*

- *He's not dealing with a full deck of cards..*

- *That chap's not got both oars in the water..*

- *She's two bricks short of a full load..*

- *They've appointed him as an OSLO - Outer Space Liaison Officer..*

nuts and bolts with an awning   Amusing but older description of a steak-and-kidney pie

nutty / Nutty
1. General term for all forms of chocolate and sweets. Someone excessively fond of either is a **nutty-*freak**
2. *Nutty* is an occasional nickname paired with the surname Edwards
3. Note that **nutty** in Australia refers to a (nut-) *brownhatter !

OSCAR

OAL　　　　Abbreviation for the *Officer's Appointment List*, a bi-weekly and numbered publication originating from the *Naval Secretary's Department* in Whitehall. It shows all the promotions and appointments (never *postings*) of *RN* Officers; an **OAL number** is usually essential for the advance of monies, tropical clothing etc.

obey the last pipe　　　　Traditional advice to the effect that if there appears to be conflict or confusion in orders that are being given, then the most recent order should be carried out

Observer *(FAA)*　　See **Looker*

OD　　　Abbreviation of *OrDinary*, the basic rate on entry for Jack being an *Ordinary Seaman*, one below the *Able Rate* or **AB*. It is the lowest rung on the promotion ladder, but also used in a wider context to describe someone of limited abilities, who is a bit slow to grasp an opportunity: *"Not 'im for Gawd's sake - the big OD.."*

odds and sods　　　General expression describing a group that is difficult to categorize exactly, eg. an **Odds and Sods Mess** in a ship that might contain *Doc, *Freshwater Tanky, the *Jack Dusty, and *Chippy

Off caps !　　　This order is only given usually at *Defaulters, but headgear can also be removed as a mark of respect at Divine Service, funerals, Services of Remembrance, or as a prelude to *cheering ship. In older times it usually led to a snowstorm of *doofers falling to the deck !

off watch　　　Not on duty; *RM* usage has **off-net** for a person who is not listening or who is just a bit *switched-off !

Office Boy   The Assistant Secretary in a Captain's Office (usually a junior *RN* or *WRNS* *Pusser)

Officer country   Jack's nickname for the *Wardroom *flat

Oggie   Traditional nickname for a Cornish pasty or anyone born and bred in Cornwall; there is also a suggestion that a Mr Edward Hogg was the name of the pie-seller who retailed these items outside the gates of Devonport Dockyard, hence also *_Tiddy Oggy_* as the nickname describing a matelot hailing from Plymouth

'Oggin / 'Ogwash   The sea; also spelt as *Hoggin / Hogwash

oh-crack-*sparrow   Common expression for very early in the morning

Old Grey Widow Maker   Also the sea: *"A sailor's grave is already dug.."*

(The) Old Man   Affectionate nickname for the Captain; see also the *Owner

Old Soaks   *Submarine Service* nickname for members of the *Submarine Old Comrades Association,* a thriving group of veterans who display a great thirst whenever and wherever they meet

old ships   Abbreviation for *old shipmate,* ie. someone you have served with before: *"'Ere, Charlie, come an' meet my *oppo Timber Woods - we're **old ships** from the *Ark in '79.."*

on board   To be physically present within the confines of a ship or shore establishment: *"*Father **on board** this evening ?" "No, he's gone *ashore with the *HODs.."* The radio call **On board** ! is also used by *FAA* aircraft on rejoining a formation or *Balbo

on the books   Held on the Ship's *muster book and therefore *victualled in for rations. The *Army* (and occasional *RM*) equivalent is *held on ration strength*

on the step *(SM)*   A nuclear *boat at speed, planing on its own bow wave. This *evolution produces more speed for less propulsive effort

on the trot   Absentee who has deserted; see also *recover and *runne

on your Jack (Jones)   Alone

one for the brow   A last drink for guests before they leave the *Wardroom, ie. the *RN* equivalent of *one for the road*; sometimes heard as **one for the plank**

one for the linebook *(FAA)*   That's worth recording !

one man band *(SM)*   Colloquial term for the one-man control system that operates a *boat's hydroplanes

one of my Lord Mayor's men   Old Navy term for a delinquent who had appeared before the Lord Mayor in his role as Chief Magistrate of the City of London, and then elected to enter naval service rather than go to prison. See also *swimmer, *Queen's hard bargain and the notes on *Impressment

one up the spout (esp. *RM*)   Live round moved up from a rifle's magazine into the firing chamber; the weapon is now cocked and ready to discharge as soon as the safety catch - and trigger - are released. This expression is also used by Jack to describe an impending state of motherhood

one yard rule   Informal regulation that can be enforced when the *Wardroom bar is busy and crowded, mostly by people who already have their drinks and are leaning against the rail. The latter are required to move away at least **one yard**, and let those with an unslaked thirst get in closer to be served

one-armed paper hanger   Nicely descriptive term for someone who is rather busy; a **one-armed paper hanger with crabs** is the next stage up !

one-eighty   Jack's equivalent of a U-turn, both figuratively and literally halfway around the compass: *"This guy then did a one-eighty right in the middle of the ruddy motorway.."* or: *"The Admiral's gone one-eighty on policy for using that new bit of *kit.."*

one-two-six   Form used to report *stores losses and then apportion blame, now used as a verb in its own right: *"Any items mislaid or not returned in full working order will be one-two-sixed against your pay account the next day.."*

once-only suit   An immersion suit that is not insulated, but only designed to prevent a survivor getting wet. It is made in one piece, with elastic wrist seals, and has no integral buoyancy

oozelum bird   Term used for any winged creature difficult to identify properly; in addition, see *spadger, *shitehawk and *arse-up duck for the sum total of Jack's concise guide to British ornithology ! Note that Shakespeare described an *ousle bird* in one of his plays (*MND*), and it can also be spelt as **oozlum** or **woozlum**. Its main identifying feature is an ability to fly in such ever-decreasing circles that it finally disappears up its own fundamental orifice

open up *(SM)*   The process of opening the hatch or *lid after surfacing; to **run opened up** usually means that the *conning tower lid is open whilst on surface passage. This is a dramatically different evolution to **open up for diving** (also *SM*) when all the submarine's ballast system valves are aligned in preparation for flooding the tanks and diving the *boat

oppo   An especial friend or chum in a ship or unit; the term is derived from **opposite number**, ie. the person who is on watch when you are off. The American equivalent is *buddy*, leading to the *buddy-buddy* system of mutual support

Ops normal *(FAA)*   Aircraft exercising or operating out of sight of their *Mother call up at regular intervals to report **Ops normal**. This can then be applied in the domestic sense when out on a *run-ashore: *"I just made an Ops normal call home - no problems.."*

Orange   An interesting trio:
1. Traditional colour of forces simulating the *Warsaw Pact* during exercises and opposing the *Blue forces of *NATO*
2. *(RM)* Adjective referring in Ulster to those of a Protestant persuasion
3. *(FAA)* *Lynx Observer; a **baby Orange** is a trainee. See also *JAFO and the *man from del Monte

(the) other half   Figure of speech which assumes that no-one ever has only one drink, and that saying: *"Would you like another one ?"* might be misinterpreted as offensive, in that there is the slight hint that the guest has had too many already. Using the usual Wardroom convention of: *"Will you have the other half ?"* directly implies that this will only be the second *wet, and thus drinks can go on being the **other half** all night - and no-one ever exceeds the limits !

out of his tree   Oblique expression doubting someone's sanity: *"If *SOBS thinks I'm volunteering for that job, then he's **out of his ruddy tree.."**

out of the range of the Service slide-rule   Older (pre-computer era) term for a problem that cannot be solved using offically-supplied data

out of station   Not in line within a formation; someone who is getting a bit, and **out of station** as well, is a married Officer involved in a spot of extramarital *bagging-off; Jack's equivalent refers to **out of watch**

Out piece and *hack ! (FAA)   *Wafu exhortation during an *Uckers game to get out and destroy the opposition, carried over into real life as a form of encouragement to tackle a task head on

Out pipes !   Curiously worded *pipe (that could easily be misinterpreted by Jack) which indicates that smoking must cease, the *stand easy is over, and it is time to get the ship's normal routine going again. The *US Navy* version of this is ***The smoking lamp is out !***

outside   Civilian life: *"Things were pretty tough **outside**. The streets weren't exactly paved with gold; in fact, most of the streets* *weren't even paved at all, and guess who was expected to get the bloody slabs down ?"*

outside wrecker　　　The *clanky responsible for all machinery and mechanical equipment on the upper deck; in a submarine, he is the chap who looks after everything mechanical apart from the propulsion machinery. The **inside wrecker** is a derogatory term for a chef !

over the wall　　　The state that pertains when either Jack or Royal have their pay stopped and enter *DQs: *"The Court Martial sentenced him to six months **over the wall** and he got *dismissed the Service as well.."*

overstretch　　　Management *wriggle stuff for the increasingly frequent state of affairs that pertains when Jack and Royal are given more and more global and local responsibilities to meet - with less and less financial and manpower resources to tackle the tasks. See also *No problem

overzone　　　An Officer who has just ceased being *in zone, and who has not been promoted is said to have **gone overzone.** In some instances of selection for transfer between *Lists rather than promotion, the *suck back of an **overzone** officer may occur

ovies　　　One-piece **overalls** of any kind; *(FAA)* **flying ovies** refer to a flame-proof flying suits also known as *green and baggies or *green and smellies

Owner　　　Pleasant nickname for the captain of a *private ship; under this convention the *Jimmy or Executive Officer in larger ships becomes the *Bloke

Dolphins

PAPA

P7R Lowered *PULHEEMS grading of someone temporarily unfit for sea or front-line duty, now used as a word in its own right: *"I'm **P7R** for the next three months with this ruddy broken arm.."*

paper Navy The administrative and clerical branches

parcel Hemp ropes had to be waterproofed, otherwise they would rot very easily and become useless in *standing rigging. The grooves in the lay of a rope were filled out by thin codline, then covered or **parcelled up** with layers of canvas strips, and the whole served with an outer coat of spunyarn applied under tension. This procedure is the origin of a modern **parcel** in the postal sense

Parish Magazine *Fleet Temporary Memoranda* (a rather serious circulating document)

paraffin pigeon Just one of Jack's nicknames for a helicopter; see also *furious palm tree, *kerosene budgie, *shuddering shithouse and *wokka-wokka

paralytic Incapably drunk; also heard as **parlatic**

Part Three (esp. *SM*) Label for an inexperienced and poorly-trained idiot, derived from the need (with current financial constraints) to provide on-the-job and qualifying experience at sea for *makee-learnees who have been drafted to a warship as part of her war complement. Part One trainees are those at *RALEIGH; note also that the *FAA* uses **to part three** something as an alternative to *snagging it

part brass rags Older term, still heard occasionally, to denote the sudden end of a close friendship; you shared your cleaning *rag bag with your close *oppo, or *raggie, up until this (literal) parting of the ways. The term can be used as a verb: *"After that little dust-up they parted brass rags.."*

part of ship   Expression used to denote an area of personal responsibility: *"Why's 'e stickin' 'is nose in ? Thass my part of ship.."*   The term **parts** refers to the male **private parts** or genitalia; whereas *Parts* (esp. *RM*) is the nickname for an individual who is well equipped with *wedding tackle

part of watch   A *Watch Bill specifies a man's place of duty, but also divides his *Watch into a First and Second **part**; at (relaxed) Cruising Stations in a non-operational area it may only be necessary for one **part of watch** to *turn to in order to meet the task

party   A female **party** who may later become one's *pash; also used for a working group as in *Buffer's party**

pash   Abbreviation for *passion* - the Number One girlfriend

pass muster   Acceptable; see *muster for other applications

Passover   To be *passed over* means that your seniority in a rank now exceeds the *zone considered by the Admiralty Board for promotion purposes; the day of your *last shot *in zone, if it is unsuccessful, becomes your personal Feast of the **Passover** !

pasting   Give or take damage to a warship in battle

paternity leave   Relatively new concept in the *Andrew; the old philosophy was based on: *"You was there when the keel was laid, Sunshine - that don't give you a ticket for the launching.."*

Pay no regard ! *(FAA)*   Classic Naval wartime version of the RAF's ***Press on Regardless***, and widely used in responding to almost any adversity - from loss of shipmates to a severe hangover. In this sense, the *Royal Marines* expression ****It's only pain !*** is identical

pay   A number of historic applications:
1. Cables or ropes are **payed out**, rather than *let out*
2. **paying-off pennant**   A long signal flag flown from the masthead at the completion of a warship's *commission, prior to her refit, sale or other disposal; it used to consist of cleaning rags tied together to show that they were now being dispensed with, and the length was in proportion to her total time spent in *commission
3. **paying off** is the process whereby a sailing ship's bows, having passed through the wind in the process of *tacking*, falls off to leeward before her sails begin to draw again
4. The seams of a wooden hull were **payed** with hot pitch (tar) after they had been caulked with *oakum; see also *loggerheads and the various entries associated with *Devil

Paybob   Jack's older term for a *Paymaster Branch* Officer, a specialization now absorbed into the many skills of the *Pusser

Pea-do
1. Nickname for pea soup
2. The *Naval Long Service and Good Conduct* medal - the origins of this usage are a little obscure, but may be a mispronounciation of the *billet-doux* grant of £25 cash (sadly now discontinued) which came with the *Blue Peter. See also *undetected crime

pear-shaped   Useful phrase employed in two distinctly different ways:
1. *"Play it **pear-shaped**.."* - be flexible, see how it goes, don't commit yourself too early on
2. *"It all went **pear-shaped**.."* - the scheme collapsed or went wrong; see *rats as an alternative

pebbledash the porcelain / walls   Suffer from profuse diarrhoea; see also *black drizzle, *scatters and *squitters

peep-stick *(SM)*   Periscope

Peggy   The *Pegasus* engine of the *Stringbag - and now also of the *Sea Harrier* (*SHAR); there is even a *Fleet Air Arm* song about the reliability of this splendid radial construction in comparison with that of its successor:

*The Stringbag relies on her **Peggy**,*
While the modified Taurus ain't sound -

So the Swordfish flies out on her missions,
And the Albacore stays on the ground..

(**Refrain**) *Bring back, bring back,*
Oh bring back my Stringbag to me..

peggy   Older word for a messenger - often a **peg-legged** old veteran

pendant number   The letter and side numbers of a warship, usually painted on the hull in big black letters and pronounced *pennant*

penguin *(FAA)*   Any non-flying *Wafu !

pension trap   Understandable reluctance to do anything remotely dangerous when approaching the end of one's career in the *mob, because an accident would save the Navy the bother of having to provide your duly-entitled pension: *"Wot, get me up in a bleedin' helicopter - with only three months left to do ? No thanks, mate - that's the biggest **pension trap** *Pusser ever invented.."* Can also be used to describe some feature of Service life that induces a person to stay in the *Andrew: *"Boarding School Allowance is a proper **pension trap**.."*

pepper-potting *(RM)*   Military *evolution for advancing tactically - the members of a rifle section move forwards under control, but in apparently random motion - as if they were being scattered from a **pepper pot** !

Per Ardua Ad Astra   *Crabfat's motto which, strictly translated, means *Through Hardship to the Stars*. Jack's version is based on the observation that most *RAF* station cinemas are named **Astras**, hence: *"After work we all go to the movies !"* Or else: *"Queue here for the upper stalls !"*

Per Mare Per Terram *(RM)*   *Corps motto of *By Land and By Sea* - but note also a *few laughs and a few beers

Perce *(RM)*   Shortened form of the generic nickname ***Percy Pongo***, used by Royal to describe anyone from the *Army* in exactly the same manner that *Jack* and *Jolly Jack* refer to members of the *Royal Navy*. See notes on *Pongo as well

perch   A seat: *"Grab a **perch**.."* Or, a position in an argument or discussion: *"This will knock him right off that ridiculous **perch**.."*

Perisher *(SM)*   Nickname for the Submarine *CO's Qualifying Course*, because if you fail this demanding test, your career in the *Submarine Service* is over - ie. *Pass or **perish** !* See also *Teacher

personal admin *(RM)*   Military-sounding euphemism for time spent attending to your own problems during the working day

Pongo

perving   Contraction of the word *perversion*, but usually employed in a gentler sense, eg. as an alternative for *glimping

Peter's Pool *(RM)*   Partially-damned stream encountered on the *Endurance course at *Lympstone which must be forded chest-high while keeping one's rifle clean and dry

Petty Officer   *RN* equivalent of a *Sergeant*, or *Senior Non Commissioned Officer.* The word **Petty** comes from the French *petit*, or *small*; hence, see also *smalley pigs

phoo-phoo dust   Talcum powder; see also *foo-foo

Phot / Phots   Standard abbreviations for the *Photographic Branch* and its members

Pi - R - squared the bastard then !   *"Work it out for yourself !"*

pick   The main anchor, hence to **drop the pick** for the process of anchoring, and **swinging round the pick** when actually at anchor in a harbour; see also *hook and *killick

pick up   The process of official advancement, already described in the passive sense of getting *made up. The same process might be described, with an identical meaning, as: *"My *B13's in and I see the *Old Man tomorrow to **pick up** my *hook.."*

pickle-jar officer   Jack's delicate and highly observant description of an individual with great intelligence but poor practical ability: *"Your* average *university graduate these days is the sort of bloke who can tell you the square root of a **pickle-jar** (or *jampot) lid to three decimal places - but then can't get the bloody thing off.."*

picturised *(RM)*   Put in the picture, usually as the result of some misdemeanour or failing: *"That useless *gob-shite Terry needs **picturising** - in a big way.."*

pied   A newer word that implies a custard pie in the face, or rejection in a dramatic or unexpected manner: *"She went and **pied** him after a year of living together.."*

pierhead jump   Draft or appointment that has to be taken up at very short notice; derived from the need to take a **running jump** from the end of the **pier** because your new ship has actually begun to *slip and proceed

Pier Cellars   An old torpedo testing station that opens onto Plymouth Sound; expedition weekends are held here by the *nozzers from HMS *RALEIGH*

-pig   A suffix to indicate something troublesome: *"It wasn't my fault that the lights didn't work - it was the ruddy switch-pigs.."* This usually indicates that the operator has had a *brainfart when making the selection

Pig / Piggery   An Officer, and the Wardroom or Officer's Mess *(RM)*. These terms are only used by disgruntled sailors or marines who are no longer in harmony with Jack and Royal's way of life

pigeon   Two different applications:
   1. Responsibility: *"That particular problem is very much your pigeon.."*   See also *part of ship
   2. *(FAA)* **Homing pigeon** derivation, where **pigeons** are given as the course in degrees magnetic to be tracked for home or *Mother in the event of a malfunction or emergency: *"Pigeons for *Culdrose are 270 at thirty-seven miles.."*

pig's ear   Upper deck urinal on a warship for Jack's use when he is unable to leave his place of duty while *on watch. Also used to describe some hopeless cock-up: *"He made a real pig's ear of the whole thing.."*

pig's orphan   Another description of some thoroughly unpleasant person (or task)

Pill   Jack's nickname for certain individuals who are small, white, round - and totally devoid of any conception

Pilot   Traditional nickname for the *Navigating Officer* of a warship, and see also *Vasco

ping   Discover something, or find out. The derivation of the word is the same as for *Pinger, but its daily use rather different, as in: *"It took us some time to **ping** him, but eventually we proved that he was fiddling the books.."* Or: *"During the honeymoon, she suddenly **pinged** the fact that her new husband was a miserable toad.."*

Pinger *(FAA)*   Anti-submarine warfare helicopter specialist, derived from the *pinging* sound made by the *Sea King's active (dipping) sonar. Note also the hybrid word *Pinglie, and a **Pinger's moon** when the skies are clear, the moon full, and the horizon nicely visible

Pinglie *(FAA)*   A *Pinger who flies ashore into what is normally regarded as *Junglie territory, and then has to map-read; see also the *most dangerous thing in the world

Pink / pink   An interesting colour in the RN !
1. **Pink** *DCI - Confidential Defence Council Instructions dealing with sensitive disciplinary matters
2. **Pink List** - projected programme of ship movements issued by Fleet Headquarters at Northwood
3. **pink chit** - formal warning issued to Jack whenever he came over the *brow in drink and the worse for wear; a second such episode meant a green chit and then *get your hat for a talk with the *Bloke. The expression is now used to denote a wife or girlfriend's prior knowledge of a night out with the boys: *"Coming on the section *run-ashore ? I've got a **pink chit** from the *dragon.."*
4. **pink gin** - Plymouth gin and Angostura bitters, drunk neat or diluted with plain water, and known also as *pinkers*
5. **pink lint** - spam, or any form of luncheon meat
6. **pink sheet** - whenever a problem is set for students at Staff College, the Directing Staff have all the relevant answers and discussion points already set out for them on pink paper. Hence the expression in real life : *"There's no **pink sheet** (solution) for this one, I'm afraid.."*

Pinky / pinky   A quartet of widely different applications:
1. *(FAA)* An artificer specializing in radar and radio equipment; its origin lies in the layout of the old *RN* Aircraft Servicing Form which used to contain pink-coloured log sheets for the radio and radar gear. The current *MoD Form 700 has no such distinction, but the label for this skilled and sea-going profession lives on. Note also the remarks made in *greenie
2. *(RM)* Nickname for the surnames White and Panther !
3. Occasional nickname for the anus - as in *fluff your **pinky**,

meaning to break wind (see Tugg's cartoon on page **P** - 217)
4. The little finger

pipe   Whistle call made to indicate various phases of a
ship's daily life such as **pipe down** at the end of the day, or to time
special *evolutions such as the saluting of visitors on arrival or
departure when ***piping the side**. Nowadays the shrill notes of the
***Bos'un's pipe** have been replaced to a large extent by the gruff voice
tones of the *Tannoy, but if an Officer is wanted urgently somewhere in
the ship, then a **pipe is made** for him

piping hot   Shoreside expression with a Naval origin; if food was
collected from the *galley as soon as the appropriate *pipe was made,
then it could be served on the *messdecks **piping hot**

piping the side   Ceremonial process of saluting important visitors
to a warship (such as foreign naval officers and distinguished
civilians) at their arrival or departure; the long rising and falling
notes were originally used to indicate the need to hoist or lower that
personage in a bosun's chair slung from a yardarm

Pirate (FAA)   *Looker's nickname for his Pilot

piso   A miserable individual who is tight with money;
derived from the unusual feature of Indian currency that one rupee
consists of sixteen annas - and each of these in turn is made up of
four **pais** or **pice** !

piss   Another word with many other meanings besides the obvious one:
1. **piece of piss** (esp. *RM*) - something easy, or no problem
   to achieve; hence also: *"You'll piss it.."*
2. **streak of piss** - tall, gangling and thin person
3. **on the piss** or **pissing up** - drinking session, sometimes
   abbreviated as a PU. Note also the term **piss-artist** as an
   alternative for *glop-head, the former defined as someone who
   can sign his name in the snow in this way
4. **take the piss** - tease or mock somebody in a bout of **piss-taking**.
   See also *extract the Michael
5. **pissed-off** - a similar meaning to *chokka
6. **piss flap** - feature of Jack's uniform trousers prior to the
   redesign of the trouser fly to allow the incorporation of a zip;
   this flap had to be unbuttoned prior to *pumping ship, and is
   still utilised in the special uniform issued to *Yachties
7. **piss flaps** - Jack's nickname for the labial lips so often
   displayed these days in the raunchier men's magazines, and which
   he may describe as being the size of *a *Buccaneer's air brakes*,
   or *John Wayne's saddlebags..*
8. **piss poor** is a traditional description of something very poor
   indeed, probably derived from (8)
9. **gnat's piss** - equally traditional label applied to weak beer or
   poorly-brewed tea

Fluff your pinky

P-217

pisser pilot   Older *FAA* and *RAF* term for an *Army Air Corps* pilot, or any Officer sporting *Army* wings; needless to say, this implied inferiority puts all the *Teeny-weenies into an immediate *high hover !

pit   Bed or bunk space; occupied around the clock by a **pit rat**: *"Sorry I'm late, sir - my duvet wouldn't let me go.."*

pitch up   Arrive; *pole up is a frequent alternative

placcy-bagging *(RM)*   The sport of sliding down a snow-covered slope while sitting or lying on a *plastic bag*

Plan B   Any alternative when things go to *rats, even when contingency plans do not actually exist: *"Aircraft cancelled ? That's *no problem. We'll just switch to **Plan B**.."*

plank   Amusing quartet of varied usages:
1. A dull individual: *"Socially, he's a complete **plank**.."*
2. *(FAA)* Helicopter aircrew's description of a normal aircraft wing, and thus **Planky** as a nickname for the pilot of any such aircraft
3. *Pusser's **planks** - wooden or fibreglass Norwegian military skis
4. Alternative word for the *brow; **plankers** *(SM)* is a declared last drink before leaving, ie. the *Boat people's equivalent of *one for the **plank***

planter's   Hot weather *rig of slacks, long-sleeved shirt, tie and chukka boots

planting *(FAA)*   Burial: *"They're **planting** him on Friday - it's a *swords and medals job, of course.."*

plastic *(RM)*   Sardonic appellation for an officer temporarily elevated to *Acting rank, ie. dressed for that rank, but not *substantively promoted to it; if the poor chap is *Local Acting* in addition, then he's not paid at the higher level either

plastic policeman   See *Modplod

play the white man   Do the decent and fair thing even when a more attractive but less honest option presents itself

player   Label for someone who is good company socially: *"You know, old *Scratch is a bit of a **player** on the quiet.."*

playpen   Another of Jack's nicknames for the vagina; you'll have to find the others for yourself !

plucky *(FAA)*   Gentle understatement for a highly demanding or dangerous job: *"Low-level troop insertions at night, high in the Lyngen Alps ? Yersst - **plucky** little number, that.."*

Plug   Label for anyone with projecting ears and/or protruding teeth; the nickname has been borrowed from a character in the *BEANO* comic's *Bash Street Kids*

pluke / plook   Any skin infection, but especially when localised into a facial boil or *zit

plumber
  1. Mechanical Engineering Officer in a warship
  2. Gynaecologist

plums   The figure 0, or a line of zeros: *"Howja get on with them birds, Taff?"* *"**Plums**, mate, nothing but bleedin' **plums**.."* Someone like this who never seems to have much luck with the opposite sex while *trapping then becomes a **plums rating**, in contrast to a *stacks rating who always seems to be *getting yards

plusher's / plusser's   Residual rum remaining in the barrel after the *tot had been distributed; usually an important perk for *Tanky

Poet's Day   Jack's alternative name for Friday: *"Piss off early - tomorrow's Saturday.."*

polar bear's arseholes   Jack's nickname for those paper reinforcing rings that come on a peel-off strip

pole up   Turn up, or arrive; see also *pitch up - the words are interchangable

poling *(FAA)*   The actual physical skills of handling an aircraft: *"You know, that boy's brilliant on poling but absolute rubbish at captaincy.."*

Polto (SM)   Nickname for the old rate of *Petty Officer (Electrical) Torpedoes*

Pom   *Father Famine's favourite - powdered mashed potato

Pompey   Portsmouth; there are a number of explanations for the origins of this term, and the least likely appears to be Jack's observation, while walking his family / wife / lady on Southsea Common, of the 18th century volunteer firemen (*pompiers*) exercising there. I very much like the suggestion that *Portsmouth Point* was the traditional landing and embarkation point for *libertymen; try slurring this geographical name as if *handcarted and listen to the sound ! In some parts of Yorkshire, a **pompey** is a prison or house of correction, so it may just have somehing also to do with the *Portsmouth Naval Prison*. The true answer seems to involve the captured French prize vessel HMS *POMPEE* which was moored in *Portsmouth Harbour* along with the *FOUDROYANT*, and used as an accomodation and *receiving ship before the present Barracks were built. Either way, the *Portsmouth Maritime Heritage*, with HMS *VICTORY* and the *Royal Naval Museum*, the MARY ROSE, HMS *WARRIOR*, the *Royal Marines Museum* and the *OVERLORD Tapestry* are all splendid and important features of the city

Pom-pom   Wartime anti-aircraft Bofors gun, mounted eight together in a *bandstand to form a *Chicago piano*; very noisy - but also rather ineffective

Pond   The Atlantic Ocean; **across the Pond** refers to the United States of America

pond life   Clearance diver's nickname for *scoobies and *bubbleheads

Pongo   Any member of the British Army - more completely known as **Percy Pongo** or (also) as *Perce. A **pongo** is a hairy African sand-ape native to the deserts south of the Med; Royal will have you believe (incorrectly) that the word is derived from *Perce's occasional failure to wash on a daily basis, so where the Army goes, the **pong goes** as well

pooh trap   Some common pitfall or easily-made mistake that one should be aware of, as in the *heffalump trap* of AA Milne's *Winnie The Pooh*

Father Famine

poodle-faking   Older term for service in a warship on a cruise designed almost entirely for some VIP's entertainment; still heard on those occasions when commerce rears its unstrategic head. The term is derived from the underlying (and rather base) desires of military men, when cultivating the society of ladies, to emulate their lap-dogs by **poodle-faking** !

pooped   Seamanship term for the dangerous event of a big sea breaking over the stern (**poop deck**) of a ship. Now also used as a word to describe great tiredness, but see also *chin-strapped and *flakers

(as) **poor as piss**   Jack's standard description for low-quality beer in a pub ashore: *"The ale in there is as **poor as piss** - and twice as nasty.."*

pop   Euphemism for the booze; a heavy drinker might be described as *being on the **pop** again* or else as *having trouble with the old **pop***

population paste   One of Jack's euphemisms for seminal fluid; see also *baby gravy and *duff(3)

Pork / Porky   The word ***pork*** is a useful basis for a number of other terms which imply gluttony, such as: *"I really **porked out** on Sunday lunch - it was excellent.."* or: *"You **porker**.."* as an insult. Someone who is looking **a little porky** is putting on weight, but just to confuse any reader who is not a native, the term **porky pies** is rhyming slang for lies !

porridge guns   Bagpipes; see also *agony bags

porthole gazer   Yet another term for a homosexual

Portland   Busy Dorset Naval base, dockyard, Admiralty research establishment, air station and sea training facility. Warships of the *RN* and many friendly navies *work-up here to a state of operational readiness. One highlight of this period is the *Thursday War

positive perhaps *(esp. RM)*   Inability to make a decision: *"I'll give you a **positive perhaps** on that one.."* See also *definite maybe

Postie   Nickname for the Ship's Postman, in past times always a *RM Corporal*

Postman's Walk *(RM)*   An interesting aerial ropeway that comprises part of the *Tarzan course at *Lympstone

pot   Diving compression chamber; a training dive will be entered into a diver's log book as a **pot dip** after the **pot run** is completed

pot mess   Any stew to which ingredients are being added constantly, but which also remains hot and ready (eg. for survivors) at all times; also used to describe any real muddle or foul-up

pouch *(RM)*   Belt-order item of a Marine's personal equipment which, for some unfathomable reason, is always pronounced as if it was spelt **pooch** !

poultice-walloper   Member of the *Royal Naval Medical Branch* - see also *scab-lifter

Pound for pound, I'd rather have the fuel.. *(FAA)*   Another put-down for the poor old *Observers, who seem to have fewer barbs to direct at their *Pirates in retaliation for this suggestion that the absence of the *Observer would mean a welcome increase in fuel load

pox doctor's clerk   The figurative lowest of the low in the Medical Branch: *"How do they expect me to run a Follow-up Clinic with the help of just two *sprog *scab lifters and a **pox doctor's clerk** ?"* In older times there was an expression referring to someone as having the **luck of a pox doctor's clerk** since he had immmediate access to all the cures for venereal disease

praise in public, rebuke in private   Eminently sensible piece of Naval man-management advice

pregnant Officers who are nearing the end of their time *In zone, and still hoping for promotion

premature Round or shell which detonates **prematurely** on leaving the barrel of a gun or mortar, with devastating effect on those nearby

presento A small gift given in return for hospitality

pressed See the *Andrew and the more general expression: *"One volunteer is always worth a dozen **pressed men**.."*

pressure-head *Skimmer's nickname for a submariner; note also *boat people *(FAA)*

previous Alternative word for early: *"We're due to run in on top at zero nine *dubs exactly, but no harm in being upwind and out of sight behind that hill some five minutes **previous**.."* Or (esp. *RM*): *"Them's that's keen gets fell in **previous**.."* meaning that you will always do well for yourself in life by arriving early

prick The vulgar slang for a penis may have a Naval origin, because one treatment of Jack's older issue of a pound-weight ***prick of tobacco*** involved stripping out the leaf stems, soaking the remains in a little rum, then rolling them all up into a cylinder which was kept tight with an outer sewn layer of canvas. The anatomical similarity is obvious

(all) **prick and padded shoulders** Jack's dismissive phrase for a *canteen cowboy, or some other social boaster without justification for his many claims

primo The male equivalent of a *prima donna*, a fussy and demanding individual who is quite good at his job on the few occasions that everything is right for him. Between the wars this word referred to any enormous person such as **Primo Carnera**, the Italian heavyweight boxer - who was eventually stretched out by Joe Louis

Procedure Alpha Ceremonial lining of a warship's side and upperworks with men for entering or leaving harbour; see also *holidays

proctoheliosis The prefix **procto-** concerns the lower bowel, while **helios** refers to the sun; someone afflicted with this condition (or, identically, *helioproctosis) is vain enough to believe that the sun shines from his or her backside

Professor Fog *(FAA)* Weather forecaster, or *Met man

proff Steal or *acquire an item

pronger See *third pronger *(FAA)* for explanation

proviso   The name of a rope - or warp - carried ashore by a vessel that has moored stern on, with a single anchor out in the stream of water; the name has also come ashore in a semi-legal sense

PU   Acronym for *piss-up, ie. a drinking session

puck   A cringle of rope used for the violent sport of deck hockey

pucker factor   Fear as a motivating force !

pud *(RM)*   Royal's term for any officer involved in Logistic supply or administration; the Senior *Loggie in any formation then becomes its **Chief Pud** !

puddle jumper *(FAA)*   Any civilian light aeroplane

puff jets *(FAA)*   *Chopper puke insult directed at the *SHAR as well as at its pilots

PULHHEEMS   Medical assessment acronym which grades from 1 to 7 the individual qualities associated with Physique, Upper limbs, Lower limbs, Hearing (R + L), Eyes (R + L), Mental capacity and Stability. These are usually a string of 1's and 2's, leading to the statement: *"The marks on his *S.206 looked a bit like a **PULHHEEMS** grading.."* (ie. not very good !)   See also *P7R

pull   Jack's equivalent of rowing, only the oars are not feathered with each stroke, but merely **pulled** through the water as hard as possible in a **pulling race**

pull pole *(RM)*   The action of dismantling a *bivvy or tentsheet shelter under Arctic conditions, only undertaken when everyone is packed and in all other respects ready to move. The expression can now be heard in use for any group activity where exact timing is crucial

pull-through *(RM)*   Device for cleaning a rifle's barrel

pulpit   Guard-rail around a raised platform

pulpit poofter   Homosexual vicar; see also *raving rev and *dodgy deacon

pump up   Another euphemism for sexual intercourse

pumping poo *(SM)*   The modern process of discharging raw sewage, as opposed to *blowing shit

pumping (the) **ship**   Polite euphemism for urination; see also *ease springs and *check the ship for leaks

punched, bored or countersunk   Mentally confused: *"By the fourth round he didn't know whether he'd been **punched, bored or countersunk**.."*   See also *Arthur, Martha or Mabel

punchy   Interesting adjective that can be used to indicate a tough, aggressive military person: *"He's one of those typically **punchy** little Paras.."*   or, when referring to a letter or position paper, it describes written text in which a logical series of hard-hitting points are developed very well

punkah-louvre   A *cabin or *compartment fitting attached to the ventilation *fan trunking and adjustable for both angle and flow

push out   Alternative for *dist, as in: *"**Push out** this memo will you, please..*

pusher   Jack's older term for his girl-friend, or the person that he **pushed** around the dance floor

Pusser   An all-purpose word to do with the Navy that is one of the most interesting used in Jackspeak. The paymaster and supplies officer of the old Navy was the **purser** (an appointment still made in the Merchant Navy) which then became slurred in daily usage to **pusser**. This word was noun, verb or adjective depending on the shade of meaning required. *The* **Pusser** is still a ship or establishment's *Supply Officer,* whereas *a* **Pusser** is any Officer of the *Supply and Secretariat* specialization. Anything of official origin was (and still is !) a **pusser's item,** or **pusser's issue,** and in the sense that **Pusser** refers to the whole Royal Navy as an organization, the word crops up in a large number of amusing daily descriptions:

pusser's camel - a *Wren
pusser's crabfat - thick warship-grey paint
pusser's daps - white plimsoll shoes
pusser's dip - candle
pusser's dirk - seaman's clasp knife
pusser's duck - Walrus aircraft (*Shagbat) or a seagull
pusser's dust - cheap instant coffee
pusser's fix-all - WD-40 fluid
pusser's grey - warship colour
pusser's grip - brown canvas holdall
pusser's hard - coarse cleaning soap
pusser's item - anything bought in *Slops
pusser's leaf - rolled tobacco
pusser's logic - any false economy
pusser's loaf - biscuit
pusser's medal - food stain on clothing
pusser's phoo-phoo - tropical foot powder
pusser's planks - military cross-country skis
pusser's red - red-painted Naval bicycle
pusser's (rum) - proper Naval rum such as *Pusser's Rum*
     (and not just a brand name that contains the
       words *Navy* or *Naval*)
pusser's shift - see *split rig
pusser's shirt - any badly-tailored garment fits like this
pusser's tally - fictitious name given in a hotel or *Aggies
pusser's wagon - battleship

A **really pusser Officer** should also be noted as a singular use of the word to describe someone who is absolutely formal and correct in both deportment and dress. The distinctions made with regard to rum may seem a little pedantic, but they are important. When speaking of proper Naval rum, Jack will refer to **a drop** of **pusser's,** without necessarily referring to the trade-marked commercial product (with a capital *P*) - although this latter liquid is exactly the same in its formulation. Stocks of Admiralty-issue **pusser's** are still held, in stone-and-wickerwork jars, for ceremonial occasions such as *splice the mainbrace. Finally, in addition to the famous *Sharks, note also the unique *FAA* application of its other helicopter display team, *The Pusser's Pair*, a Gazelle duo that is sponsored up and down the UK during the summer season by Messrs. *Pusser's Rum* !

Put me down for some of that !   *"I fancy her !"*

putting the Queen to bed   Nickname for evening *Colours and/or
the *Sunset ceremonial

putty Sticky or muddy shallows - as opposed to rocks; placing a warship **on** or **in the putty** is still an embarassing *graunch in that the vessel goes aground

PVR *Premature Voluntary Release*

QUEBEC

QRs / QRRN   *Queens' Regulations* (for the *Royal Navy*); these used to be called *KR's and AI's* (*Admiralty Instructions*)

QT   **On the QT** means *on the quiet*, or *unofficial*: *"On the QT, old chum - could you slip me a *towpath copy of the minutes of that meeting ?"*

Quack   Medical officer - as distinct from the *Doc who is traditionally the ship's *Medical Assistant* !   *Avquack is a *FAA* variant, but see also *chippy, *gasman, *plumber, *Dick Doc, *fanny mechanic and *quim quack

Quarterbill   A *Watchbill showing the place of duty in action - or *Action Station - of every man borne in the ship. In older times the ship's drummer would **beat to Quarters** when action was imminent, using the rhythms of *Hearts of Oak. Nowadays the *pipe *Action Stations !* accompanied by an urgent klaxon or bell sound is used for this purpose, although the *US Navy* still sounds *General Quarters*

quarterdeck   The spiritual heart of a warship, and where a religious shrine was positioned in the sailing vessels of yesteryear. The custom of removing one's cap, or *saluting the quarterdeck* in passing, is a tradition that is maintained to this day by all *RN* and *RM* personnel crossing the *brow to enter or leave one of *Her Majesty's Ships*

quartermaster / QM   The senior helmsman - or **Master** of whichever course that a vessel is sailing on, the latter dictated by the wind's direction or *quarter*. The wheel or steering mechanism was also located on the **quarterdeck**. When a warship is alongside, the **QM** runs the *brow and is responsible for the *station card routines, *piping the side, and all other relevant ceremonial. A *Royal Marine* employed in this role is called the duty *Ship's Corporal; this is because Royal thinks of a **Quartermaster** as the officer responsible for all *Unit stores and transport, an appointment similar in function to that of the *Pusser

quarterly report   Special three-monthly reports *rendered on an Officer who is not apparently performing to the required standard

Queen Mary *(FAA)*   Large articulated lorry and trailer used to move an aircraft by road

Queen to bed   See *put the Queen to bed

Queen's   Any residue of rum left in the *fanny after everyone in the *messdeck had drawn his *tot, similar to *plusher's and *plusser's in this respect. This was usually the *rum bosun's perks, even though his judicious use of a large thumb had caused short measure to be given. When referring to *neaters, any **Queen's** was on occasion (illegally) stored in a *ready-use bottle, supposedly for visitors and guests to the Chief and Petty Officer's Messes, but very occasionally for a *Black Mass

Queen's (from King's) **hard bargain**   Jack's (much older) description of a fellow sailor who has elected to join the Navy rather than go into prison. Now used for a sailor who serves his time to pension without doing anything really very spectacular or useful during his twenty-two years - and then goes on to draw his pension for twice that length of time

queen bee A *Flag Officer's wife, or the Commandant of the *WRNS; - or the senior *WRNS officer of a shore establishment. The term was also used for a pre-WW2 radio-controlled aircraft

quick burn   Rapidly (and silently) smoked cigarette

quick coat of paint   Lovely euphemism for a rapid *legover

quickfix (esp. *FAA*)   An urgent solution that, in the long run, may not be the best one

quiet number   Another version of *cushy number, but especially so when there is little or no supervision involved

quim quack   Alternative for *fanny mechanic or gynaecologist

ROMEO

RA Abbreviation of *Rationed Ashore*, ie. an Officer or rating who is feeding ashore and not living *on board; see *bean stealer in this context. Note also the term **RA's clock** to describe a timepiece that is running slow - in order to allow late arrival at the place of work. The *RM* equivalent of someone **RA** is an *outlier

rabbit(s) Frequent descriptive term for a gift - or something that has been *proffed. The word originates from Chatham Dockyard, where a small island inside the harbour area was overrun with rabbits. These were often taken home as a welcome (and free) source of fresh meat. A **rabbit run** describes an excursion ashore in order to buy presents. To say that something has *got ears on it means that the article being described is a **rabbit**, or is something that has been **rabbited** or *proffed. **Rabbitwork** is material made in a workshop on a semi-official basis

racing snake A person who is extremely thin: *"During the *yomp across East Falkland, both the *Cherryberries and the *Booties found that their **racing snakes** and marathon runners were unable to hack the distance under load.."*

rack out Go to sleep; see also *hit the pit and *turn in. The *SM* world also describe the interesting phenomena of **rack reversal** - to be half-asleep on watch, yet half-awake in one's bunk. Also note **rack rejection** - being satiated with sleep and unable to lie down any longer

racking and tracking *(FAA)* Fighter-pilot terminology for the process of turning hard under *G* acceleration forces (**racking**) while trying to get a gun or missile-firing solution on the target (**tracking**)

radhaz   Abbreviation for *radio-frequency emission hazard,* painted as a warning sign near radar aerials and at microwave transmitter sites

(The) Rag   The *Army and Navy Club* in Pall Mall, London

rag-bag   Untidy and messy individual: *"You look like a *teased-out **rag-bag**.."*   See also *scran-bag as an alternative insult

rag-head   An Arab

rags / raggie   Older term for *oppo in the sense that the person you shared your brasswork *cleaning rags* with tended to be a particular chum. hence the expression *parting **brass rags*** used to describe the sudden break-up of such a friendship

RALEIGH   HMS *RALEIGH* is the shore establishment near *Torpoint, Cornwall, where all basic new-entry training in the *Royal Navy* is carried out. The *nozzers spend six weeks here before moving on to their Part Two courses; also the home of *Supply and Secretariat* as well as WRNS training. See *DAUNTLESS* in addition and *Royal Navy School of Dancing

Ram it ! Jack's way of saying: ***Get stuffed** !*   The phrase is used to perfection in the *RDP song

rampstrike *(FAA)*   Older *stovie term for a misjudged carrier approach in which the landing aircraft's wheels hit the curved lip of the flight deck's edge. The violent deceleration was disconcerting, and the impact occasionally severe enough to destroy the undercarriage

ranged *(FAA)*   The process whereby an aircraft is brought up from (or out of) a hangar and made ready for *launching; the opposite procedure (following *recovery) is *striking down

RAS / razz   Abbreviation for *Replenishment At Sea*, but the terminal *S* is usually pronouced as a *Z.* Can also be used as an alternative for *proff as in: *"Where did he get those bindings from ?"* *"Dunno, sir - reckon 'e must have **razzed** 'em from the *Noggies.."*

Steaming bats

rat-arsed (esp. *RM*)　　Also heard as **ratted**, or **ratters**, but in all cases meaning drunk

rate　　Naval equivalent of rank, gained on being rated by the Commanding Officer: *"I got rated up to *killick during my time in BOXER.."*

ratpack *(RM)*　　Compaction of the words **ration pack** to describe either tinned rations (*compo), or the dehydrated and foil-packeted **Arctic rats**

rats / ratshit (esp. *RM*)　　Term used to describe the collapse or failure of some scheme: *"Then it *clamped and began to rain, so the plan went to rats.."*

rattle　　To be **in the rattle** is to be in big trouble, ie. receiving professional attention from the *Reggies

raving Rev　　A homosexual cleric; see also *pulpit poofter and *dodgy deacon

RDP　　*Run Down Period,* usually prior to a ship's paying off, but also used for an Officer or sailor who is about to leave a job (or the Navy) and hence is not interested in what's going on. Cleverly used by the singer *Shep Woolley* in his song - **Ram it - I'm RDP !*

ready-use　　A small stock of something held near to its point of use, eg. an ammunition **ready-use** locker near a gun, with the rest of the ammunition down in the Magazine

rear party *(RM)*　　Those left behind to maintain security or keep things ticking over during a *Unit's deployment or seasonal leave. The *RN* equivalent refers to *retard leave

reasons in writing　　Moderately serious lapse in behaviour, following which a hand-written and formal letter of explanation is required. The phrase has now become an adjective in its own right: *"When the boys got the Commander's Mini up the steps and into the *Wardroom foyer, it was - as you can imagine - a reasons in writing job all round.."*

rec space　　A compartment or *flat *rigged for recreational purposes

receiving ship　　An old and decaying hulk permanently moored in a harbour as temporary accomodation for newly-entered or *impressed men before they were sent off to sea

receiving swollen property　　Sexual intercourse; the phrase may be used in conjunction with *assault with a friendly weapon

Recommend (esp. *RM*)　　Semi-formal expression of praise: *"I think he deserves a Recommend for that.."* or: *"You all did well, so take an*

R - 234

official **Recommend** *!"* Note also the subtle put-down implied in: *"A miserable old boot ?   Saying **that** about her would be a **recommend**.."*

recovery   The process of landing an aircraft back onto a carrier or the runways of a *Naval Air Station*; a *runner or deserter is also **recovered** when back in custody

Red Dragon *(FAA)*   *Captain The Prince of Wales KG KT Royal Navy,* a fully qualified and operationally-experienced *Junglie

Red Duster   The Merchant Navy ensign

Red Endorsement *(FAA)*   This older system of official comment in a pilot's logbook following the perpetration of some serious error does not seem to be practised nowadays in the *FAA*, but the *Green Endorsement certainly is. A **red ink** entry in an aircraft's log book refers to an acceptable problem which will be dealt with as soon as practicable

red ink
1. Colour traditionally used by the Captain when writing on minutes or memoranda; see *spilled blood as well
2. The underlining of any adverse comments written in a man's Divisional documents, done to signify that his attention has been officially drawn to these

red lead   Tomato sauce; ***worms in red lead** refers to tinned spaghetti

Red Plum   Affectionate nickname for HMS *ENDURANCE*, the *Royal Navy*'s Antarctic ice patrol ship

red recommend   Older term for an especially good report on a senior *rate which, in a system no longer extant, had the top 10% of candidates' names on an alphabetical list typed out in red

Red Sea rig   *Wardroom evening wear in hot climates featuring a cummerbund and an open-necked white shirt with rank shoulder-boards

redemption by *pusser's hard   Old system whereby items from the *scran bag could be recovered on payment of one inch of Naval-issue soap, which was then used for communal purposes

redders (esp. *RM*)   Really hot, abbreviation of red-hot, but also used to describe sunny weather. The phrase *gangs of redders* is often used when talking about a plentiful source of heat such as an oven or a sauna

regain *(RM)*   An exercise undertaken over the static water tank at *Lympstone; the special technique of recovery after falling off and hanging from a rope must be demonstrated. Also used in a wider sense: *"After a mistake like that he'll have to do an enormous regain if he wants to get back in the CO's good books.."*

Reggy / Reggies   Polite abbreviation for a member of the *Regulating Branch*; see also *crushers, *Gestapo, *Jaunty, *Jossman and *Master-at-Arms

relaxed rig   Informal (recreational) clothing

relief   The person who takes over your duty, watch or job

religious experience (esp. *FAA*)   Something that you would like your enemy to have in war, so that he suddenly changes his outlook on life - and then either surrenders or *bangs out !

remuster   In an official sense, to **remuster** something is to check it for a second time; in practice, the word is often used to describe someone who has changed trades or vocations: *"After the attack on Two Sisters, one of the Rifle Company officers asked to remuster as a padre.."*

render   Submit a report or *return; note also that a rope **renders** to a block rather than passing through it

Rentaset   The *Royal Navy School of Education and Training Technology*

Report your position and depth at midnight..   Jocular and traditional telegram sent to a Naval Officer on his wedding day - to be read out at the wedding breakfast by his best man. The *Royal Marines* equivalent might be the piece of fieldcraft advice which states: *"Don't fire the first time up.."* Either way, the maiden aunts are usually horrified

request chit (esp. *RM*)   Written request seeking formal permission to do something: *"You want a slot on that *exped up to the Hardanger Vidda ? OK, can't promise anything, but put your **request chit** in.."* In the *RN* this idea has more to do with reminding a senior officer of a discussion, after he has had time to think about the problem

Requestmen   Captain's *table for the hearing of **requests** by his men for advancement, redress or recognition following success in academic or sporting matters. Usually a happy occasion, in contrast to *Defaulters

required on board   Formal punishment awarded by the Captain to an Officer or rating who has drawn unwelcome attention to himself, eg. by drinking too much. If he is **required on board,** then he will be unable to participate in a *run ashore, or accept any invitations to go *up-homers; an Officer may also find himself *watch and stop on for duties, and might also have a *stoppage of wine-bill to suffer into the bargain

re-scrub   Repeat something, especially an inspection after failing it the first time around

rest of your natural   The **rest of your natural-born** days, ie. the rest of your life

retard leave   Staying back for security or administrative duties during main leave, thus **retarding** your own leave (or even taking it earlier !) and forming the **retard party;** the *RM* equivalent uses the phrase *rear party

retinue   A *Flag Officer's household staff

re-tread   Someone who is doing a job for the second time, usually after a long absence from it; can also be used as a descriptive adjective for a person who has *remustered from another skill: *"Joe's a re-tread *Looker - he bust his back ejecting from a Vixen and is now a really excellent *Air Tragicker.."*   A **re-tread bachelor** is a divorcee

return   A written report, usually listing names or quantities of stores. *Nil returns are required* means that, even if you cannot reply positively to a request, the mere fact that you are replying is important

RFA   The *Royal Fleet Auxiliary,* an afloat organisation that supplies stores, fuel and ammunition to HM warships at sea

RHIP   *Rank Hath Its Privilege* - a nice way of deferring to a senior officer in some matter. Note also *boat routine

rice
1. *(RM) Give it rice !* is like saying: *"Let's have more effort !"*
2. *Feed 'em rice, Jimmy !* is similar to: *"Give them a piece of your mind, James !"*

riff-raff   Term derived from the rather unsavoury **Riff** and Berber pirates of the Barbary Coast of North Africa

rig   Several distinct meanings, depending on context:
1. **Rig of the day** - the uniform laid down in Ship's Daily Orders as appropriate for wearing that day. A **split rig**, in which items of uniform are mixed with *civvy kit must always be avoided; another name for this is a *pusser's shift !
2. **Shore rig** - civilian attire, which may be *planter's or *dog robber's, but will undoubtedly be a **clean rig** - and a **smart rig** as well
3. **Jury rig** - old sailing term for a temporary get-you-home form of mechanical repair, perhaps derived from *de jour*
4. **Rigged like a** _____   See *Nagasaki
5. *"Excuse my rig, please ?"*   Traditional and polite request to the senior uniformed officer present in a *Wardroom for permission to use the facilities despite not being in uniform yourself. This permission is almost always granted - providing that your **rig** is not too weird !
6. **Scruff rig** is not particularly smart, and inappropriate to the formal surroundings of a *Wardroom, so there is often a **scruff's** bar to cater for those dressed in this manner after sport or study

right   An adjective which emphasizes the meaning of the noun which it is applied to: *"He's a right *knacker, he is.."*

ring eight bells   Older term meaning to die, hence the underlying significance of the *Alistair Maclean* novel's title - *When Eight Bells Toll*

ring off   Derived from the engine telegraph system of **ringing off** to finish with main engines, hence this usage to imply that a task has been completed and it's now time to do something else

ring out the old year   Pleasant custom in *RN* ships whereby the youngest man on board - Officer or rating - rings sixteen bells at midnight on New Year's Eve to **ring out the old year**, and then **ring in the new**

ring piece   The anus, hence **ring stinger** as a very hot curry; see also *chicken Chernobyl in this sense. Jack may also use the phrase *I puked my ring piece* to describe persistent vomiting. The phrase can also be used, almost inevitably, for a *Looker

ring the bell *(RM)*   Small brass bell hanging in the *Senior's bar, usually with embroidered and fancy ropework attached to the clapper. Sounding this bell, whether by design or curiosity, will bring a host of new friends to your side - because you have just indicated your willingness to buy a drink for everyone present

ringbolt   A zero, as in *820 Squadron* becoming *Eight-Two-**Ringbolt,*** or oh-crack-**double ringbolt** (0-00) as midnight ! There is another occasional use to describe the anus, hence a **ringbolt kicker** is a homosexual; note also note the term **ringbolted** for someone who is hopelessly drunk

Rip van Winkle   Legendary *kip *merchant whose legacy is celebrated in the accusation: *"You've had more time off than **Rip van Winkle's** bunk light.."*

Ripple *(FAA)*   The maintenance of a squadron's aircraft in the air around the clock; a **Ripple three** means that three aircraft are continuously airborne, day and night - a punishing requirement that taxes aircrew and maintainers alike

ripshit   A wild colonial boy

Rise and shine !   Traditional call when making the pipe *Call the hands..* It is repeated once and usually followed by the words: *"You've had yours - now I'll have mine.."*
Other versions are:
"Rise and shine - the morning's fine !"
"Rise and scowl - the morning's foul !"
"Rise and sweat - the morning's wet !"

RM repair kit   *Black maskers and a big hammer

robbing chit *(FAA)*   Written authority to *acquire some spare part off a *Hangar Annie or *Xmas tree

rock ape
1. Member of the Royal Air Force Regiment
2. *(RM)* Occasional nickname for a *ML (Mountain Leader)* or a member of the *M and AW (Mountain and Arctic Warfare) Cadre*
3. The phrase *a real *three-badge **rock ape*** describes someone of low intellect who can lift heavy weights

rock up   General expression similar to *turn up* or *pole up; note that getting one's **rocks off** has a completely different meaning - to do with giving *the ferret a run

rocket fuel   Any really strong drink, but especially brandy mixed with Benedictine

rocket shop *(SM)*   The missile compartment of a *bomber, as opposed to the *bomb shop up for'ard; see also *Sherwood Forest

rocking horse droppings / manure   Form of comparison for something rare or unusual; one politer alternative might concern the rare event of a *Fleet Jossman's sea draft !

rocks (esp. *RM*)   Censure or criticism as when *bollocking someone: *"That approach was OK but I got **absolute rocks** for the landing.."*

Rodneys   *RFA nickname for *Royal Navy Officers*

Roger D   Informal alternative to *OK* when agreeing to do something; a shortened form of the alliteration *Roger Dodger*

rogue's yarn   Coloured jute thread laid up in the strands of a rope to identify its source and thereby stop thieving; Naval rope commanded a particularly high price ashore if it could be smuggled out of the dockyards and sold

rolls on wet grass   Description of a ship with poor *sea-kindliness

ROMFT !   *Roll On My (Flipping) Twelve !* Expression used by someone who is on *RDP and impatient to get *outside after the twelve year engagement of old

rompers   Underpants, or *keks

roof *(SM)*   The surface of the sea

roof rats   Those personnel working up on an aircraft carrier's flight deck, and especially the *chain gang

Root'n'Toot !   Expression of disbelief; see also *Boogaloo !

Rose Cottage   Euphemism for a venereal diseases clinic, possibly because of the rose-pink sores of syphilis - now very rarely seen. Another explanation may lie in the special messdeck set aside for *CDA men* in the old Navy - those who had *Contracted Disease Ashore* and had their own *heads and tableware which were over-painted with roses. And as if that wasn't bad enough, the inhabitants of **Rose Cottage** also had their *tots stopped

roster   Duty list, and also the waiting list for advancement that is kept by *Drafty; a **dry roster** is one with no names on it, so promotion or advancement is automatic when the necessary qualifications have been obtained, in contrast to a **wet roster** which may be very wet indeed

Rosy Dawn   Potent hang-over cure served up in a number of variations, depending on the skill and experience of a warship's *Doc. The ingredients can vary, but are usually based on a red-coloured proprietary tonic which is mixed with aspirin and Alka-Seltzer and then served freshly fizzing

Rotate ! *(FAA)*   Expression of exasperation: *"So now the Admiral wants us to *scrub round that new procedure and carry on doing it the old way ? Well, **bloody ro-tate**!"*

roughers   Rough seas: *"I enjoy a spot of **roughers** - no queues in the *galley for a fried breakfast.."*

roughy-toughy   Descriptive term for Royal, or anything to do with the Corps, derived from Winston Churchill's famous observation: *"The Royal Marines have a **rough, tough** and glorious history.."*

round-down   The aft end of a carrier flightdeck; this is hit in a *rampstrike

Rounds   Formal tour of inspection through some designated area of a warship or establishment. These may be **Captain's Rounds** or **XO's Rounds**, or simply called **Evening Rounds**

Royal Naval Air Service   This organization, the forerunner of today's *Fleet Air Arm*, was founded in 1912 as an unofficial naval air branch of the *Royal Flying Corps*. Although it developed independently, the *RNAS* was often in conflict with the *RFC*, and to resolve these problems the Smuts Committee recommended their amalgamation to form the *Royal Air Force*, which came into being on April 1st 1912. On the last day of its existence the *RNAS* had 103 airships, 2,949 aircraft and over 67,000 officers and men !

Royal Navy School of Dancing   The *Harbour Lights* discotheque in *Torpoint, where the young *nozzers from *RALEIGH* stand and watch the girls dancing together around a pile of handbags in the middle of the floor

royal   Adjective used occasionally as an order of magnitude: *"He's a royal pain in the arse.."*

RPC   Abbreviation that has now become a word in its own right - *Request the Pleasure of your Company*

RT   Radio-telephony - voice transmission, as opposed to the *WT of wireless telegraphy and Morse

rub / rubber   A loan of money: *"Anyone give me the rub of a tenner ?"*

Rubber   Older nickname for a *Physical Training Instructor* - or an *India-rubber man*

rubber dicked (esp. *RM*)   Unfairly beaten; see also *dicked

rubber Henry   Another version of the above. When you are heavily defeated in some contest, someone will probably have *hit you with a big rubber Henry*

rubber hubby   Jack's nickname for a vibrator

rug rat   A small child. See also *ankle biter and *carpet crawler

rum baron   Similar meaning to *beer baron, ie. someone who stored the stuff illegally, and wielded power and influence on the *lower deck as a result, particularly among the **rum rats** who would do almost anything for an extra *tot

rum bosun   The man who draws the spirit ration for his *messdeck in a rum *fanny, takes the *three and one *grog, tries not to get it *gofferred, and then dishes it out to his messmates, usually ensuring that something extra is left for him as *plushers

rum bum and 'baccy   Summary of Jack's social interests in the old Navy

Commando

R - 243

rumbled   Found out

Rumour Control   Legendary source of good *buzzes: *"I'm not sure what my next appointment's going to be, but Rumour Control says it's something to do with *number-crunching up in the *Madhouse.."*

run / run in   To **run someone** or **run him in** is the same as putting him in the *rattle, ie. placing that person on a formal charge of disobeying or breaking some section of the *Naval Discipline Act*. Can also be used in the sense of trying something out, as in: *"**Run this up the flagpole** and see who salutes it.."* Or: *"**Run this past** the Boss and see if he's happy with it.."*

run-ashore   A social visit, with various shipmates, to a series of pubs or clubs; those who are your regular companions in these endeavours become your **run-ashore oppos**

(do a) runner   Desert or go *AWOL (Absent Without Leave)*. After 30 days absence, the Service Certificate is marked **R** for **Run**. Note also that a **runner** was also a WW2 term for an exercise torpedo that had no warhead

Rupert   Generic term for an *Army* officer, but especially one who is from a Cavalry outfit

Rusty   Occasional nickname for the surname Steele, or someone with red hair

rusty bullet-hole   The anus

SIERRA

S.206   Confidential reporting form raised on all officers at regular intervals and thus vital to their promotion prospects. A combination of textual comments and marking points for various personal qualities gives an overall picture and score which is used to make up ranking lists at the six-monthly Admiralty Promotion Boards. Naval officers do not see their **Forms S.206**, but receive a *flimsy instead. Note also the ironic comment: *"His **206** was so bad, it looked like a *PULHHEEMS.."* There are a number of other classic comments listed under *two-oh-six

sack rat   Another pithy label applicable to an individual who is addicted to his *pit. See *canvas back for a complete listing

sad on   A bad mood, usually caused by a subordinate's failure in some task: *"The first time that happened, the *Boss got a *right **sad on** that lasted for the rest of the week.."*

Safeguard   Code word used to prefix a message about casualties during an exercise to indicate that they are genuine and not simulated

sailing orders   An enhanced state of preparation for sea; when a ship is **under sailing orders**, shore leave becomes somewhat restricted and the penalties for breaking that leave then become much more serious

sailor's sarnie   Jack in a horizontal mode with two lady friends

salad gear   Traditional collective description of the *bunny grub, celery and tomatoes etc. that go to make up a salad

sale before the mast   Older term for a *kit auction

salthorse   A *Naval Officer* who has remained a seaman throughout his career and has not sub-specialized in aviation, submarines, mine warfare, engineering, instruction, navigation, hydrography, aircraft direction or any of the other black arts denoted by a special symbol in the *Navy List. The term is derived from *salt horse*, the old method of preserving meat at sea, and it used to apply almost exclusively to destroyer captains

Sandy bottoms *!*   Rare privilege, (or the settlement of a considerable debt) involving the *tot; this is a specific invitation to *see off the contents of a glass or mug, ie. until the *sandy bottom* is showing

sangar *(RM)*   Defensive position constructed with stones, rocks and sandbags: *"I was only away for three days, but by the time I got back to my desk, the In-tray had turned into a ruddy **sangar**.."*

santan man *(RM)*   A Marine trained in field hygiene duties, or a *civvy tasked with emptying chemical toilets. The latter may also be responsible for operating the *honey monster

SAR   Well-established acronym for Search and Rescue; this can be part of the national service to which the *Fleet Air Arm* contributes at a number of locations around Britain's coastline (along with the *RAF* and certain civilian contractors) - or out at sea. While **SAR Flight** helicopters are specifically dedicated for this job, **SAR** itself remains an occasional (and welcome) task for all rotary-wing aircrew

sarnie   A sandwich, probably Liverpool in origin. A **knuckle sarnie** is a punch to the face, and note also *sailor's sarnie

Saturday night at sea   Traditionally relaxed mood and routine in RN *Wardrooms afloat; the junior officer present proposes the *Toast to *Sweethearts and Wives*. During the era of the *Tot, it also meant an extra issue of *Nelson's blood for the *lower deck

Sawbones   The process of limb amputation in the old Navy, now preserved as a nickname for the *Principal Medical Officer*

scab-lifter   Perjorative label for any member of the *RN Medical Branch*, but also a description specially reserved for the warship's *Doc: *"Our **scab-lifter** is an excellent *hand - spent the first six years of his career with the *Booties, and knows more about fieldcraft than most of the ship's *Detachment.."*

scatters   A dose of diarrhoea; see *squitters for the main listing

scend   The quick vertical rise of a ship's bow out of a trough between two waves, as opposed to its pitching down; the bow in this condition was ***a-scending***

Crabs

School of Dancing   See *grab-a-granny night or *widow's hop, as well as the *Royal Navy School of Dancing

schoolie   Abbreviation for schoolmaster and thus the commonest nickname for an *Instructor Officer*. See *chalk bosun for a listing of alternatives

scooby-dooby / scooby-doo   Jack's name for a civilian sport (*SCUBA*) diver

scope   The length of chain *paid out to allow a ship to swing safely to her single anchor. This has given rise to the shoreside expression *plenty of scope*

Scotchman   Older term for any piece of wood, metal, leather or canvas used as local protection against chafe or wear, such as the metal plate found at the head and foot of a *companionway to protect the decking

Scouse / Scouser
1. Any Liverpudlian (native of Liverpool) - derived from the word *lobscouse
2. Frequent nickname for the Chinese *dhobeyman employed in HM Ships - because, like his Merseyside counterpart, it's often quite difficult to understand exactly what he's saying !

scram *(SM)*   Emergency shut-down of a *boat's nuclear reactor

scrambled egg   Nickname for the gold wire braid on the peak of a senior officer's cap

scran   Food: *"I'm going down the *galley for scran - you coming ?"*

scran bag   Any personal possession found *sculling around the ship is placed in a **scran bag**, to be redeemed only on payment of a small fine, with overall proceeds to the ship's *Welfare Fund*. In older times the fee for *redemption was a square inch of *pusser's hard (soap) per item. The term can also be used to describe an untidy or scruffy person

Scratch   Traditional nickname for the Captain's Secretary

scratcher
1. A bed; see also *pit, *rack, *sack and *green slug for variants
2. *(SM)* The bosun's mate

screaming skull   Label applied to a senior officer who is thin, gaunt and generally rather humourless

screwdriver *(RM or stoker's)*   A hammer

Scribes　　Standard nickname for a rating of the *Writer* specialization

scrimshanker　　Older term for a workshy individual

scronk / scronky　　Untidy and generally grubby individual whose appearance may be described by the adjective **scronky**

scrote　　Marvellous term of abuse which rolls well off the tongue, particularly when it is combined with a descriptive qualification such as *born-again*

scrub round　　Cancellation of some previous arrangement due to sudden change in needs or circumstances: "*Culdrose is *clamped, so we'll have to **scrub round** that trip.."

scruff rig / scruffers　　Clothing suitable for the garden or building site, or any so-called fashionable style that, at great expense, achieves the same untidy effect.　See also further comments under *rig

sculling about / around　　Something that is lying or rolling about on the *deck: "Get your kit stowed as soon as you can, lads - and don't leave anything **sculling about**, or it'll end up in the *scran bag.."

scum bag　　A more general term of abuse, but the phrase also implies a particular dislike of the person concerned

scuttle
1. The *RN* equivalent of a circular window.　A **scuttle run** is a dangerous expedition that passes along the outside of a ship using a **scuttle** for both exit and re-entry
2. Sink a ship by opening her sea-cocks and **scuttling** her
3. Break open a barrel by **scuttling** it, as in a *scuttle(d)-butt

scuttlebutt　　Gossip; the original **scuttlebutt** was an open (*scuttled*) fresh-water cask (or *butt*) between decks, from which issues were made to the messdecks.　It served as a focal point for the exchange of rumours, *buzzes or other daily information.　The term is particularly used across the *Pond

SD List　　Abbreviation for *Special Duties List*, Officers commissioned from the *lower deck somewhat later in their careers than the *Upper Yardsmen

sea boat
1. Term used when referring to a vessel's handling qualities: "She may not be very pretty, but she's an excellent **deep sea boat**.."
2. Small workboat that can be lowered quickly while its parent ship is still under way, eg. to rescue a survivor: "Man overboard - **seaboat's crew** *close up *at the rush.."

sea daddy　　A well-respected older rating or officer, sometimes self-appointed to educate younger men in the ways of the world - and the Navy. Up until recent times this term had no other connotation, but it has now become confused with *sugar daddy*. See *Bugis Street for an example of its correct application. A **Sea Daddy** scheme has now been started to improve officer recruitment, whereby boys still at school can write to, and then visit *RN* Officers who were at that school themselves. The idea is still in its infancy but appears to be working well

seagulls *(RM)*   Any group of *(Army)* Guards or Cavalry officer's wives talking amongst themselves - so named because of the collective sound that emerges, in marked contrast to the lower-pitched *wah-wah noise made by their spouses !

Sea Jet *(FAA)*   Nickname for the *SHAR

sea-kindly   A ship which moves and handles well in a seaway

Sea King   Long-serving and versatile twin-engined helicopter built by Westlands to an original (American) Sikorsky design. This all-weather aircraft serves the *Fleet Air Arm* in *Anti-Submarine (HAS)*, *Commando (HC)*, *Airborne Early Warning (AEW)* and *SAR (HAR)* variants, all subject to occasional upgrading and changes of Mark number. It is due to be replaced in service by the EH.101 - to be named the *Merlin - early in the next decade

sea lawyer   Jack's (older) nickname for a shark. All lawyers are sharks; sharks live in the sea, so all sharks are **sea lawyers** ! Also an alternative term for a *messdeck lawyer

seamanlike   Any action or procedure carried out in a neat, yet functional and practical manner. The phrase ***seamanlike** precaution* is in particular use for any aspect of sensible planning that takes account of possible delay, disaster or damage

seaman's eye   Quality of judgement and perception possessed by an experienced *hand when gauging the effects of wind and tide on a ship's movement relative to something else

Sea Queen *(FAA)*   Nickname at *Culdrose for the *Royal Air Force*'s *SAR version of the *Sea King - a machine of really enviable performance and function, except that it has no weapon systems

sea rider   Member of *FOST*'s staff *(Flag Officer Sea Training)* on temporary detachment to join ships *working-up at *Portland for instruction and assessment purposes

searoom   Manoeuvering space when handling a ship in a seaway. Note also Friday's *Toast to: *"..a willing foe - and **searoom**.."*

sea squire   A Warrant Officer of the *Royal Navy*

sea story   An exaggerated tale containing variable amounts of the truth

Sea Vixen   Twin-boom and twin-engined all-weather jet fighter which served the *Fleet Air Arm* well during the Sixties before being replaced by the *Toom. A **Sea Vixen** *Looker sat in the darkened *coal hole, offset below and to the right of his *Pirate

second thing I'll do when I get home *(RM)*   Lovely phrase, much-heard at the end of an exercise or deployment, indicating a certain base enthusiasm to see one's missus: *"..and the **second thing that I'll do when I get home** is - take my pack off !"*

secret squirrel *(RM)*   Anyone employed in an Intelligence role; see also *sneaky beaky

secure
1. Finish work: *"**Secure** is at 1645, and not a minute earlier.."*
2. Cease an *evolution, or change from one work state to another, as in the *pipe ***Secure** from *flying stations !* or the classic order: *"**Secure** for sea.."*
3. Make fast to something; ships and *boats are **secured,** whereas shoelaces are tied up

see
1. **See over the brow** - welcome arriving guests, or take leave of those who are departing
2. *Seen off!* - complaint made when someone has got the better of you, or some injustice has befallen you
3. **Seeing-to** - vigorous sexual activity: *"What that woman needs is an occasional good **seeing-to**.."*

selected   For promotion: *"Francis was **selected** for his *brass hat in the June *List.."*

self-adjusting cock-up *(RM)*   The best-laid plans of mice and men are always going wrong, but especially so when the military become involved. Good plans should always allow for an element of luck in their execution; sometimes the development of a new problem suddenly provides the solution for another pre-existing difficulty. In this way the original error or divergence from the plan suddenly becomes a **self-adjusting cock-up** !

Senior / senior
1. The **senior engineer officer** (usually a *two and a half) below the Commander (Engineering) or *Chiefy
2. *(RM)* A Senior NCO. Also, the Command course at *Lympstone which all Sergeants must pass before being promoted is known throughout the Corps as **The Seniors**
3. Degree of severity or size: *"Quite honestly, what we're dealing with here is an error of fairly **senior** proportions.."*
4. **Senior Coward** *(RM)* Unfair, but still-awarded label for the most senior member of the Corps without any campaign medal ribbons on his uniform

Sergeant-Major *(RM)*   The senior *NCO* of a ship's *detachment, irrespective of his actual rank

Sergeants   Nickname in a ship for those of Commander's rank, because they also have three stripes on their sleeves: *"How many **Sergeants** are coming to the party tonight ?"*

sesh (esp. *RM*)   Heavy beer drinking session

set   A *full set of facial whiskers, ie. beard and moustache. Permission must be sought to grow a set, and if this looks uneven or stunted after two weeks, the rating may be ordered to *shave off

set of papers   Jack's *Divisional documents or *comic cuts; a really good rating who is doing well will have an ***immaculate set of papers**

set up the backstays   Conceal or make good an *oppo's mistake in order to prevent disciplinary action being taken against him. In contrast, a fair-weather friend is a *shifting backstay

Full Set

seven bells   A total of eight bells are struck to end a
*watch; to knock **seven bells out of** someone implies some pretty severe
handling - without actually finishing him off. A **seven beller** is also
a nice cup of tea taken just before the end of a *watch

seven navies   Figure of speech used as a means of comparison:
*"That man is the biggest *skate in seven navies.."*

sew-sew   A Hong Kong Chinese tailor carried on board; see also
*jewing firm

shacked up with ___   Living with someone who is a **shackeroo** or
shackerelle depending on their gender

Shady   Traditional nickname for someone with the surname Lane

shafted   Politer version of *screwed* when describing someone who has
been *royally *seen off

Shagbat *(FAA)*   Lovely nickname for the old and much-loved Walrus
aircraft, which was amphibian and also known as a *pusser's duck

shagged-out   Very tired indeed, derived from the word ***shag*** - which
has connotations of vigorous sexual activity

shag-nasty   Term of abuse that contains an element of affection

shake down   Traditionally, a short cruise undertaken immediately
after refit to ensure everything is bedded down and working correctly

shake / *Shakes*   To **shake** someone is to wake him or her up; ***Shakes***
is the polite nickname for the person in charge of the **shakes list**, a
book containing the name, Mess number, bunkspace and time
requested. This book has to be signed by whoever is being **shaken**

shambolic   Nice term that combines the words *shambles* and
diabolical rather cleverly to describe either a scene of organized
chaos, or some event that has gone badly. Can also be described as a
shambollocks if a noun is needed

shamfered   Older term for a ship damaged in action, now used to
describe the process of tidying up a messdeck for *Rounds, or getting
ready to go ashore. The expression: *"**Shamfer up** !"* is an exhortation
to do better

Shammy leather !   Spoken with a heavy French accent, and
accompanied by a pronounced Gallic shrug, means: *"That's life.."*

SHAR *(FAA)*   Standard acronym for the versatile and highly effective
Sea Harrier (jump-jet) fighter currently serving at sea with the *Fleet
Air Arm*: *"For air combat in the Falklands, the final scoreline was*

SHARs *22, Mirages and Skyhawks nil..."* Also referred to as a *Sea Jet, and note *ski-jump and *Yeovilton

Shareholders *(FAA)* Briefing and planning meeting held in a squadron which all **shareholders** - squadron personnel - are supposed to attend

Sharks The *Fleet Air Arm*'s premier helicopter display team, a four-ship Gazelle outfit based at *Culdrose that flies the White Ensign throughout the UK and Europe during the summer season

sharp end The bow of a warship (as opposed to the *blunt end !) but also used to describe the front line, ie. the place where all the action is

sharpener A drink taken on a cold morning in order to **sharpen** one's wits

shave off
1. The process of removing a *full set
2. *Shave off !* is a frequent cry of disgust, disbelief or frustration expressed in response to some unexpected event or a setback
3. Rant and rave: *"Fer Gawd's sake don't tell 'im that - 'ave you ever 'eard 'im shavin' off about them pop singers ?"*

shebang *(FAA)* An incident that involves explosive activity or wartime action: *"Then the whole shebang mushroomed in a ball of flame.."*

shellback A sailor who has been at sea so long that *limpet shells* and barnacles are encrusting his *back*, like a ship's hull. The term appears to have been derogatory at first, but later took on an admiring tone similar to that of *Sea Daddy

Sherwood Forest *(SM)* The missile compartment of a *bomber; see also *rocket shop

shifting backstay A supposed *oppo who, instead of supporting you through a crisis by *setting up the backstays, wavers weakly instead and therefore cannot be relied on in future

shifting tack Alter one's thinking or opinion on some matter by adjusting the line of argument; see also *suck back ten

Shiner Traditional nickname for someone called Wright or Light

shiny burbs Oilskins; see also *burbs

ship husbandry The business of maintaining, provisioning and generally looking after a warship in order to maintain her at a peak of efficiency; this process is still performed by the **ship's husband** or *boat swain* - hence *bo'sun

Shipmate   Honorary rank of all members of the splendid *Royal Naval Association* which has branches all over the UK and Commonwealth

shipped his *killicks   Promoted to *Leading Hand, ie. a naval term for putting up the fouled anchor (***killick***) badges on a uniform

shipping it green   Bad weather at sea, with mountainous waves passing unbroken along the ship's length

Ship's Corporal *(RM)*   Title now applied when the duties of *quartermaster are being carried out by a junior NCO of the ship's *Detachment

ships that pass in the night   A rather nice way to take your leave of someone without using the ordinary platitude of *see you again sometime*; Jack's alternative is: *"**Ships that pass in the night** will no doubt pass again.."* This is a more modern usage than the older meaning of ships passing in the night, their names not known - and more than likely *never* to meet again. So it is with certain ladies !

shipshape   Neat, tidy and generally seamanlike in functional appearance; the term has passed into general usage, occasionally in the more complete form based on the days when Bristol was the country's premier western coast port, as ***all shipshape and Bristol fasxhion***

shipwreck   Someone suffering the next morning from *CSB rash, or feeling rather *hen-pecked, may well be greeted by his *oppo with a hearty slap on the back and a loud cry of: *"Hello me **old shipwreck** - how's yer head ?"*

shirtlifter   Yet another term for a *brownhatter !

shit   Vulgar but common expletive employed by Jack in a number specific ways:
    the **shits** - diarrhoea
    *"..he gives me **the shits**" - "I don't like him very much.."*
    shit bits - haemorrhoids
    shit chute - geographical feature of an *Uckers board
    shiters - drunk
    shitting conkers - the combined effects of adrenalin and fear
    Shitty Death ! - "Well, goodness gracious me !"
    shit faced - totally drunk
    shit-fer-brains - a person who is not very bright
    shit hot - brilliant
    shitkicker - cowboy film
    Shitloads ! - "There is a plentiful supply !"
    shit locker - the rectum
    shit or bust - messdeck card game, or an expression of
       great determination
    shit on a raft - devilled kidneys on toast
    shit on your oppo - messdeck card game where success comes
       from looking after yourself alone; also used for any
       really anti-social behaviour
Note also the synonym of **shite** as a variant to all the above

shit-shower-shampoo-shave   Almost slurred into a single word, these four **S**'s are a neat summary of Jack's usual pre-breakfast activities. Royal will clean his boots in addition, so the fifth **S** of **shine** is usually added to the description in his case ! An optional extension of -**shandy-shag** (or **short time**) then leads the **seven S**'s of a complete *run ashore, as an alternative to *beer, big eats, bag-off and back on board

shitehawk
  1. A seagull
  2. An enemy reconnaissance aircraft operating just out of
    gun or missile range
  3. General term of abuse
  4. The Senior *Rates' bar at *Culdrose is called
    The Shy Talk Inn

shock   Older term for the process of cooking something; a dish would be taken down to the *galley with the request to **give it a shock** !

shonk / Shonkey   Nose; someone with a significant nasal adornment to his *fizzog may well be nicknamed *Shonkey* - whatever his surname !

shoot a line (esp. *FAA*)   Exaggerate or boast when recounting some incident involving yourself. To **shoot the breeze** with someone is to engage them in general conversation

shoot through   Fail to keep an appointment or rendezvous. The phrase can also be used as an abusive noun: *"We were there at least ten minutes *previous, but Shiner didn't turn up - the useless ruddy shoot through.."*

shop   Service or technical naval matters: *"Please don't talk shop in the *Wardroom.."*

shore leave   Permission granted to leave the ship when alongside in harbour; Jack will then change or *clean into his **shore rig**

Shore Patrol   Special Duty *Watch policing the conduct of Jack while on *shore leave - and in some cases protecting him from assault or injury

short arm inspection *(RM)*   Medical Officer's examination of the *wedding tackle, usually undertaken in *Rose Cottage

short arms, long pockets   Tight-fisted individual ungenerous with his hospitality, ie. unable to reach down far enough to find the money for a round of *wets !

short arse   Any person of slight stature, or suffering from *duck's disease

short course   Any brief introduction to some complex subject, often used in a mocking sense: *"I don't know how he has the nerve to call himself a doctor - it's quite obvious that he's only done the *scab-lifter's short course.."*   By contrast, see also *long course

short haircut and over the wall   Slang term for the process of being sent to *DQs: *"Stealing from the ship's Welfare Fund ? That ought to be a short haircut and over the wall job, I reckon.."*

short rations   Reduced issues of any *stores item

shot away   Drunk: *"By the time he'd had *sippers from about twenty people, the poor chap was completely shot away.."*

shot line   Rope or cable to which a bottom *sinker or *lazy shot is attached during diving operations

Shotley shuffle   Older term for doubling with the minimum effort while under punishment. **Shotley** was the Boys Training Establishment of HMS *GANGES*, near Ipswich, which was closed down in the 1960s

Show a leg!   Traditional exhortation to wake up, derived from the old days of sail when women were allowed on board and to stay overnight while in harbour. The females could also linger an extra hour in their hammocks, providing they could prove their gender by **showing a** (hairless) **leg** to the Bosun's Mates as they did their rounds

show the flag   The diplomatic aspect of Jack's visits to foreign ports; by entertaining local VIPs and *CIPs and allowing others to visit the ship, the image of Great Britain is enhanced

shrapnel
1. Metallic fragments from a bursting bomb or shell
2. Any otherwise useless foreign coins (see *klebbies and *ickies) that still remain in Jack's pockets as the ship sails from some foreign port. This original definition has now expanded in general usage and applies to almost any loose change; see also *washers

shreds / shreddies (esp. *RM*)   Underpants

shtum   Keeping quiet; saying nothing

shuddering shithouse *(RM)*   Any *RAF* Chinook heavy-lift helicopter, but especially the fantastic *Bravo November* of 1982 Falklands fame

shuff duff *(SM)*   Older term for an intelligence-gathering mast which was direction-finding at super-high frequencies, or *SHF/DF*. **Huff duff** similarly applied to high frequency electronic emissions

shufti   Arab word used in the sense of taking a look; the fibre-optic and highly flexible endoscopes originally designed for medical use that are now used for looking inside jet engines are known as **shuftiscopes** !

shut-down *(FAA)*   Stop the engine(s) - and helicopter rotor blades

Sick Bay   The *compartment occupied by a warship's *Doc, or the generic name for a collection of medical buildings in a shore establishment. Note also the following specialist applications:
    sickbay ranger - hypochondriac, or malingerer
    sickbay shackle - safety pin
    sickbay *Tiff - Medical Assistant, or *Doc

sidelight   Circular glass fitting of a *scuttle for admitting natural light to a *compartment, usually a fixed structure in modern warships with efficient air-conditioning, but it may also be hinged when part of a *scuttle. Always coverable with a *deadlight in order to *darken ship

sidestepper   See *shirtlifter

siff on his donk *(FAA)*   Tactic employed in an *Uckers game played according to *Wafu rules; this particular move is designed to prevent the final home run of an opponent's counter

sighter / sighting shot   First attempt to do something, so that corrections can then be made and the action repeated with a greater chance of success

sign on   Extend one's service for a longer period: *"I've just signed on for pension.."*

silent copy   Extra carbon- or photo-copy of some letter or document whose existence and destination are not recorded in the *Dist(*ribution*) Annex

Silent Service   Traditional nickname for the *Royal Navy*, resulting from the quiet and self-effacing modesty of the *Andrew - and the fact that they don't stamp around the parade ground when doing drill

silent hours   The (night) period between *pipe down and *call the hands; during this time watch bells are not struck, and only emergency *pipes can be made

silent routine *(SM)*   Submarine operating in a manner intended to create the absolute minimum of noise; see also *sock-footed

simulated *(FAA)*   Sleeping on top of your bunk rather than in it; see also *actual

sin bosun   A vicar; see *amen wallah for the main listing

Singers   Singapore; **Singers rules** state that the last man out of the taxi pays for it

singing from the same hymn sheet   Everyone in agreement about some point to be discussed at a meeting or presentation

sinker
1. Lead or iron weight on the end of a diving marker line
2. Suet dumpling !
3. *(FAA)* A target submarine's *snort mast or periscope disappearing off radar

siphon the python   See *pump ship

sippers   Small mouthful of an *oppo's *tot taken in repayment of some favour or debt. Note also the *framework of hospitality where two sippers equal one *gulpers

sitrep   Abbreviation of **situation report**: *"Can anyone give me a **sitrep** on those casualties that we heard about at midday ?"*

six *(FAA)*   Shortened form of **six o'clock** in the clock code, or right behind you. Hence, the traditional fighter pilot's advice: *"Watch your **six** !"* ie. remain alert at all times for someone coming up to attack you from *astern

six-throwing sod   Difficult opponent to beat in an *Uckers game

sixteen bells   Traditionally rung on the ship's bell at midnight on December 31st, in order to welcome in the New Year

skate   Ne'er-do-well, workshy individual who appears unable to accept the normal self-disciplines of Jack's life; *scrote is a useful alternative. Interestingly, **skate** (as in fish) was the common nickname in old *Pompey for any *matelot

'Skers / **'Skurrs**   Abbreviation of *whiskers*; Jack's *ready-use nickname for any bearded rating or officer whose real name is not known at that exact moment

ski-jump   Upwardly angled forward deck ramp of the three *RN* carriers; this brilliant British innovation devised by *Lt Cdr Doug Taylor RN (rtd)* markedly improves the safety margins as well as the weapon and fuel loads of a *launching *SHAR

skidmark   To be found in a pair of *keks that need *dhobeying

Greenie

skimmer *(SM)*   The *Trade's disparaging nickname for any surface vessel: *"All **skimmers** are targets as far as I'm concerned.."*

skin   Young and unmarked, ie. in a virginal sense. Can be used either as adjective or noun: *"Leave 'im alone - the poor kid's just a bit of **skin** ! Someone get him back to the ship.."* Also used with the word *essence for someone young and really lovely: *"She's all **skin** and essence.."*

skinful   Of drink: *"Look after Nobby - he's had a real **skinful**.."*

skirmishing
  1. *(RM)* Controlled fire and movement of ground troops
  2. Cleaning up an area by picking up all litter and rubbish while **skirmishing through**

skrinser *(FAA)*   All-purpose substitute word like *doobrey, *doofer or *johnson

sky artist   Psychiatrist !

sky pilot   Another word for a vicar or padre: see *amen wallah for the full list

skyscraper   Originally a small triangular sail, set seventh in ascending order from the deck, but used only in fine and steady light weather. The name has come ashore now to describe the tall multi-storey buildings found especially in America

Skywegian   Older term for anything of Scandinavian origin; see also *Noggie

slack
  1. Not taut - lazy and indisciplined; a **slack arse** is also a feature possessed by a *sleaze
  2. **slack in the programme** - space for adjustment or delay
  3. **slack hammocks** - punishment for oversleeping and failing to *turn to on time

slag off   Say something unpleasant about somebody behind his or her

slammer   Prison, or *chokey, also an alternative name for *DQs

slap in   Make a written *Request by filling in a request chit; *"I'm going to **slap in** to see some bastard.."* is the same as saying: *"I intend to make a full and formal complaint about this matter.."*

sleaze   A *party who offers little or no resistance on being *trapped

sleepy juice   Any strong drink or *vino collapso

Sling your hook !   A slightly less than polite invitation to go away and **sling your hammock** *clew **hook**s somewhere else ! To **sling**, as to *turn in, is the process of retiring for the night

slinger / *Slinger*
1. A *yardie's particular skill and trade of moving a heavy item or load with slinging wires and a crane
2. Occasional nickname for the surname Wood or Woods

slip
1. **slip right** - when the target time or completion date for some project is getting later and later; this process is called **slippage**
2. **slip left** *(FAA)* What happens to the *flypro when a sortie is cancelled
3. **slip and proceed** - leave a mooring or jetty, then head for sea and the next task

slips *(FAA)*   Slip ***watches** running from 2200 to 0800 the next day. The *first, *middle and *morning watches all **slip** into each other in this shore routine that equates to being *on nights* in the *civvy sense

SLJO   Frequently-heard acronym for *Shitty Little Jobs Officer*

Slops   Cash clothing store, where items of slops can be purchased from what used to be the traditional seaman's **Slop chest**

slop chit   List of responsibilities; should someone or something be **on your slop chit** then he / she / it is down to you in all respects. The term originated from the clothing list (*chit*) which recorded Jack's issues from the *Slops chest*

slop out   Wash a place through (with **slops of water** from a bucket)

slope
1. Leave a place furtively, by **sloping off**
2. Pass a problem on to someone else by **sloping shoulders** (generally with a brushing motion) to them. See also *Coke-bottle shoulders as an anatomical feature of those unable to carry any form of responsibility
3. American import for **sloping eyes** - any person with an Oriental *fizzog; may also be heard as **slopehead**
4. **slot** *(FAA)* *Stovie procedure for rejoining an airfield or carrier circuit to land

slug *(RM)*   A sleeping bag, especially a ***green slug**

slush   Originally, this was a term for the fat skimmed off by the cook from his cauldrons of boiled meat. This was compacted, and sold to the *purser for making candles. The monies made from this process constituted the very first **slush fund**, a term now in widespread use ashore

smalley   Little, as in **smalley eats** for cocktail-type snacks, **Smalley Pigs** for Petty Officers, and (esp. *RM*) **smalley girls** for under-age jail-bait. **Smalley boys** are Sea Cadets; **to go for a smalley portion** is similar to a *legover or a *quick coat of paint

small ships   Minesweepers and fishery protection vessels, rather than frigates and destroyers: *"I've been a **small ships** man for most of my time in the *Andrew.."*

smalls   Underwear, as in *crash out your **smalls***

Smartie tube *(RM)*   Long, filthy tunnel on the *Endurance course at *Lympstone, made of concrete piping and containing mud, stones and running water. This obstacle has to be negotiated on your back, in semi-darkness, with the rifle barrel kept dry at all times - or else you go through again !

Smashex
1. An exercise which simulates a submarine accident, with all the relevant responses being taken.
2. *(RM)* Decriptive term for a really good party

Mr. Michael Heseltine became Secretary of State for Defence in January 1983.

smeggers   Semolina pudding

smell   *"You smell like a zoo-keeper's boot.."*

smellies *(FAA)*   Nicknmae for maintainers; *green-and-smellies are flying overalls

Smoke   London: *"I'm off up the Big Smoke for *extenders.."*

smoked *(FAA)*   Crash into the ground, leaving only a smoking hole to mark your passing: *"Then I fell behind on cockpit workload, got a bit distracted, and almost smoked myself and my wingman.."*

Smudge / Smudger   Nicknames traditionally associated with the surname of Smith: *"Yessir, that's right - Smudger Smith, sir - and that's Smiff spelt with two f's.."*

SNAFU   WW2 acronym for *Situation Normal - All (Fouled !) Up.* Some would say that this is the normal situation pertaining to most military endeavours, but see also *self-adjusting cock-up and *FUBAR*

snag *(FAA)*   Process of rendering an aircraft temporarily unserviceable by reporting a defect and logging this fact in the MoD Form 700

snake pit
1. Any untidy messdeck
2. The *Wardroom at *Dartmouth
3. *(SM)* Forward lower section of a *diesel drainpipe's engine room
4. A temporary Ladies' *heads set up in a ship during a function
5. **snake and pygmy pie** is a steak and kidney pudding !

snake's honeymoon / wedding   An unholy tangle of lines and ropes on the *deck

snap one off
1. Defaecate; see also *crimp off a length
2. *(RM)* Salute

snap roll *(SM)*   High speed turn in a dived submarine which creates a large angle of heel into the turn

snapper   See *brownhatter - again

snarley   A mess of some kind, although *RM* usage also has this as a the *green grolly hanging like candlewax from a *snot gobbler's nose. A **snarleypig** is any particularly unpleasant individual - of either sex, whereas a **snarley *crocadillapig** is a really fierce animal - of any size

sneaky *(SM)*   A covert patrol carried out under semi-operational and highly classified conditions. The word can also be an adjective as in **sneaky beaky** for someone who is employed on intelligence-gathering duties; see also *secret squirrel in this respect

snifter
1. Smell something: *"Have a **snifter** of this.."*
2. Drink: *"Give us a quick **snifter** of your *wet.."*

SNLR   Acronym meaning *Services No Longer Required*: *"This geezer reckons 'e served during the Falklands punch-up, but I've 'ad a little *buzz that 'e went outside **SNLR** the year before.."*

Snobs   Older nickname for an amateur ship's cobbler, now replaced on larger ships by a Chinese *Tap-tap; this is a shortened form of the term *snobber

snookered on red   Discovering that one's wife or girlfriend is at the wrong time of her menstrual cycle

snorker   Sausage

snort *(SM)*   The process of running a diesel *boat's engines while at periscope depth in order to charge batteries; the air is drawn down through a **snort mast**

snot gobbler   Interesting term of abuse, derived from the description of a young child whose nostrils are festooned with *green grollies or candlesticks

snot box   The nose: *"He gets right up my **snot box**, he does.."*

Snotty   Older word for a Midshipman; apparently, these young men used to have three buttons sewn onto their jacket cuffs to stop them wiping their noses on the sleeves. Their uniforms were designed without pockets so that there would be no temptation to stand around idling, but there was also nowhere to stow a handkerchief. Many officers still carry their handkerchieves up one sleeve of the uniform jacket; those who are *Communicators* traditionally sport silk - which is allowed to show ! Note that **snotty** also has the adjectival meaning of someone who is short-tempered and rather conceited

snotty heap (esp. *RM*)   Anyone who trips and falls over, usually does so in a **snotty heap**; can also be used to describe the manner of collapsing after a really good *run ashore

Snowy   Nickname for anyone with the surname Winters or Winterbottom; also for anyone with particularly fair hair, or even - (and esp. *RM*) as an abbreviation of **Snowball** - for a black *oppo

snurger   Another name for a *toggle-oggler

Soapy   Traditional nickname for anyone called Watson

SOBS *(FAA)*   The Senior Observer of a squadron: *"**SOBS** 706 is off to the West Indies as the *guardship's *Jimmy - the *jammy git !"*

'GUNS'
The Gunnery Officer

social handgrenade *(RM)*   An individual whose general lack
of the social graces makes him really bad news at a party

sock-footed *(SM)*   Moving very, very quietly in a *silent routine

Sods opera   Ship's concert arranged, performed and appreciated by
Jack, usually on *Channel night. Some old scores are settled
painlessly, and tradition dictates that *Father should sit in the
front row of the audience, take some *stick, and then perform himself
after due encouragement from the audience:
*"Sing, you bastard, sing - or show us your *ring -*
We don't want to see your ring, so SING !"
The word **Sods** is supposed to stand for *Ship's Operatic and Drama* Society

soft   A number of uses:
  1. **soft option** - easy way out of a problem, but may not be the best
  2. **soft number** - a really cushy job
  3. **soft tack** - bread
  4. **softwood wedge** - suppository

(The) Soldier   The junior of two *Royal Marines* Officers, if two
are carried a part of a warship's *Detachment

soldier's farewell   To obtain good riddance of something worthless

Someone's on our side !   Remark made when things have been going
badly, and then the luck begins to run the other way; rather like saying
"Well, at least God is with us !"

son of a gun   Rough *hand but a good chap nonetheless. Debauchery
on the gundecks in older times was a common feature of life in harbour
after a long stint at sea. With women on board in this way, there were
even babies born 'tween decks; a male child, born on the gundeck
and father often unknown, became the **son of a gun**. Collectively, they
all became **sons of the sea**:
*Begotten in the *galley and born under a gun,*
*Every hair a rope yarn, every tooth a *marline spike*
Every finger a fish-hook -
And their blood right good Stockholm tar..

SOP   Acronym of *Standard Operating Procedures*, hence: *"The only*
way to tackle this problem is according to SOPs.."

Sort that bastard out !   Traditional exclamation made as you give
up trying to solve a complex muddle or problem, and pass it on to your
*oppo instead; also heard when a punch is landed on an adversary

sound off
  1. Play a bugle call or make a *pipe on the Tannoy
  2. Express an opinion loudly

soup jockey *(SM)*   Nickname for a *Wardroom steward

spacehopper   A short, fat, adolescent *smalley girl: *"Any talent down the disco, Bill?" " "Nah, mate - just *gangs of **spacehoppers**.."*

spadger   One of the four types of feathered bird recognized by Jack; see also *shitehawks, *arse-up ducks and *oozelum birds !

spanner wanker   Rude nickname for a *Mechanician

Sparks / Sparkers   Radio operator, the modern version of the old Telegraphist and his *sparking* wireless set

sparrowfart   Dawn, or at first light; ***oh-crack-sparrowfart*** is very early indeed, ie. when the sparrow wakes and breaks wind, ong before first light

spasm chasm   Another of Jack's nicknames for the vagina; find the ohers yourself !

spazz *(RM)*   Marine or recruit who is temporarily sick or injured

spear in *(FAA)*   Crash in an aircraft, usually with terminal results; also the process of hitting the *pit when extremely tired

Special Duties list   Officers selected for promotion from the *lower deck and therefore limited in their ultimate prospects unless they manage to transfer *GL; see also *SD List. Note that Special Sea Dutymen (or *Specials*) has a completely different usage in respect of responsibilities undertaken when entering or leaving harbour

Speechless One *(FAA)*   Callsign used by *Air Traffic Control* for an aircraft which has sufferred partial or complete radio failure; the term can also be used for an Officer who is unusually taciturn and quiet

speed march *(RM)*   Technique of double-marching on the flat and downhill, and quick-marching uphill, which forms the basis of the *nine-miler *Commando test - nine miles in ninety minutes as part of a formed squad wearing boots, *fighting order and carrying a weapon

spewing his ring / toenails   Vomiting excessively, especially when suffering from *nautical nausea

Spick   General nickname for a dark Latino type, but especially a native of Argentina: *"**Spicks** ? Well, as far as I can tell from the history books, they're basically Italians who speak Spanish rather badly - and also think they're English !"*

Spike / spike
  1. **marline spike** - pointed tool on a sailor's knife for ropework
  2. Nickname for the surname Hughes or Milligan !
  3. Foil a plan by **spiking it**, as in the older ploy of **spiking** (an enemy's) **guns**

spilled blood   *Father's amendments to a draft *S.206 made in *red ink, usually in disagreement to some high opinion expressed, or to the general overmarking

spin a yarn   Elaborate story to cover up some misdemeanour, or reminiscences that have been fabricated or exaggerated

spine-shattering *(RM)*   Qualifying adjective indicating extremely pleasurable sexual congress and the subsequent dramatic relief of what might be termed *pelvic tension*; can also be used to describe the similar effect of *coiling a really good one down

spit and polish   The ingredients for success when making your uniform boots and brasswork bright, shiny and clean

Spithead   An area of sea between the Isle of Wight and the entrance to *Pompey harbour which has given its name to the **Spithead pheasant** - a kipper, and a **Spithead nightingale** - the *Bosun's mate's *whistle

spitting distance   Ships that are very close, as when *Razzing, are said to be within *spitting distance* of each other

spitting feathers   Enthusiastic, or rather anxious to get a particular job: *"What do you mean **keen** to go ? I was **spitting feathers** to get selected.."*

spitkid   Bucket, *barrico or old brass shellcase, used as a *gashbin on a messdeck; originally used for spitting into, especially when chewing a plug of tobacco. Now most commonly seen as a large, round aluminium ashtray-cum-*gashbin

splashed *(FAA)*   Shot down (even used over land): *"The Seawolf missile system **splashed** three of the four Argentine Skyhawks as they ran in to attack us.."*

splash-target *(FAA)*   Floating framework towed on a raft behind a warship, but at a safe distance; diving aircraft can then fire rockets or cannon shells at the device. See also *bite !

splice
  1. Join something to something else
  2. Marry: *"When you gettin' spliced ?"*
  3. **Splice the mainbrace** is a special Navy-wide celebratory issue of *pusser's by Royal prerogative. It is also the only time that Officers were allowed a *tot. The last **Splicers** were at the wedding of *Lieutenant The Duke of York RN*, the birth of *Prince William* in '82 (coinciding with the restoration of freedom to the Falklands), the wedding of *Commander The Prince of Wales RN*, and The *Lord High Admiral's *Silver Jubilee* in 1977

split pin   Jack's nickname for a lady who has little trouble in parting her legs

split-arsed matelot   Crude, anatomically-based nickname for a member of the *WRNS; sometimes known more simply as **splits**; someone who *cracks up may also be said to have **split right down the middle**

split-arsed turn *(FAA)*   Tight turn that begins with a half-roll and ends with the second half of a loop in order to reverse course quickly. The term ***split-arsed*** can be used for any reckless manoeuvre

Splot *(FAA)*   The *Senior Pilot* of a squadron: *"I hear that Nick's off to be **Splot** of 849.."*

spoil the ship for a ha'porth of tar   Older phrase that has come ashore to mean that anything that is worth doing should be done properly, and not skimped just to save a small amount of money, because both efficiency and appearance will be affected

spoil your whole day *(FAA / RM)*   Lovely understatement, probably of American origin: *"And above all, please don't walk into the tail rotor while it's turning, because that will **spoil your whole day** - and mine with the paperwork.."*

spondoolicks   19th century Jackspeak word for money: *"Can't go on a *run-ashore tonight - no **spondoolicks**.."*

spoof
  1. Trick or device designed to get a really good *bite; some
     really classic examples include asking for names for:
              - *the famous *Malta dog shoot*
              - **splash-target cox'n*
              - *a Haggis hunt*
     Or sending a new boy for:
              - *a fuse for a *deadlight*
              - *some red and green lamp oil*
              - *the key of the starboard *Watch*
              - *five metres of Fallopian tube*
  2. Deliberate ploy to distract and mislead the enemy
  3. *(FAA)* Guessing game played to establish who buys the wine
     at dinner. See also *horse

sports pages   The romantic or sexy bits of a letter written to Jack
by his *pash

spotted dog   Any *duff with currants or raisins (may therefore
also be known as Dalmatian pudding or duff)

spout   As in *toggle

spring a leak   Pass water, or urinate

springer *(RM)*   Physical Training Instructor

springs   Ropes resricting the *surging or fore-and-aft
movement of a warship when she is *secured to a quay or jetty; these
may need *easing as the ship rises and falls with the tide

sprog   General description of any novice, either to the Navy
or to some branch of the Senior Service, eg. a **sprog pilot.** Said to be
derived from the word for a *baby gannet*, but may also be a portmanteau
word for *frogspawn*, or a confusion between *spocket* and *cog*

Spud   Nickname for the surname Murphy, but note also **spud barber**
- anyone on potato peeling duties

spur-lash   Wonderful excuse for pushing young *middies and *subbies
overboard: *"Ever seen a **spur-lash**, young sirs ? No ? Well, come and
have a look over here then.."*

square   Word used in a number of phrases:
  1. **square meal** - decent *scran; in earlier times, the sailor's
         plates were square and made of wood
  2. **square number** - nice, easy, undemanding job
  3. **square rig** - sailor's uniform (below Petty Officer) with
         square jean material collar, jumper and

buttoned trousers, in contrast to the
*fore-and-aft rig of Petty Officers and above
4. **square yards** - reconciliation process with somebody after a disagreement
5. **squared away** - stowed and secured in a *seamanlike fashion
6. **squared off** - tidied up

Squat, Jack !   Dismissive phrase used to describe official indifference to a sailor's problems: *"An' even if you did ask *Pusser, nine out of ten times the answer would be **Squat, Jack** ! - so what's the point of askin' in the first place, eh ?"*   See also *face aft and salute

squawk *(FAA)*   The semi-automatic process of sending out a numerically coded identification signal to assist the *Air Tragickers

squawk box   *Bulkhead-mounted speaker of a ship's *Tannoy public address system, or any inter-office intercom

squeeze box   Accordion

squeeze up   See *catch the boat up and *blob up(2)

squirt *(FAA)*   Older term for a carrier catapult which **squirted** the aircraft off the front end

squitters   Diarrhoea and frequent, loose bowel motions.   See also *black drizzle, *scatters, *pebbledash and *trots as alternatives

stab   Attempt something, as in: *"Go on - have a **stab** at it.."*

stab out *(FAA)*   Most Naval helicopters have some form of gyroscopic stabilization system which can be switched off: *"By this time he was well *ratted, lurching around the bar, totally **stab out**.."*

stabbing arse   Euphemism for homosexual activity

stack *(FAA)*   Cancellation of the flying programme for some reason, followed by a mass movement to the *Wardroom bar; also an older name for what are now called *funnel uptakes*

stacks *(RM)*   Abbreviation for *stacks of effort*, hence: *"Come on lads, give it **stacks**.."*

stacks rating   Someone who is successful with the ladies and who is *getting yards as opposed to *plums

staff officer   An Officer who has trained at a ***Staff College*** (usually) and who works in an Admiral's or *(RM)* Major-General's Headquarters.   They are members of a general breed which can be either be helpful or unhelpful: *"If you ask him for the time he'll just tell you, in enormous detail, how his watch works.."*

The List

Staffy (FAA)   The **staff officer** - usually *WRNS - of a second-line or training Squadron

stag (esp. *RM*)   Guard duty, or intensive study for an examination: *"He's away **stagging** for his *killick's.."* *This word was* in recorded use during the 18th century for the process of observing, watching or detecting

stagger juice   Any strong spirit, but especially rum

stamps   Of no importance, without power or influence: *"*Reggies are **stamps** when you're home on leave.."* (Not strictly true !)

stanchion   Fixed *deck structure; see also *barrack stanchion

Standard !   Sentry's warning shout on sighting the approaching *Royal Standard* on a car or motor launch

stand by
1. Naval order to get ready to do something
2. Request for someone to wait: *"**Stand by** for just a minute, will you ?"*
3. To be appointed to a warship or submarine that is still in her builder's hands and has yet to be accepted into HM Service: *"I **stood by** CORNWALL while she was building at Yarrow's.."*

stand down   Return to a more relaxed state of alertness after *Action stations, (RM) *standing to or: *"We stood by to assist, but an hour later the Rescue Co-ordination Centre **stood us down**.."*

stand easy
1. *(RM)* Order to relax further after: *"**Stand at ease**.."*
2. A specific period of relaxation built into the normal work routine: *"I'm going to the shop at **stand easy**.."* Interestingly, the *Army* equivalent is a *NAAFI break
3. The **big stand easy** or the **permanent stand easy** are both euphemisms for death

stand fast   Substitute for *except* in conversation, or as in the following typical emergency *pipe: *"For exercise, for exercise, **stand fast** the *Sickbay and medics - FIRE ! FIRE ! FIRE ! - FIRE in the hangar - Attack party and Damage Control teams *close up to the canteen *flat - This is for exercise.."*

stand over   Formal decision for a Captain or Executive Officer, while hearing a disciplinary case at *Defaulters, to close the proceedings and re-open them later - after a specified delay

stand to *(RM)*   The process of manning defensive positions rapidly when under attack, or when attack is expected at the traditional times of first and last light

standing into danger   Maintaining a course that will take the ship into hazardous conditions. To say to someone: *"Listen, you're **standing into danger**.."* implies that if he carries on doing what he is doing, he will get into trouble fairly soon

Standing Orders   The Captain or *HoD's written orders and instructions for what is expected during a normal working day. Any regularly performed *evolution may become a **standing routine**, while a **standing watch** is a period of duty undertaken at the same time each day rather than in the rotation of a normal *watch system

star jumps (esp. *RM*)   In an excitable state; see also *Wall of death and *low hover

star system   Method of denoting seniority within *Flag rank; this runs from **one star** (*Commodore*) up to **five stars** for *Admiral of the Fleet*

starbolins   Older term for members of the starboard *watch

starters *(RM)*   Any lubricant or easing fluid, but especially one designed for personal use on the skin, such as *Vaseline*; see also *stoppers in this latter context for the vital components of Royal's *run-ashore kit

State of the Nation   Traditional nickname for the overall message given by *Father at *clear lower deck when he attempts to explain some new *MoD directive, or a recent Defence White Paper

station card   Small coloured card with Jack's name, messdeck and normal place of duty written on it. This is left on board with the *QM when going ashore, and is also rather wryly known as the *licence to breathe*

stats sheet *(FAA)*   Daily record of all flying undertaken in a squadron; the **stats sheets** are collated and analysed each week

steady   Adjective describing someone who is a reliable *hand; also a word used just prior to the command to cease pulling (or pushing) something

steamer   Jocular nickname for a warship

steamie   Mechanical engineer of any rank or rate who specialises in the fast-disappearing methods of steam propulsion

steaming bats   Shoes with steel toe caps and non-slip moulded soles

steam-shy   A *steamie who has become reluctant to enter the engine-room and its associated machinery spaces

steel-beach barbie   Barbecue held on the ship's flightdeck

steely *(FAA)*   Tough and resolute: *"Two *SHARs against six F-15s ! That's a bit steely, isn't it ?"*

steer   Take up a heading; not confined to ships, but also used for Naval aircraft and in a more general sense: *"Could you give me a steer on this one please - how do I do it ?"*   A **bum steer** refers to bad information, rather than the activities associated with *botty bandits

stick
   1. Punishment of any kind: *"He didn't half give their bowling some stick.."*
   2. A group of passengers formed up to board an aircraft, such as a **stick of parachutists**; the term is derived from a **stick of bombs**

stickler   Someone who insists on the exact letter of any regulation being obeyed; see also *by the book

Sticks   Nickname for a *Royal Marine Bugler*; traditionally, drums were used to beat out orders, followed by a bugle call. All *RM* drummers are trained in these skills, which can be seen to great effect in the *Sunset ceremony or *Beat Retreat

sticks out like ____   Both Jack and Royal have a number of favourite descriptive comparisons for items such as nipples that are especially prominent:
   - *a racing dog's bollocks*
   - *a blind carpenter's thumbs*
   - *organ stops*
   - *brass check fire gong buttons*
   - *chapel hat pegs*

sticky   **Sticky greens** are drinks with a base of *creme de menthe*; tea and **sticky buns**, or **tea and stickies** are both descriptions of any friendly domestic get-together. To Royal, the **Stickies** are members of the Official *IRA* (as opposed to the Provisionals or *Provos*)

Stiggins *(FAA)*   Spotty, immature and rather ill-mannered jet pilot from John Winton's novel *HMS LEVIATHAN*. A caricature of the *Fleet Air Arm* needless to say, but a revealing one: *"Our new Commander seems to think that all Sub-Lieutenants with wings on their sleeves are called Stiggins.."*

Still !   The *pipe made for *Silence and stand still* at *Colours

Stills   Nickname applied to *Bennies soon after a local order came out in the Falklands banning the use of the latter term, because - as the logic ran - whatever else you called them, they were **still** *Bennies. However, note the locals' superb riposte concerning *Whens

Stimulator *(FAA)*   *Sea King and *SHAR cockpit simulators with excellent visual and motion systems that can actually convince a pilot he is coping with a real emergency and get his *adrenalin flowing !

stitch up   Any procedure, trick or *spoof which sets an *oppo up for embarrassment or trouble. Derived from the old trick of **stitching up** the legs of a pair of trousers; getting a good *bite has much the same intent: *"They promised me a gorgeous blonde, which is what I got, but nobody said anything about her husband ! I was well and truly* **stitched up**.." Or: *"'Oo put me down fer duty on New Year's Eve ? It's a bleedin' **stitch-up**, that's what it is !"*

stocious   Angry, unreasonable, drunk, or all three at the same time

Stokes   Nickname for any stoker; **Stokie boy** is the *SM* equivalent

stone frigate   Any Naval base or shore establishment with a ship's name

stoned   Despite the *civvy connotation with drugs, Jack still uses this word in relation to drunkenness

stonker   Erection; see also *lob and *lazy lob

stonking *(RM)*   Heavy artillery or mortar barrage: *"3 PARA suffered seriously from Argentinian 155's in an all-day* **stonking** *of Mount Longdon after they had taken this objective.."*

stoofed   An aircraft crash into the sea or ground, but may also be used in the non-aviation sense: *"He tried to *trap that gorgeous *Wren-O who's the Admiral's PA - but stoofed in completely.."*

stooge around   Cruise or fly about in an area while observing

stoppage   Punishment characterized by the withdrawal of some privilege, as in **stoppage of leave** etc. May also be used in a social sense: *"Didn't enjoy the weekend much - the Missus had me on stoppage.."* **Stoppage of wine bill** is a specific punishment that denies any alcoholic drinks to an officer; the jamming of an automatic weapon leads to the performance of **stoppage drills**

stopped his clock   Another euphemism for death; see also the big *stand-easy

stoppers *(RM)*   Local anaesthetic jelly used to delay onset of the *vinegar strokes; see also *starters

stopping   Anything used to seal a leak, or to secure a furled sail

Stores   Items designed to be left on the shelf because, according to *pusser's logic, if they were meant to be given out, then they would have been called *Issues*!

stovie *(FAA)*   Member of the fast jet community, so-called because of the **stove-pipe** appearance (and flaming afterburners) of their jet engine exhausts

stow   Put an article away in a secure and safe manner; *Stow it !* or *Stow your tits !* are both ways of saying: *"Shut up and be quiet !"*

straddle   The process in Naval gunnery of getting hits on both sides of a target, ie. the salvo is *Bang on target !*

straight rush   Older term for boiled meat and vegetables, all cooked, served and eaten in a great hurry

Straight up ? / Straight up !   *"Is that true ?"* or: *"Honest, that's exactly what happened !"*

strapadicktomy   Jack's description of Lesbian activity

strap-on job   Another rude name for a *split-pin

strapped   Very short of some commodity, eg. **strapped for cash**

streak of piss   A long, thin and generally weedy-looking person

striker   Usual name for an assistant, perhaps a title inherited from the sailing-ship days of Second Mates who used to hit hard - and often

Heads

strike   The process of lowering anything that has been elevated or hoisted, hence **strike your colours** - to surrender

striking down
  1. Lower cargo or equipment into a hold using a crane or lifting tackle
  2. Term used in aircraft carriers to describe the removal of aircraft (at the end of *Flying Stations) from the flight deck, via the main or side lifts, into the hangar below

Stringbag (FAA)   Affectionate nickname for the WW2 *Swordfish* naval torpedo carrier aircraft that slowed the *BISMARCK* and also badly damaged the Italian battle fleet at *Taranto

stripe basis   Method of *divvying up the cost of a *Wardroom function so that a *Subby with one stripe pays a single share, whereas a *Sergeant (*Commander*) pays for three

Stroll on !   *"Well I never..!"*

strop   Any made-up rope used for lifting purposes - or a strap used in helicopter winching, but note also the word **stroppy** as an abbreviation of *obstreporous* - someone who is in an argumentative mood and spoiling for a fight. See *Jack Strop in this latter context

struck down
  1. (for action) Anything that can be tied down or thrown over the side before battle is **struck down** to avoid its conversion into flying and potentially lethal splinters
  2. (*FAA*) The opposite of *ranging, ie. the process of moving aircraft from the flightdeck down into the hangar as in *strike down

stuck in   *Get stuck in !* is a traditional exhortation to do better, whereas to get **stuck across** someone has connotations of a *legover

study for Staff College (*RM*)   Fall asleep !

stuff of greatness   Sardonic but traditional remark directed at poor quality *Wardroom food

stumper   See *wolverine for definition; *coyote and *wildebeeste are alternatives

Sub / sub
  1. A **Sub-Lieutenant** *RN* (may also be a **Subby**)
  2. Stand in, or substitute for an *oppo in a *watch bill: *"Do me a sub this afternoon will you, Shiner ?"*
  3. A loan of money: *"Anyone got a fiver to sub me ?"* (See also *rub)
  4. (rarely) A submarine !

submariner's shower / dust bath　　Rapid once-over with a tin of *foo-foo powder before going ashore; a **submariner's dhobey** refers to a similar procedure, but with a bottle of deodorant instead

substantive　　Confirmed in a rank or appointment, usually after a period in the *Acting rank

suck back　　An *Uckers ploy according to *Wafu rules which drags an opponent's counter backwards just before it can reach home; if this is achieved around the corner it becomes a **bendy suck-back**. The process of changing your mind about something or reversing a decision can be announced with: *"Suck back ten..!"*

sucker's gap *(FAA)*　　Temporary improvement in poor airfield weather conditions; those aircrew eager to *commit aviation can then find themselves unable to return when the weather *clamps soon afterwards

sucking on the hind tit　　At the bottom of the promotion ladder, or the last in a line

sucking the monkey　　Wonderful *dodge pulled in the West Indies by Jack in older times when he would fill coconuts ashore with rum and then bring them back on board, thus leading to bouts of unexplained drunkenness that must have had the *crushers going spare !

suds　　Beer

sun over the yardarm　　Traditional observation made at midday on the Equator; it has now become a more general cue for the first alcoholic drink of the day

Supplementary List　　Officers entered on limited duration Commissions, only some of which are pensionable (unlike the *General List) but whose specialist skills are in particular demand; **SL aviators** of the *Fleet Air Arm* form the biggest group. Note also the traditional descriptions of **SL shag** and **GL smoothie**

surge　　Move with a wave

survivor's tot　　Similar to an *arduous duty tot, and still available for issue to the rescued survivors of *ditching or shipwreck

SUSO　　American importation directed at those who are not trying hard enough - *Shape Up or Ship Out*; see also *FIFO for Royal's version of these sentiments

suzzies (a word usually uttered with a low growl)　　Suspenders

'swain　　Abbreviation for *boatswain (bo'sun) or *coxswain (cox'n); the **'swain** element means *husband*, as explained in *ship husbandry

swallow the anchor   Retire from a career at sea

swamp / *Swampy*   Nocturnal enuresis, ie. bedwetting, which can also occur in older men who have been drinking heavily and **swamp** their *pits. The nickname *Swampy* often sticks unfairly in these cases, but is also traditional for anyone with the surname Marsh

swanning about   Wandering around in a generally aimless way, usually while awaiting orders or instructions

swapping spit   Graphically accurate term for kissing !

sweating neaters   Very anxious state; a Captain who is **sweating on his Flag** is involved in and highly concerned about possible promotion to Rear Admiral

sweeps   Any cleaner, but especially the *RM* *block sweeps; also the mine-sweeping cables towed by mine warfare vessels

swept-up
1. De-luxe: *"I've got the **swept-up** version of that estate car.."*
2. Knowledgeable: *"You'll need to be pretty **swept-up** on fuel control systems when the *Trappers arrive next week.."*

swig   Short pull on a rope or a drink: *"C'mon, Barney - let's have a **swig** of yer *goffer.."*

swimmer   Old Navy term for a sailor who was once a prisoner, but chose a life at sea rather than in gaol; nowadays the **swimmer of the watch** is a life-saver dressed to enter the water if required

swindle sheet   Any expense claim !

swing
1. **swing it** - arrange or achieve something
2. execution - *"I'll see you **swing for it.**"*
3. **swing the lead** - malinger, or pretend to work
4. **swing around the buoy** - have nothing much to do
5. **swing the lamp** - tell stories, usually highly coloured

switched-on   Alert; *RM* usage also has **switched on to custard** for someone who is particularly dozy. Jack may be described, in an opposite sense and when in *Pompey, as being **switched to Brickwoods** (ale) but **switched-off** is the commoner term. See also *thumb in bum, mind in neutral; a **switch-op** is a *WRNS* telephone operator

switched to transmit   Someone who always talks and never listens

swopsies   Something that has been acquired in an exchange

swords and medals   Formal occasion for an officer, eg. for a ceremonial parade but also used in another, almost disciplinary sense:

"I stood my ground with the Admiral's staff, and it almost became a **swords and medals** *job until someone high up, maybe even the *Flag Officer himself, realised that I might be right after all.."*

syphon the python   Yet another way to *pump ship

TANGO

(the) Table   Generic name for a *Defaulter's parade. usually qualified by the title of whichever Officer is investigating the charges or conducting proceedings, eg. **Captain's Table, XO's Table, OOD**'s (*Officer Of the Day's*) **Table** etc. Note that the *United States Navy* equivalent is a *Mast*

table money   Entertainment allowance made to Flag and Commanding Officers to ensure that providing the traditional and official hospitality of the *RN* does not leave them too far out of pocket

tack in a pint of water   A really handy sailing ship; nowadays reserved for sailing dinghies that are particularly responsive to the helm

tactical   Taking precautions not to be detected, ie. maintaining radio silence, getting blacked-out and moving as quietly as possible: *"Sssh ! We've gone tactical !"*

Taff   Nickname for those with the surname Evans, Williams - or any Welshman

TAG *(FAA)*   *Telegraphist Air Gunner*, and the salt of the wartime *Fleet Air Arm*; in the *Stringbag the **TAG** was responsible for *WT communication and air defence with a single machine gun. The **TAG**s are the forerunners of today's *Aircrewman* branch and have a thriving Association, with regular get-togethers

tailor-made   A factory-manufactured *tickler as opposed to the roll-your-own product

take charge (esp. *RM*)   Expression used in a personal, rather than in a leadership sense: *"Breathe properly, you *big girl's blouse ! Come on, take charge of yourself !"*

take the con   Assume directional control of a warship or submarine

taken aback   Expression that has come ashore for surprise or the effect of something unexpected; this stems from a sudden wind shift at sea that struck the sails from the wrong direction and caused the ship almost to stop

taken off / on charge   A valuable, attractive or important stores item is **taken on charge** when issued, ie. the event is recorded in a *Permanent Loan Record* book and the item must be then be accounted for at regular intervals. The more dramatic form of **struck off charge** may be used to describe a *FAA* aircraft that has crashed (or been put up for disposal by sale)

talent   Quality *clacker in a pub, disco - or at a party

talk into the big white telephone   Euphemism for the procedure of vomiting into a lavatory bowl, usually whilst promising never *ever* to drink again

talking baggage / Nav bag *(FAA)*   Rather disparaging Pilot nicknames for their Observers

tally
1. **Cap tally** - the blue cap ribbon bearing the ship's name blocked out in gold lettering. An exception to this is the *SM* world where the **cap tally** simply states *HM SUBMARINES*. Note also the expression **different ships - different cap tallies*
2. A **Pusser's tally** is any *nom-de-plume* used by Jack when staying ashore in a place like **Aggie Weston's*

tame Crab *(FAA)*   *RAF* officer serving in a Naval aviation billet on an exchange basis, usually excellent men who enter into the spirit of things by developing a shaving rash that can only be resolved by growing a *full set

tampion   Ornamental plug for the barrel of a gun, a name that has been modified and commercially adapted elsewhere

(the) Tank *(SM)*   Nickname for the *Submarine Escape Training Tower* at HMS *DOLPHIN*, a prominent feature on the Gosport skyline near Portsmouth. All those who aspire to *Dolphins must make a free ascent from the bottom (120 feet) wearing escape gear. The instructors are splendidly fit men capable of free-diving (just like dolphins !) in the opposite direction, which they all do once a year for an underwater photograph

Tank   Inevitable nickname for anyone with the surname Sherman

Black-catter

tanked up   Drunk or inebriated: *"Johnno was getting tanked-up, so we *scrubbed round the other nightclub and dragged him back to the ship.."*

Tanky   Old nickname for the *Navigation Officer* who, amongst his other duties, is responsible for the storage of fresh water and its effect on the ballast trim of the ship. ***Fresh-water Tanky*** is generally the *Navigator's Yeoman*, and is the *killick who is responsible for the condition and maintenance of all these drinking water storage tanks and filters, as well as the daily sounding of their contents. In the era of the *Tot he also had another equally crucial role as part of the team that *mustered outside the Spirit Room when **Up Spirits !* was *piped

Tannoy   A internal main broadcasting system in a ship or shore establishment; the name is applied indiscriminately even if that system is not actually made by *Messrs. Tannoy plc*

Tap tap   Nickname for the ship's Chinese cobbler, if carried; *Snobs was the nickname for an amateur cobbler in a previous era

taped   Abbreviation of **tape-measured**, in the sense that someone who has a job **taped** has it measured in all respects and can now complete the task with both speed and certainty

tapped   Two different applications:
1. To be **tapped for** a fiver means that some *oppo has borrowed £5 from you
2. To be **tapped up** implies that some *brownhatter has made an approach or advance to you

Taranto *(FAA)*   The Fleet Air Arm's epic night attack on the Italian naval base at **Taranto**; twenty *Stringbags from the carrier HMS *ILLUSTRIOUS* equipped with long-range tanks, and dropping bombs, flares and eleven torpedoes (fitted with newly-designed *Duplex* magnetic firing pistols that allowed the *tin fish to pass beneath torpedo nets before exploding *under* the steel hulls) took out the anchored Italian battle fleet as an effective force, despite their many defensive precautions. Only two of the *Swordfish* aircraft were lost; one crew survived to imprisonment. The ***Men of Taranto***, and their justly-celebrated feat are remembered on or near the anniversary of ***November 11th 1940*** wherever *FAA* and former Royal Naval aviators gather around the world. The message behind Churchill's summary: *"By this single stroke the balance of naval power in the Mediterranean was decisively altered.."* was one also well-heeded by the Imperial Japanese Navy. *Nearly thirteen months later they staged something of a* repeat performance - at **Pearl Harbor**, Hawaii, on Sunday ***December 7th*** 1941

tarbreeks   Jack's older name for a sailor whose speech was laden with *Avasts* and *Belays*

target *(SM)*   According to submarine lore there are only two kinds of vessels that go to sea - other submarines, and **targets** !

tarmac tiff   Parade ground instructor; see also *tick tock tiff

tarpaulin   Originally *tarpawling*, this was old sailcloth dressed with tar and cut up by Jack to make waterproof clothing for wet or heavy weather. Later on the name described, as it still does today, a heavy waterproof material used to cover hatches and deck cargo. A **tarpaulin captain** was a 17th/18th century officer who had risen to his command position on merit and experience rather than influence at Court like a *Gentleman Captain; a **tarpaulin muster** was the precursor of the modern day *kitty, because it refers to Jack's pooling of resources prior to a *run-ashore

Tarzan course *(RM)*   Agility and co-ordination test conducted against clock as part of the *Commando course at *Lympstone; not for the faint-hearted or those frightened of heights

'tash *(RM)*   A **moustache**, the growing of which is strictly Royal's privilege - except on those ocasions when Jack decides to have a **'tash growing** competition, for charity, while at sea

tatticks Tactics: *"Doan' listen ter humm - 'e couldna fight hus way o wet pepper bag, boot the boogger's allus talkin' **tatticks**..."*

taut ship   An efficient, smart and well-disciplined ship in which there is very little slack: *"He ran a **taut ship** down South and it really showed in the results.."* A **taut hand** is a general expression used to describe someone possessed of these same qualities

tea and stickies   Formal afternoon tea in the sense that cake, sandwiches or *sticky buns are served, hence its current usage to describe generous hospitality, perhaps as a precursor to a *bramah *Up Homers

tea boat   Originally a pot of tea, now the kitty, or a money pool collected for provision of tea *makings

Teacher *(SM)*   Nickname for the Officer in charge of the *Perisher course who lives cheek-by-jowl with his students, as they put the *Perisher boat through the increasingly complex *evolutions that he demands of them. All the while **Teacher** is watching, correcting, encouraging, worrying - and then, if necessary, sacking

teased-out   Well-worn, rather like a frayed rope's end: *"What's up with Chiefy ? He's been looking rather tired and **teased-out** recently.."*

Technicolour yawn   An episode of vomiting; see *Dockyard omelette for a complete list of alternatives

Teeny-weeny airways *(FAA)*   *Junglie nickname for the light helicopters of the *3rd Commando Brigade Air Squadron* based alongside them at *Yeovilton

tell-tale   A repeater instrument (eg. the compass in the Captain's *cabin)

Tell that to the Marines !   When *flying fish* were being described to general disbelief at *William IV*'s Court, it was a *Captain of Marines* who confirmed the traveller's tale. The Royal response was that, henceforth, when the truth of a story needed verifying, his Marines would do this job

telling-bone   Telephone; see *bone for an interesting assortment

tender to _____   A smaller ship lying alongside a larger one in harbour, or a small Naval establishment linked administratively to a larger one nearby

tent peg *(FAA)*   Euphemism for crashing fatally on land; *smoked, *spear in and *stoof are alternatives

(the) **texture never varies, only the depth**   The material referred to is *manure* and the phrase describes someone who is always in trouble !

Thames barges   Very large shoes or steaming *bats. Another expression in this context: *"Those aren't shoes, sunshine..they're the boxes that they came in.."*

That is all !   Traditional phrase used to end any *pipe that begins with the words *D'ye hear there ?

thickers   Condensed milk; see additional reference under *B's

thief's cat   A special *cat'o'nine tails in which the ropes were knotted along their length to inflict extra damage; a thief might also be punished by *cobbing or the *gauntlet for less serious crimes

thing *(RM)*   Lovely label for a useless individual: *"What's my opinion of him ? Well sir, that man - that man is a **thing**.."*

thinks bubble *(FAA)*   Cartoon device carried over into real life: *"Approach told me to report when I was passing south *abeam the field. When I reminded them that we were twenty miles to the north, you could almost see a big **thinks bubble** forming in the distance over the Control Tower.."*

third nostril   Amusing simile: *"It will be about as much use to you as a ruddy **third nostril**.."* See also *ashtray and *chocolate

third pronger *(FAA)*   Pilot who goes to *Lynx and a Ship's Flight after gaining his *Wings, thereby leaving the two other training pipelines that flow towards the *Pinger or *Junglie worlds

thirst after righteousness   Paraphrase of the Biblical expression, used in this context to describe the first *wet taken in the *Wardroom after Church service on Sunday !

thirty miler *(RM)*   Final *Commando pass-out test for the *green beret; a *thirty mile* group *yomp aross Dartmoor, in fighting order, while carrying weapons, safety stores and a radio. The time allowed is eight hours for recruits, seven-and-a-half hours for *YOs

thousand miler   A piece of *kit that has seen much service during its time, or an item of clothing that gets *dhobeyed at these intervals

threaders (esp. *RM*)   Run ragged, or about to blow one's top in a very big way: *"On the bus, off the bus - and then on the bloody bus again - the boys were getting really **threaders** by now.."* A contraction of the word **threadbare**

three and one   Three parts water to one of rum, ie. *grog; note that this was this was originally **two and one**

three badge   In possession of three *Good Conduct Badges*, displayed as three chevrons (not to be confused with those of an *Army* /

RM Sergeant) and worn on the sleeve of Jack's uniform suit up to, and including, the rank of *Petty Officer*. An *AB who is a **three-badger** is often a stalwart of great experience and character who has not sought promotion during his career

three sheets to the wind   Older description of a sail that is almost out of control because its **sheets** - or control ropes - are flapping in the wind. Now used to describe someone who is drunk; see *legless for a complete listing of the regular terms

three-Yankee   A very high *Damage Control condition of watertightness. When Jack describes a fellow rating as being in **three-Yankee** he implies that the chap is a bit *piso and reluctant to damage the contents of his pockets by paying for a round of drinks

throbbing   Socially active and exciting: *"Fort Lauderdale in June ? The place was absolutely **throbbing**.."*

throw off   Deflection in gunnery practice which must be incorporated into any calculations in order to avoid actually hitting and thus destroying the (expensive) target

throw the book at ___   When referring to *QRRN the expression implies that someone has committed a number of misdemeanours, or a single offence so serious that a number of charges can be *framed against him: *"Of course that was the last straw, so *Father **threw the book** at him.."*

throwing   Adjective used to mock someone being pompous about wine: *"What would you like to drink after dinner ? I've got a rather nice little **throwing** brandy.."*

thruster   Ambitious and determined officer: *"Mike's being a typical *In Zone **thruster** at the moment. Hope he gets promoted and back to normal soon.."*

thumb up bum, mind in neutral   Apt description of someone who is day-dreaming while on a task, and therefore not paying the necessary attention; may be abbreviated as *TUBMIN. See also *switched-off

thundie   *Thunderflash*; an enlarged banger used for simulating the explosion of a hand-grenade, or for emergency signalling underwater as when recalling divers to the surface. *Bopper is an alternative

Thursday War   Combined air, sea and sub-surface exercises held on *Thursdays* off *Portland as part of a warship's *work up to operational readiness

tick in the box   Some routine stage in a ship or officer's progress: *"I went and did that course, but it was only to get a **tick in the box**.."*

tick tocking   Marching badly on a parade ground, swinging the right arm with the right leg in a very awkward-looking motion; a **tick tock tiff**, like a *tarmac tiff, is a Naval drill instructor

ticket
1. Certificate of Qualification: *"I got my Officer of the Watch ticket in BRILLIANT.."*
2. Expression of approval: *"That's just the ticket !"*
3. *(FAA)* Instrument Flying qualification

ticklers   Shredded or cut tobacco - also known as *pusser's leaf - issued to the old Navy in half-pound tins at duty free prices. The scale of issue was one pound per person per month, as cigarette or pipe tobacco. Cigarettes which were self-rolled in this way also became known as **ticklers**. The actual origin of the term is most interesting, because around 1904 jam preserves became *issue, and one of the main suppliers were **Messrs. Ticklers** ! A new class of rating joining for only twelve year's service was also created at about this time; these men much preferred the shredded baccy to the tough plugs of pipe tobacco smoked (or chewed) by the old salts, and they were themselves immediately and rather disdainfully labelled as *Ticklers*. The actual creation of these traditional plugs is discussed at the entry for *prick. The shredded tobacco could also be made up into *tailor-mades, by a contractor with a cigarette-making machine mounted on the back of his truck which came round the larger shore establishments. These cigarettes would incorporate the ship's crest in the paper, obviously the antecedents of *blue liners ! Note also the term *Jack-me-tickler - a sailor who knows all the answers

tiddly   A bit tiddly - slightly drunk or merry

tiddley
1. Tidy, of neat appearance. A **tiddley suit** is Jack's Number One uniform suit, often tailor-made rather than issued from *Slops, and always kept clean and neatly pressed in a *messdeck locker or hanging space
2. Details, often of ceremonial or procedure: *"The *Master-at-Arms will precede you on *Rounds to do the tiddley bits.."*

tiddy oggy   Traditional nickname for a Cornish pasty, and an older name for a sailor born and bred in Devonport

tide over   Another old sailing term that has come ashore to a wider meaning. Ships beating down the English Channel against the prevailing winds could not also make headway against a flood tide; instead they would drop the *pick until the tide began to ebb, thus **tiding over** the temporary difficulty

Tiff / Tiffy   Nickname for an Artificer

Grog rat

Tiger / tiger
1. Nickname for a big strong lad
2. Occasional nickname for a steward: *"I was the *Captain's tiger in ARROW.."*
3. **Tigernuts** are prolapsed haemorrhoids - see also *bumplums

'tilly   Shortened version of the (Bedford) **Utilicon** van, now a word used in its own right for almost any kind of light transport

Timber   Nickname associated with the surname Woods

timbershifting   Cheating; originally from moving the matchsticks used to score with at cribbage. The word is now employed in *Uckers as well. See also **fifteen-two that bastard !*

timberwolf   An ugly lady or *gronk; the **timberwolf** is supposed to eat through its own leg if caught in a snare or trap. Should Jack or Royal *trap a **timberwolf**, he would rather do the same thing than wake her up by removing his arm from around her the following morning ! *Coyote, *stumper, *wolverine and *wildebeeste are variations on this rather cruel theme, but then see *booze as well

tin fish   Torpedo

tin man   Older expression for someone trying to dominate any conversation or discussion without having the necessary knowledge or experience, and therefore in danger of being knocked down like the **tin** and **man-sized** targets on a rifle range: *"Don't you come / go the tin man with me !"*

tin trousers   A Captain's Mess Dress uniform trousers embellished with *lightning conductors

titfer   Hat; Cockney rhyming slang

tits
1. Tomatoes in tomato sauce - see *-ITS
2. Expression of annoyance: *"He gets right on my tits.."*

3. *"It's about as much use as **tits on a bull**.."*
4. A **tit hammock** is a 44 inch D-cup brassiere

tits up (esp. *FAA*)   Lying on its back, ie. broken or useless: *"We were due to *launch at *oh seven dubs, but the aircraft went **tits up** as we taxyed out.."*

Tizzysnatcher   Very old nickname for the Paymaster (now part of the *white empire); a **tizzy** was Cockney slang for a sixpence

Toasts of the week (*Sotto voce* additions in brackets !)
Monday : *Our ships at sea*
Tuesday : *Our men*
Wednesday : *Ourselves* (since no-one else will think of us)
Thursday : *A bloody war or a sickly season* (and quick promotion)
Friday : *A willing foe - and sea room*
Saturday : *Sweethearts and wives* (may they never meet !)
Sunday : *Absent friends*

toddy   Rum (or whisky) with hot water and lemon

toe-rag (esp. *RM*)   Frequent term of abuse: *"Just look at him working on the *Boss - the snivelling **toe-rag**.."*

toe rot   Athlete's foot, or any other fungal infection of the skin - often used with the qualification *chinky

toe the line   Older Naval term that has now come ashore. When the ship's company was *mustered for *victualling or pay, each sailor stepped forward to a line marked on deck and then gave his name and place of duty in the ship. This has developed ashore into an expression which indicates an acknowledgement of authority and a willingness to obey the rules

toggle and two   The male genital apparatus: *"Well - wozzit a baby boy then?" "Fink so - at least it 'ad a **toggle an' two**.."*
A **toggle pin** can alo be found opposite a *becket on a duffle coat

toggle-oggling   Gazing at someone else's *parts, eg. in a stand-up urinal: *"Shiny shoes you've got !"* Or: *"New shoes ?"* *Snurging is another name for this activity

tombola   Shipboard version of bingo or lotto: *"You've got skin like the lee side of a **tombola ticket**.."*

tonsil varnish (older)   Strong tea

took the wind out of his sails   A *windward vessel steals the wind from another to *leeward*; this can be seen in the *covering* tactics that are supposed to make the *America's Cup* races exciting. The expression is now used ashore for someone who is rather *taken aback and splutteringly speechless

Crusher

UNIFORM

UA   Entry made in the ship's *Victualling Book,* in the days of the *Tot, against the names of all ratings **Under** twenty years of **Age** who were not entitled to draw a *tot of *grog

Uckers   The old family game of ludo, modified by Jack to include strategy and tactics, and played at all levels throughout the *Royal Navy* from minesweepers to the *Yacht. The piling up of counters creates *blobs which, depending on their size, require varying challenges to overcome. A *mixy blob loses those challenge rights. *Wafu rules are not played in *General Service, but include such subtleties as *suck backs and *siff on his donk. See also *double six, *Out piece and hack !, *Look for the rules !, *Up table !, *Up tit !, and *eight piece dicking

Ugh man *(FAA)*   The grunt of effort *Ugh !* associated with a big, strong individual lifting a heavy weight; usually involved *stovie *bombheads of a past era who all seemed to be well-built *muscle bosuns

ugly   Some choice figures of speech used by both Jack and Royal when describing a certain lack of feminine beauty:
- *She wasn't ugly, she was _____ing ugly !*

- *Her mouth looked like a torn pocket..*

- *Her *moosh deserved its own *Hurt Certificate..*

- *And her teeth ! They reminded me of a row of condemned houses*

- *Helen of Troy's face launched a thousand ships - this one would have caused the boys to *scuttle the fleet..*

- *Trying to describe her face is difficult, but she looked a bit like a bulldog chewing a wasp..*

- *Every time she stood up, I thought someone had switched the bleedin' lights out..*

- *She told me she worked for an airline - if it's true, then she must bump-start them Jumbo jets..*

- *She was as ugly as a robber's dog..*

- *'Er teeth stuck out so far it looked like 'er nose was playin' a piano..*

- *Honest, her face was enough to stop a clock*

ullage   Worthless residue in a beer barrel, can also be used to describe the overall quality of a group

ulu *(FAA and RM)*   The Malay word for *jungle*, sometimes written incorrectly as *ooloo*; now employed conversationally to describe any remote location that might be occupied by *Junglies or *Booties - even in Arctic Norway

uncork   Older term for decoding a signal

under way   Strictly speaking, no longer secured; a ship that *slips and proceeds is **getting under way** as she starts to move, and **making way** when well established in forward motion

undetected crime   In Jack's eyes, fifteen years of this is what the *Blue Peter or *pea-do is awarded for

unhook   Older term for *proffing

Unknown Warrior   Used, without any disrespect intended, to describe a total *sack rat: *"He spends more time in his bunk than the Unknown Warrior.."*

unlatched   Term used for someone on detached and loan duty away from his normal appointment

unscheduled sunrise *(FAA)*   The effect of detonating a nuclear weapon; see also *bucket of sunshine and *CND

Up Spirits !   *Pipe made in the era of the *Tot to initiate the daily collection and issue of *pusser's from the Spirit Room

Up table !   Ploy in *Uckers, used to end the game by lifting the table and causing the counters to slide off. As in *Look for the rules !* the fist size and degree of inebriation of your opponents should be very carefully considered before employing this tactic

Up tit !   Exhortation to move a counter forward on the *Uckers board after dice have been thrown

up homers   Any family hospitality shown to Jack when he is away from his own home; see page U - 313

up my nose   Frequently heard expression indicating annoyance with someone: *"Usually he's a really good *hand, but his whole attitude to this particular problem gets right up my nose.."*   See also *tits

up sticks *(RM)*   *Turn to, strike camp and get *yomping; see also *pull pole

up the line   Up country somewhere from *Guzz or *Pompey, but generally at home

up to speed (on something)   Briefed and fully aware of the facts or details of a case: *"Are you up to speed on the latest developments concerning the replacement amphibious ships ?"*

up top   On deck or *topsides

uphill gardener   One of the many alternatives for *brownhatter

Upper Deck   Collective noun for the officers in a ship; *Clear Upper Deck !* implies a gathering of all those officers in the *Wardroom for a briefing - or *bollocking.

Upper Scupper   Technically, this is the weather deck, or No. 1 Deck, but the term is often used by the *lower deck to mock some piece of deliberately Officer-like behaviour: *"I say, old chap - that was just a bit **upper scupper**, don't you think ?"*

Upper Yardie   A rating under 21 who has been commissioned as an Officer, ie. someone who is rising quickly through the ranks, rather like the specially selected **Upper Yardsmen** in the sailing ships of old, climbing rapidly up the masts in order to reef or trim the topsails

upside-down head   A bald man with a beard; see also *VFR

upstairs *(SM)*   The surface of the sea

uptake   Correct name for a warship's funnel

U/S (esp. *FAA*)   Abbreviation for **unserviceable** - an expression that is rather difficult for American exchange officers to come to terms with !

uselessness   Note the terms *ashtray on a motorbike, *chocolate fireguard and *third nostril, but in a more general sense of describing a totally useless person these gems may occasionally be heard:
- He couldn't pull the skin off a rice pudding

- He couldn't spot a new sixpence on a chimney-sweep's backside

- He couldn't fight his way out of a wet paper bag

Up homers

VICTOR

Van Heusen   Famous clothing manufacturer who advertised a *semi-stiff collar* as a feature of his shirts; quickly adopted by Jack to describe a *lazy lob, or incomplete erection

Vasco   Classic nickname for the *Navigating Officer*, from **Vasco da Gama**, the 16th century Portuguese explorer

Velcro back   Someone who is stuck to his *pit; a similar expression to *canvas back

Velcro rating   A man who has been promoted to and then demoted from the same rank on several occasions in his career: *"He's been made up to *killick and then busted down that many times, his badges must be backed with **Velcro**.."*

verbal   Encouragement or vocal support: *"Don't just stand there and watch your team, lads - give it some **verbal** !"*

vertrep   Amalgamated word for *vertical replenishment,* now widely used for any stores ashore or at sea that are delivered by helicopter

Very good, sir !   Affirmative and positive response to a steering order

very seldom up top   Bald as a coot; may also be termed an *upside-down head

vetting   Screening process for an appointment; all Naval personnel are supposed to be *Normally* **Vetted** to a certain degree. Some, in sensitive appointments, are also *Positively* **Vetted** or **PV**'d

VFR on top, IFR below *(FAA)*   The acronyms stand for *Visual* and *Instrument Flying Rules,* and the whole phrase refers to a bald, bearded man.   See also *upside-down head

vicky verky   Jack's traditional mis-pronounciation of the Latin phrase *vice versa*

victualled
1. On the ship's **Victualling Book,** ie. living on board
2. **Well victualled** - first class food and drink
3. *"Is our Caterer competent ? I tell you, the fellow couldn't victual two woodpeckers into Sherwood Forest.."*
4. Note the special *RM* application of *vittled up

vin d'honneur   Formal invitation by the *Wardroom, for an Officer who is leaving the ship, to attend for lunchtime drinks as their guest

vinegar strokes   The phase immediately prior to orgasm, or as Jack would put it: *"Almost there !"*   This is also the last opportunity to get out at *Fratton

visual *(FAA)*   Single word used in radio traffic to indicate that something is in sight: *"Roger, visual the tower.."* Or: *"I have you visual, James !"*

vino collapso   Any rough, strong local wine

virginity screen   Canvas *dodger rigged across a ladder or *companionway to stop Jack looking up the skirts of lady visitors to the ship. This is the polite version of a much cruder phrase

virgins on the verge   Jack's amusing nickname for a group of Officers who seem collectively unable to make their minds up

vittled up *(RM)*   Special application of the word *victualled* to describe the impact of machine-gun bullets or cannon fire, as in strafing: *"We were in HMS PLYMOUTH on June 8th when she was vittled up good and proper by a gaggle of Argentinian Air Force Mirages.."* *Some of those bullet marks can still be seen on the old war horse,* now alongside as memorial and floating museum at Millbay Dock, Plymouth

VMT   Abbreviated signal group for *Very Many Thanks*

vodka & Windolene   Jack's wry description of an imaginary *wet which gives you much the same headache the morning after as any other mixture, but at least with this one you can see clearly !

volret   (Premature) **voluntary retirement**; composite word which can also be used as a verb: *"I'm volretting next year.."* See also *PVR

Hurt Certificate

Whisky

wacky baccy   Cannabis

wafter   WW2 term for a convoy escort vessel which wafted the ships in a convoy from place to place. The word achieved public recognition in a recent television advertisement: *"Were you truly **wafted** here from Paradise ?" "Nah, mate - Luton Airport !"*

wah-wah *(RM)*   Royal's generic name for a cavalry officer - based on the noise that a group of them make in conversation; see also *Rupert

Wafu   *General service nickname for a member of the *Fleet Air Arm*, or anything to do with the *FAA*; the acronym is supposed to stand for *Wet And (Flipping) Useless*. It is in fact derived from the *Pusser's stores category of **WAFU** which used to be applied to the sleeveless, anti-static and sheepskin-lined leather jerkins for issue only to *Weapon And Fuel Users* like *chockheads, *bombheads and Air mechanics, especially when they had to work up on the cold, windswept and spark-dangerous spaces of an aircraft carrier's flight deck. Some authorities spell the word as **Wafoo** and state that this is because the embarked squadrons in a carrier have the operating philosophy of *We always fly off - offshore !*

waister   Older term used by Jack for an incompetent novice, incapable of doing anything really useful on a ship such as climbing the mast and getting out on the *yards. Instead, all he could do usefully was swab the deck in the ship's **waist** and pull on ropes

Walcheren *(RM)*   *Corps memorable date of 1944 now commemorated every November 1st; this difficult amphibious assault cleared the entrance to the Scheldt river and was crucial to Allied operations in the Low Countries

Wall of Death (esp. *RM*)   The excitable state of a Senior NCO or officer when he is responsible for something that's either about to go wrong - or has just done so. See also *star jumps and *high hover

wall-safe   At sea, the equivalent of a *File 13. The request to *put* something in the **wall-safe** is much the same as saying: *"Chuck it through the *scuttle!"*

Wakey, wakey!   Traditional early morning *bosun's call, heard in the *Royal Navy* long before *Billy Cotton* made the phrase his trademark, and classically followed by: *"Rise and shine, You've had yours - now I'll have mine!"* See also *rise

wallop
  1. A resounding blow
  2. Beer: *"Pint of **wallop** please.."*

Wanchai burberry   A *burberry is a quality raincoat; the **Wanchai** version is a Chinese oiled paper umbrella available in *Honkers

wangle   Obtain something by craft, trickery or deception: *"'Owja **wangle** that then?"*

war canoe   Affectionate nickname for a warship

Wardroom   Technically, this is a collective term applied to all the officers of a warship or establishment above the rank of *Wart; it is also the *compartment wherein a ship's officers dine - the *Royal Naval* equivalent of an *Officer's Mess*. Note that the latter term is still used by the *Royal Marines*

Wardroom 2 *(FAA)*   Alternate **Wardroom** in an aircraft carrier for aircrew relaxing or eating while still in their flying clothing. The term is also used to describe any particularly favoured local pub

warmers into the butts *(RM)*   A few rounds fired deliberately down a range, without really being aimed, purely in order to heat up the rifle's barrel prior to competitive shooting. Now used to describe a few drinks taken prior to some event, ie. the *RM* equivalent of getting up *flying speed

warming the bell
  1. Heating the bowl (*bell*) of an hour-glass to make the neck expand slightly - so that the sand falls through slightly faster, thus ending the *watch prematurely. An older but exactly similar expression is to *flog the glass
  2. Now in general use to describe any early arrival, for instance at a party, or the process of preparing the way for the introduction of some new idea or concept. Often used also to describe a baby born less than nine months after a marriage because its parents had **warmed the bell** a bit!

warn in / warn out   The process of making a *Movement Occurrence Report* in a special *Wardroom book, so that proper allowances can be paid (or deductions made!) by *CENTURION*

Warrant Officer   New title which previously existed in the *Royal Navy*, but was revived in 1986 to replace the rank of *Fleet

Chief. This is now standard throughout the three services, but is no longer uniquely Naval - except in the sense that there is no *first or second class* applied, as in the **WO1** or **WO2** *(RM)*. However, the **WO** abbreviation has produced a small crop of dark-blue *funnies such as the **WO(OPS)** of *Operations*, and the **WO(CK)** *Chef*

warry   Abbreviation for **warlike** or a **war story**: *"Wow - you look really warry in that gear.."* Or: *"You tellin' warries again - or just *swinging the lamp ?"*

warshot   An explosive-filled torpedo or missile, as opposed to a dummy or practice round. Someone who is firing **warshots** is not taking any contraceptive precautions when *giving the ferret a run; after a successful *bricking these **warshots**, rather like a submarine simulating the discharge of a torpedo, become *****watershots**

Wart   Historic nickname for a Midshipman or *Snotty, because each one is generally held to be an unwelcome and persistent excrescence on the face of Nature

wash-out   Cancel something; also a description of someone or something totally useless

wash-up   Post-exercise analysis and discussion; a **hot wash-up** is just such a meeting held immediately after *Endex, and not something to do with dirty dishes

washers   Newer name for *klebbies - foreign coins of little real value that might just as well be drilled through and then used as **washers**

waste of rations   Someone who is not worth having on board; also heard occasionally as: *"He's a complete **waste of space..**"*

watershot (esp. *SM*)   Release of compressed air from a dived submarine's torpedo tube, thereby simulating a firing during exercises. See detail on *warshot for another more general application

watch   Spell of duty undertaken by Jack in order to **watch** (out) **and ward** (off danger) therby ensuring the ship's safety.   Note also the following:
1. **watch and watch** (about) Duty in alternate watches of four hours on and four off throughout a twenty four-hour period. When *closed up in this state while at war, the ship's company is said to be in **Defence Watches**
2. **watch on stop on**   Jack's rueful description of any continuous duty undertaken without relief
3. **Watch Bill** A schedule of the whole ship's company, setting out in vertical columns where a man works, his station in the event of abandoning ship, his cleaning duties and any *special sea duties he may have when entering or leaving harbour. The **Watch Bill** covers the general working routine of a ship, whereas the Quarter Bill deals with her fighting functions
4. ***anchor watch** - special **watch** kept when anchored in rough weather to detect any signs of the anchor's dragging
5. **watch keeper** Formal description of someone **standing a watch**, or as Jack would put it, a sailor who works irregular hours on a very regular basis !
6. **watching**   A buoy, float or paravane is said to be **watching** when just visible
7. **watch doggy** Older term for a warship on convoy escort duties
8. ***Watch my lips !*** Encouragement to pay close attention, derived from the fire-control order ***Watch my tracer !***

water-hen   Jack's description of Jenny when she is employed in boatwork or seamanship duties

waterlogged / waterwedged   Unable to consume any more alcohol, even if not yet totally *handcarted

Wave   The *US Navy*'s equivalent of a *Jenny Wren

Wavy Navy   A *RNVR (Royal Naval Volunteer Reserve)* Officer's rank was denoted by a narrow and **wavy** gold *lace braid, but this is now used only by *Sea Cadet Force* Officers. The *RN Reserve* Officers of today have the same braid as their regular counterparts, but with a gold *R* sewn inside the curl

ways of the Navy   The often unwritten traditions and customs of the *Senior Service* which one learns by experience - sometimes painful

wazzing *(FAA)*   Low flying without any purpose, or any unauthorized aerobatics; note that in *RM* usage a **feat of waz** can describe something brilliant, similarly a **wazzer**

Goffered

wearing a *Flag   A warship that has become a *Flagship as opposed to a *private ship, because she has an Admiral embarked

weasel out   Excuse oneself from some duty or task: *"How on earth did you **weasel out** from that one ?"*

weather eye   Watch any situation carefully for change or deterioration

weather guesser   The Met*(eorological)* Officer - who may be WRNS; see also *Professor Fog

webbing check   The process of establishing, by a Braille technique, whether or not a lady is sporting *suzzies

wedding garland   An evergreen garland is hoisted to the masthead when an Officer or rating of the ship's company gets married. This was originally the signal indicating that women were welcome on board - in the days when Jack was *pressed and likely to go on the *trot if allowed ashore

wedding tackle   The male genitals, also known as **marriage tackle**

wedge technician *(FAA)*   Newish term for a *chockhead

weed a pack   Remove any non-current or superfluous papers from a file docket

weejie   A word similar to *bazzy, in that to *get a **weejie** on* implies that the person involved is both angry and upset

weekend Admiral   An amateur yachtsman who visits a warship and then dispenses advice on nautical matters; **weekend sailors** are members of the *RN Reserve* but this time the name is far from derogatory

weighed-off   The meaning of this phrase depends on the context that it is used in:
 1. *"He had the whole thing completely **weighed-off**.."* implies that at least someone knew what was happening and how to cope with the problem
 2. *"*Father's just **weighed** Johnno **off** for seven days *chokey.."* means that some bad lad is about to spend a week in cells

(the) weight   Refers to the *weight of responsibility*. Thus: *"Who's got the **weight** this evening ?"* means: *"Who's the Duty Officer ?"*

welly
 1. Hit something
 2. Try harder *(esp. RM)* as in the expression: *"Give it some **welly** !"*
 3. **wellies from the Queen** are condoms held by the *QM at the *brow during foreign port visits and available (free) to Jack on his way ashore

Wendy   Excitable and upset in a rather womanish way: *"*Jimmy the One's got a **Wendy** on about smoking in the canteen *flat.."* Or: *"Their *Splot's a great big **Wendy**.."*

Wessex / Wezzy *(FAA)*   What used to be the *Fleet Air Arm*'s main workhorse helicopter, initially in the anti-submarine, but latterly in Commando and SAR roles. Very sadly, the aircraft retired from *RN* service in 1988: *"I reckon the only suitable replacement for a* **Wezzy 5** *is another one, whatever the Staff say.."*

wet   Many applications !
1. **wet a stripe** - celebratory drink on promotion, similar to **wetting the baby's head** at its birth in rehearsal for the christening !
2. **wet as a mess deck scrubber** - totally useless
3. **wet behind the ears** - a complete novice
4. **Wetdream** *(FAA)* - Jetstream training aircraft
5. **Wet List** - officers who are selected and in line for a seagoing command appointment
6. **wet Navy** - either the *RN*, *RAN* or *RNZN*, because alcohol in various forms may be consumed on board, under strict control
7. **wet nurse** - officer or senior rate in charge of first-timers in a sea training ship
8. **wet of tea** or **coffee** - a mug of either fluid, as in: *"I don't care what it is - just as long as it's **hot and wet**.."* Or: **"Tea's** wet !"
9. **wet ship** - a really hard-drinking outfit
10. **wet your whistle** - have a drink
11. **wetting ship** is the process of automatic hosing down of a ship's upperworks with sea water in order to minimise contamination by chemical agents or radioactive fallout

whack   Unit of quantity, based on punishment of older times, but now used for any share: *"Come on - you've had your fair **whack**.."* Note also the nickname **Whacker** associated with the surname Payne !

whanged into   Collided with something; see also *graunch

whaler   Double-ended wooden rowing boat designed on **whaleboat** lines; these were powered by oars or sail at first, but later on small engines were fitted. There are three oars on one side, two on the other

Whaley   *Whale Island*; see *Guns

wheaties   All-purpose nickname for any form of breakfast cereal

Wheel   A fairly important person such as a *Head of Department*, or *big wheel*; see also *mudguard

wheeze   An idea, usually something with an underlying humorous intent

Whens   Falkland Islander's nickname for British servicemen impolite enough to call them *Bennies or *Stills. This is based on the newcomers' tendency to precede most discussions with the phrase: *"**When** I was in.."*

Which wax ? *(RM)*   Traditional Arctic battle cry referring to the many compounds available to smooth (or retard) the progress of a pair of *pusser's planks through snow

which way it's screwed on   Someone who is possessed of *common dog, as opposed to pure intelligence, is described as knowing **which way it's screwed on**; see also *pickle jar and *jampot lid in this context

whip   Single rope *rendered to a block for hoisting and lowering something, hence a triple, or **three-line whip** used where additional power is required. This has led up the Thames to the Parliamentary meaning for the importance attached to a Vote or debate, as well as the actual office held by those responsible for enforcing this interest

whipper-in *(FAA)*   A formation leader's assistant who flies above the *Balbo while it assembles, and then calls with advice (and names !) on tidy and correct positioning

whipping   Yarn lashed neatly around a rope's end to prevent it *fagging and becoming frayed

whistle up   Call someone forward or create something quickly. Whistling has always been banned at sea because of possible confusion with the *boatswain's *pipes - except for the ship's cook while he was stoning prunes, who was required to whistle and thus show that he wasn't actually eating them ! To **whistle for a wind** was a superstition that, in order to get a breeze going when becalmed, all one had to do was whistle loudly and stick a knife into the mainmast

whistling handbag *(FAA)*   A portable filter and blower unit carried by aircrew wearing chemical warfare protection equipment

white around the gills   Seasick; see also *nautical nausea

White Empire   The *Supply and Secretariat* Department, based on their old *distinction cloth; note also ***White Mafia**

white gloves   A Captain's *Table at which there are no *Defaulters; this expression commemorates the rare event at County Assizes when the visiting Judge had no cases to try and was presented with a pair of **white gloves** instead

white-knuckle *(FAA)*   Frightening: *"Constant-attitude *autorotation ? It was a complete **white-knuckle job** from start to finish.."*

White Mafia   Collective nickname for the *Supply and Secretariat* Branch; see *distinction cloth for explanation. May also be heard as *White Empire

white rat   Older name for an informer on the messdecks

white silk   Collar tape and bow (from his tropical white uniform) traditionally worn by Jack when he gets *spliced to whichever *pash is destined to become his *CINC-NAG-HOME

white telephone   Toilet bowl; the confusion is usually induced by excess alcohol, but may be secondary to *nautical nausea

Whitehall Warrior   An Officer who is appointed to the *MoD in London for Staff duties and therefore slightly divorced from the practical realities of life at the *sharp end

whizzer *(FAA / SM)*   A helicopter's rotor blades, or a submarine's propellers

widger *(FAA)*   Either a perspex protractor used on maps and navigation charts, or a word used as a substitute for *doobrey, *doofer, *skrinser or *johnson - in other words, practically anything

widow's hop   See *grab-a-granny night and the *RN* *School of Dancing

wife and kids *(FAA)*   Phrase used to describe caution induced by family responsibilities: *"I've calculated the fuel required, and added three hundred pounds extra - for the **wife and kids**.."*

wife's best friend   The *toggle or *bedroom boatrope: *"I'm going to shake hands with the **wife's best friend**.."* is a less than polite announcement that you intend to *pump ship or *syphon the python

wigging   Any severe reprimand

wiggle   Escape: *"Just try and **wiggle** out of that one !"*

wiggly amps   Electricity of the alternating kind

Wiggy   Traditional nickname for the surname Bennett

Wilco *(FAA)*   *"**Will comply**.."* ie. the response to a message or order that indicates it is understood and will be carried out

wildebeeste   Alternative to *stumper and *coyote when describing those in attendance at a *grab-a-granny night; see also *wolverine for a more complete definition

win   Similar meaning to *proff or *acquire

wind up   Teasing someone in an attempt to get a *bite: *"You're really **winding me up** now, aren't you ?"*   Note also the extended version of **winding** (someone) **up a treat**, meaning that the response generated has been a really *senior one

Wind yer neck in !   *"Shut up !"*

windward   **Getting to windward** of someone, as in all sailing, implies gaining an advantage of some kind

Windy / windy
1. Traditional nickname for the surname Gale
2. Frightened: *"Fran got a bit **windy** about the whole thing, so he cancelled.."*
3. **windy hammer** - pneumatic drill

winger   A term applied to a sailor who helps voluntarily in another department; the rating who helps a *sin bosun to rig the chapel for a service is the **chaplain's winger**. The word originated from WW1 when all *Active Service* personnel were encouraged to take a *Hostilities Only* rating **under their wings**, but the term is also used now for a regular *run-ashore *oppo

Wingnuts   Traditional nickname for someone with large or bat ears; note also the label *assy when the condition is only one-sided

Wings *(FAA)*
1. General nickname for a *Commander (Air)*, the Officer who is in overall charge of all flying, deck or runway operations in a carrier or *Naval Air Station*
2. Pilot, Observer, or Aircrewman's *Flying Badge*, worn on the left uniform sleeve and presented at a ***Wings Parade*** following basic flying training. In older times, if a pilot was grounded, he was said to have **folded his Wings**, not by ceasing to wear them, but by having his flying pay withdrawn. Note also that some Naval Officers are parachute-trained, and also wear **Wings** on their sleeves as a result

winker   Marginally more polite version for the common term of abuse which implies self-abuse !

wiped out   Drunk, or severely *frapped at sport

wired *(FAA)*   Two applications:
1. Simulated attack by fighter aircraft: *"The Sea Harriers **wired** the airfield very effectively from two directions.."*
2. Description of a *Balbo: *"The whole formation **wired up** nicely - and stayed that way for a change.."*

wiring diagram   An organizational chart

WMP   Standard affirmative response to an invitation or *RPC. The acronym stands for *With Much Pleasure*; a badly-organized ship might also add *PSB - Please Send Boat* !

wobbleheads *(FAA)*   Another *stovie term of derision for *chopper puke helicopter aircrew

wobbly   Adjective applied to anything containing alcohol, such as **wobbly coffee** or **wobbly pie**. When used in the sense of **throwing a wobbly**, it implies a severe sense of humour failure

wokka-wokka   A helicopter, especially one of American manufacture with this characteristic blade-slapping sound; see *paraffin pigeon for some alternatives

Foo-foo powder

wolverine   The **wolverine** is an animal of great determination in that it will gnaw through its own leg to escape if the limb is caught in a steel trap. Jack now uses this label, along with *stumper, *coyote and *wildebeeste, to describe a *gronk who he has *trapped for a spot of *all-nighters, but then would rather gnaw through his arm than wake her up the following morning !

Wombat *(RM)*   Obsolete 105mm recoiless anti-tank weapon with an open rear venturi which produced an enormous noise and back-blast when fired - hence the expression: *"She *bangs like a *belt-fed **Wombat**.."*

wood butcher   Carpenter; see also *chippy

wooden topsails   Oars

Woodbury rash *(RM)*   An infectious skin condition apparently unique to *Lympstone

woof run   Going *ashore specifically to eat large quantities of food in some facility where quantity matters more than quality

woofter   Homosexual (rhyming derivative of **poofter**)

woolly pully   Blue or green *(RM)* woollen jersey pullover with reinforced elbow and shoulder patches in the same colour. Widely adopted now in the *RN* as a standard working *rig. Interestingly, Lord Nelson wrote to their *Lordships of the Admiralty* in November 1804 about his seamen's *Guernsey jackets*

word salad   Any statement, whether written or spoken, which fails to make sense when closely examined

work one's ticket   Exploit the appropriate regulations quite deliberately in order to get *outside

work-up   Period of increasing activity for a newly-built or refitted warship when all systems are thoroughly tested, then *evolutions run through repeatedly until the ship is at maximum efficiency and assessed capable of operational deployment. The words are also used to describe any gradual process of moving from slow to top speed, or *(FAA)* a squadron **working up** to operational standards before deploying to sea in a carrier

worms
  1. Older nickname for sailors employed on gardening duties ashore
  2. **worms in red lead** - tinned spaghetti in tommato sauce
  3. turned into a **can of worms** - everything went disastrously wrong

Wot sir - me sir ?   *"No sir, not me sir - not me never sir !"*

wrap   Give up, also applied in this sense in the phrase **wrap your hand** (or *tits*) **in**

Wren The basic rank of the *Women's Royal Naval Service*, or *WRNS*. Collectively they are known as *Wrens*, although a group of more than two or three may be specifically described as a **wriggle of Wrens.** A **Wrenlin** is an older term for a *Fleet Air Arm* **Wren** for whom nothing ever seems to go right (compounded from **Wren** and *gremlin*) The **Wrennery** is where the girls live; any job or appointment that has been given to the **WRNS** in order to free male sailors for sea duty is described as having been **wrennified** or **wrennerized.** Note also the frequent description of **WRNS** Officers as **Wren-Os**

wriggle stuff Management bullshit associated with an unwillingness or inability to speak or write the truth

wrinkle A **nice little wrinkle** is a short cut, or some hint or tip that makes a task easier to carry out

write The expression *May I write for you* ? is explained at the entry concerned with the *no treating rule

write-off Useless, when used to describe a person, generally when they have become incapable through drink; **written-off** is the process whereby non-consumable stores held *on charge have been destroyed for some accidental reason and must be removed from the accounting books. Note also the specific application of **writing your name astern** - the inablity to steer a steady and straight course

Writer Rating employed on clerical duties: *"*Scribes ? He's been working his trousers to the bone.."* See also *cross-dressing

WT Abbreviation for the *Wireless Telegraphy* of Morse code, rather than the radio-telephony and **RT** using voice

Homeward bounders

X-RAY

X-chaser   Older name for the Navigator, especially a *dagger N chasing a row of pencilled X's across his chart

X-factor   A pseudo-additional component of Jack's pay which is supposed to compensate him for the uncertainties and exigencies of Service life

Xmas tree *(FAA)*   A well-robbed *Hangar Annie that people with *robbing chits keep taking *presents* from

YANKEE

Yacht   The Royal Yacht, HMY *BRITANNIA*; when Jack refers to a **Yachtie** or a **Yachtsman** he is not talking about the off-shore racing fraternity, but about a member of the *BRITANNIA*'s crew

yam seng   Drinking toast that has persisted since Royal and Jack's Singapore days, now used in a direct sense to mean draining a glass in one continuous swig: *"So, seein' as it was 'is birthday, the bleeder went and **yam senged** it.."*

yammering   Complaining

yaffling   Eating voraciously; note these additional applications:
  yaffle fish - a barracuda or shark
  yaffling irons - knife and fork
  yaffle gear - mouth and teeth

yardarm   Outer portion of the horizontally-positioned spar attached to a mast from which signal flags and - in the days of capital punishment at sea - condemned men were hung from. Note also the term *****clear** (your / his) **yardarm**

yellow   Another interesting colour with several Naval applications:
  1. **Yellow List** - old Admiralty list of those officers for whom no further employment was planned
  2. **yellow Jack** - a quarantine flag, not a sailor with hepatitis !
  3. **yellow peas and trees** - sweetcorn and broccoli
  4. **yellow peril** - smoked haddock

Yeoman of Signals   Descriptive rank of a senior *bunting tosser

Yeovilton   Headquarters base of the *Fleet Air Arm*, and spiritual home of all *Junglies as well as the *Sea Harrier*. Immediately adjoining this busy *Naval Air Command Fighter Station* is the excellent *Fleet Air Arm Museum*. From the steps up to the entrance one can appreciate the massive bulk of the *Bucc, then view the *Toom, *Concorde* and some fascinating exhibits on both current and historical themes. Spot the author's contributions in the Falklands section ! Then, if the weather is reasonable, your picnic in the Museum car park should be enjoyed to a backdrop of the sound of Falklanders' freedom - the *Rolls-Royce *Pegasus* jet engine of the *SHAR

Yes and no !   The question: *"Are Royal Marines Officers any good at taking quick decisions ?"*   Answer (after a very long pause): *"Well - yes and no !"* See also *positive perhaps

yeti *(RM)*   Royal's description of falling over while ski-ing; if the resulting **yeti-hole** is big enough (as a direct consequence of carrying a *chacon for instance) then it can be described as an *elk's nest: *"You should have seen us on that hill ! Carl **mega-yettied** into a ditch and broke his skis, while I did a *tree-stop that shook all the snow off its branches and buried me completely.."*

Yin Yang   Allegedly *yin* is the Chinese word for a vagina, but along with the word *yang* it has now become a portmanteau word for a foreign river somewhere out in the *far-flung: *"We're completely up the Yin Yang now on manpower.."*

yockered   Spat, a slang word originating from Liverpool that is based on the sound made at the back of one's throat when clearing it, or when expressing disgust at something revolting

yodel in a bucket   Vomit copiously; see also *pavement pizza, *dockyard omelette, *technicolour yawn and *white telephone

yomp   A word that has always had, as its principal meaning, the rapid consumption of food; *yomping your meal* in big mouthfuls then became adapted to Royal **yomping** across the ground with huge strides. It was this latter sense which caught the British public's imagination during the Falklands campaign, rather than the Paras' equivalent activity of *tabbing*, and the former has now become part of the vernacular

yonks   A long time

you-can't-bend-it   Optional extension of the *all-singing, all-dancing, **you-can't-bend-it** label applied to some new piece of *kit

Young Officer / YO *(RM)*   Royal's officers are trained alongside other recruits at *Lympstone, although their training is twice as long, and they must achieve all the *Commando tests to a higher standard. They are known as the **Young Sirs** by their NCO trainers, and collectively as The *Batch. This latter phrase is always used when describing a colleague: *"He was in my *Batch.."* and not: *"We went through training in the same year.."*

You have the ship ! Formal expression of handover from an *Officer of the Watch* to his *relief. In the **FAA** this is modified to *You have control* when changing pilots, but in either case the transfer is confirmed by the response: *"I have the ship / I have control.."*

Young Butcher Junior Surgeon/Deputy PMO or Little *Doc

You're a scholar and a gentleman, sir ! *"Thank you very much.."*

ZULU

zap lead *(FAA)* Grounding wire carried by helicopter winchmen, and designed to conduct static electricity earthwards by a route other than the crewman's body

zeds General purpose word for sleep; the word is used in a number of expressions such as *racking up **the zeds**, piling up **the zeds**, **zeds** *merchant or: *"I'm off to crack out a few zeds.."*

Zeebrugge A specific *Corps memorable date for this harbour on the Belgian coast, long before the ferry tragedy that shocked the world in 1987. This *St. George's Day* attack on 23 April 1918, against what was then a German naval base, was designed to block the harbour entrance and destroy the outer Mole. In this aspect the operation was only partly successful, but tremendous gallantry under withering enemy fire was shown by personnel of the 4th Battalion RM. There were heavy *RN* and *RM* casualties; two of the eight *Victoria Crosses* awarded went to *Royal Marines*

Zero *(FAA)* Newish nickname for an *Observer based on his (O) description in the *Navy List, and according to some *stick monkey (Pilot) opinion, also indicative of overall value !

zero crack zero *ringbolt Really early in the morning

zip lip (esp. *FAA*) Radio silence: *"From then on in we're zip lip.."*

zit See *pluke; supposed to be derived from the sound made when the thing is squeezed and its contents hit the mirror; note also **zit bar** as Jack's description of a large piece of *nutty

zizz Alternative to *zeds when describing sleep. A **zizz *duff** is a particularly heavy and coma-inducing pudding

zonk   As for *zeds and *zizz

zoomboots *(FAA)*   Jack's nickname for *Royal Marine* pilots who, sadly, are no longer trained by the *Fleet Air Arm*

zoomies   Another rotary-wing aircrew nickname for *stovies

Zulu
1. **Zulu time** is *Greenwich Mean Time*
2. **Zulu Warrior** - a ritual male strip routine performed when most of the participants are fairly well *handcarted
3. Battle cry of **Z Company** of 45 *Commando *RM* when they did the necessary business on the twin peaks of *Two Sisters*, 11/12 June 1982 in the Falkland Islands

NOTES

All additions and suggestions to:

Surgeon Commander Rick Jolly OBE RN
c/o Palamanando Publications
PO Box 42
Torpoint
Cornwall PL11 2YR

(Mark envelope PLEASE FORWARD
TO 'JACKSPEAK' AUTHOR)

NOTES

NOTES

NOTES

NOTES